Gianluca Vialli is one of the most famous Italian footballers in the post-war era. He won league titles with Sampdoria and Juventus and captained Juventus to Champions' League victory in 1996. At international level he won fifty-nine caps for Italy, scoring sixteen goals and leading them to the semi-finals of both the 1988 European Championship and the 1990 World Cup. As a manager, in two and a half seasons at Chelsea he won more trophies than any other manager in the history of the club, including the FA Cup, Cupwinners' Cup and League Cup. He currently divides his time between London and Italy where he is the top analyst for Sky Italia's Serie A and Champions' League coverage.

Gianluca is donating proceeds from *The Italian Job* to the Fondazione Vialli e Mauro per la Ricerca e lo Sport (www.fondazioneviallimauro.com), a charitable foundation set up by Gianluca and Massimo Mauro, which raises funds for research into cancer and amyotrophic lateral sclerosis (ALS), better known as Lou Gehrig's disease.

Gabriele Marcotti is the UK correspondent for *Corriere dello Sport*, and World Football columnist for *The Times*. He has also written for the *Financial Times*, *Sunday Herald*, *Daily Mail* and *La Stampa*. He co-presents two weekly radio shows on TalkSport and is a regular analyst on Bravo, Setanta and SkySports News. He is also a columnist for *Sports Illustrated*.

THE ITALIAN JOB

A journey to the heart of two great
footballing cultures

Gianluca Vialli
& Gabriele Marcotti

BANTAM BOOKS

LONDON • TORONTO • SYDNEY • AUCKLAND • JOHANNESBURG

TRANSWORLD PUBLISHERS
61-63 Uxbridge Road, London W5 5SA
a division of The Random House Group Ltd
www.booksattransworld.co.uk

THE ITALIAN JOB
A BANTAM BOOK: 9780553817874

First published in Great Britain
in 2006 by Bantam Press
a division of Transworld Publishers
Bantam edition published 2007

A CIP catalogue record for this book
is available from the British Library

Addresses for Random House Group Ltd companies outside the UK
can be found at: www.randomhouse.co.uk
The Random House Group Ltd Reg. No. 954009

The Random House Group Ltd makes every effort to ensure that the papers
used in its books are made from trees that have been legally sourced from
well-managed and credibly certified forests. Our paper procurement policy
can be found at: www.randomhouse.co.uk/paper.htm

Typeset in 11/14pt Berling by
Falcon Oast Graphic Art Ltd.

Printed in the UK by CPI Cox & Wyman, Reading, RG1 8EX

2 4 6 8 10 9 7 5 3

To our families and to all those who love football
in a passionate, sincere and honest way, and who
believe that, as beautiful as the sport is today,
tomorrow can be even better.

Acknowledgements

This project began with a phone call from me in London to Gabriele, who, fittingly enough, was at UEFA headquarters in Nyon, on the banks of Lake Geneva. That was way back in November 2003, two and a half years before the book came to life in print, which should give you an idea of just how long and laborious a process it has been.

I am not the first manager to write a football book, nor is Gabriele the first journalist to do so. But as far as I know, it is the first time a journalist and a manager have collaborated on a project like this: a work which is only marginally autobiographical and instead focuses on research. That's why I am grateful to the people who, from the start, believed in the concept. My literary agent, David Luxton, was honest and blunt from the start, telling us: 'Some publishers love it. Others just don't seem to get it.'

Those who got it, thankfully, were the men and women at Transworld. Thanks therefore go to my editor Doug Young, Emily Furniss, Katrina Whone, Vivien Garrett and Hazel Orme, an extraordinarily tough, but very gifted copy editor.

In the time it took to write this book I became a father, set up a charitable foundation, earned my UEFA Pro Licence coaching badge, moved house three times, spent what seemed like days in television studios and logged more Air Miles than I will ever know what to do with. Keeping my life straight while all this was going on would have been a real challenge without the invaluable support of my personal assistant, Virgina D'Amore, as well as that of Stella Andretta, who replaced her when she went on maternity leave.

Gabriele and I conducted most of the research ourselves, but we are grateful for the precious help we received from Lorenzo Amuso, Alberto Corral, Antony D'Angelo, Tom Edwards, Dave Farrar and Jennifer Marcotti.

My proceeds from this book are going entirely to the Fondazione Vialli e Mauro, which raises funds for research into cancer and amyotrophic lateral sclerosis (ALS). It is a cause in which I believe and I must give thanks to everyone at the foundation, particularly Grazia Micarelli, as well as everyone who has supported us since our launch. You can find out more at www.fondazionevialliemauro.com

A special thank you also goes to my family, who were patient and who supported me at every turn, and an extra special thank you to Ken Hayward, my 'grandfather-in-law', who was among the first to read the manuscript and provided valuable feedback.

Finally, my gratitude goes to all the very busy people who donated their time to speak to us about football. Their insights allowed me to better understand this wonderful sport and the way it lives and breathes in the two countries I love: Italy and England. In strict alphabetical order, a big 'Grazie' to: Carlo Balestri, John Barnwell, Dave Boyle, Andy Cale, Tony Colbert, Pierluigi Collina, Marcel Desailly, Paolo Di Canio, Matt Dickinson, Sven-Goran Eriksson, Sir Alex Ferguson, Ciro Ferrara, Franco Ferrari, Gianni Grazioli, Richard Hughes, Luca Locatelli, Arturo Lupoli, Giordano Maestroni, Massimo Mauro, José Mourinho, David Platt, Graham Poll, Gordon Taylor, Giovanni Vaglini and Arsène Wenger.

Foreword

Read on and you will join me in a journey. A journey that began out of curiosity and ended up consuming the best part of two and a half years. But, then, that's not such a long time when you consider where I was trying to go: right to the heart of football.

I had been given a gift, the physical ability to make my living from this wonderful game. And I had also been given the mental strength to pursue that gift and make a career out of football. Yet twenty-five years in the game had left me with more questions than answers. I figured there must be others in my position, people who have asked themselves the deeper questions about this sport. It seemed only right to me to try and give something back, to discuss, if not answer, some of those questions. I figured I had three crucial points in my favour: a boundless curiosity, a good cause and access to some of the finest minds in football today.

That's what this book is about. My thirst to learn more about this game. My desire to help my foundation, which raises funds to combat cancer and amyotrophic lateral sclerosis. And my picking the brains of some of the cleverest football people I know.

This book is not an autobiography. There is no kiss-and-tell, no stories about what was said in a dressing room or on the pitch. This is about me spending thirty months criss-crossing Italy and England, meeting people and talking football, life, Mars and Venus. These managers, players and officials, all among the busiest people I know, generously donated their time and brainpower because, more often than not, we deconstructed together what many feel is a very simple game.

We begin with the footballers, the basic building blocks. Where do they come from? Why are they different in Italy and England? How do we teach them? How can we make them better?

Then there are the managers and coaches, those who bring it all together. How do we choose our managers? How do we decide when to let them go? Why do they use certain tactics?

Finally, in the third part, we look at all the extraneous factors, the 'other' which makes football special: money and agents, referees, fans, the media, clubs and institutions, all of which colour the game and how we experience it.

Do I know more now about football than I did before I started? Yes. Do I know more about the Englishman and the Italian? Absolutely. Do I feel like one of those philosophers who, the more questions they ask, the more questions they generate and ultimately find themselves surrounded by unresolved issues? A little.

But it doesn't matter. It's been quite a ride. Please join me.

Veronica, Mary and Me: A footballing love triangle

Football is love and passion – like that for a woman. Those who live this sport – whether as fans or players, club officials or referees, managers or groundskeepers – end up hopelessly in love. But there is a world of difference between England and Italy. It's an entirely different kind of love.

If I had to reduce my feelings for the game in either nation to how I might feel about a woman, I would describe two very different women, Mary and Veronica. By the time you finish reading this book, you'll know which is Mary and which is Veronica.

Mary is faithful, bubbly, comforting. She may not be a natural beauty, but, when you are with her, she gives everything she has and makes you feel special. Sometimes you think it might be nice if she took more pride in her appearance – maybe she could spend a few more hours in the gym, perhaps she could dress elegantly instead of in high-street jeans and top, and perhaps a touch of makeup wouldn't go amiss. When you argue, which happens even in the best relationships, it's over quickly and she is always eager to forgive and forget. She only remembers the good times, and never casts up past events to use against you. Your intimacy with her is usually brief but intense: she never holds back and uses every ounce of her body to please you. You leave in the morning and you might not see her for several days. You don't hear from her and, frankly, you don't mind, because you don't often think about her. Or, rather, you don't think about the last time you were with her, but you might fantasize about your next meeting. Mary is innocent and direct: she tells you exactly what she's thinking, she has no ulterior motives. She's the girl next door, the one you know you can always return to and be welcomed with open arms. The one who will always satisfy you, at least for a short while.

Veronica is passionate, vain and envious. She is drop-dead gorgeous and she knows it. In fact, she uses her beauty to intoxicate and manipulate. She gives you just enough to keep you coming back, but she preys on your insecurity, messing with your mind. She's obsessed with detail, impeccably made up and elegantly dressed, always glamorous and enticing. But your relationship is never easy. She disappoints you, she ignores you, she cheats on you. When you're with her, you're rarely happy, yet you always go back. And you can't be with her for just a few hours: you remain captive, minutes turning to hours, hours to days. You can't get away. Each time, just before you see her again, you are torn, every neuron in your brain trapped in a mental civil war. On the one hand, you know exactly what will happen: odds are, she'll mistreat you, humiliate you, let you down again. But on the other hand, you *have* to go back to her. By the time you finally see her, you're an empty shell, drained by the agony and mental effort you've put yourself through in the anticipation of your liaison. And, when it's over, you simply can't leave. Especially if you've had a row. She'll analyse everything that was said and done in excruciating detail, resurrecting long-forgotten suspicions. She never forgets and rarely forgives. Veronica is moody, irritable and always ready to deceive. In your rare moments of clarity, you consider ending your relationship, freeing yourself from those unhealthy and suffocating bonds. But you always go back. You can't help yourself.

The Footballer

Chapter One

The First Few Kicks

It all begins with a ball and a child. The ball is usually some kind of plastic/rubber compound (leather is for the big kids) and, these days, it originates somewhere with cheap labour. The child, of course, is flesh and blood, yet he or she is drawn to this artificial object, mesmerized by its shape and its unfamiliar smell. It looks solid and inert but as soon as it's nudged, a wonderful thing happens – it moves!

Anyone who has seen a child approach his or her first football may relate to the wonder they experience as the little leg stretches out to kick, and, magically, the ball rolls away.

It may sound clichéd, but at that age, that moment of first contact between child and football, everyone is the same. The Italian child is like the English child, and they are no different from a Venezuelan or an Inuit. What is striking, though, is how quickly the footballing paths diverge when the outside world crashes in. Even in the earliest kickabouts with parents, siblings or friends, footballing differences begin to emerge, and grow with the child, particularly in those who, like me, have the good fortune to turn their relationship with the ball into a life-long profession. Climate, culture, social class, economic conditions, all play their part. They divide the footballing world – but that is not necessarily a bad thing. In fact, it enriches us. Without it, there would be no 'Italian football', 'English football' or 'Brazilian football'.

We all have a sense of what those terms mean. We know that football is different in different countries. In fact, we have a mass of stereotypes: German football is disciplined; Italian football is defensive; English football is direct; Brazilian football is full of flair.

I wasn't satisfied with these descriptions. To me, they seemed like convenient short-cuts to explain a far more complex reality, one which is rapidly changing.

I wanted to dig deeper. I wanted to understand, as best I could, the way things really were and how they were evolving. I wanted to figure out how, when and why those differences developed. Understand where we are, where we came from and where we're going. And, perhaps, destroy a few myths, unravel a few mysteries and offer one or two suggestions along the way.

We spend a lot of time talking about football – all of us, whether we're players, coaches, the media or fans. We talk about it pretty much incessantly. We've got twenty-four-hour television sports channels, radio stations, daily sports newspapers in Italy, lengthy sports sections in the English papers and, of course, the constant chatter in bars and pubs from Rome to Rotherham. It struck me that much of this discourse is both immediate and specific. We are drawn to it because it's so vast and colourful. We think about who won or lost and why, which player or team is better, whether the foul was inside or outside the box, how it made us feel. And that's all wonderful.

But we don't generally think about what lies beneath: why we see and experience football as we do. Why do some places produce certain types of player? Why do some supporters prefer a certain kind of football? Why do some countries prefer certain tactical schemes?

If we all start in the same place, why do we end up all over the footballing spectrum?

Of course, I am only one man and I don't have all the time and resources in the world, so I have focused here on the two footballing schools I know best: Italy, the country of my birth, where I lived and played until I was thirty-two, and England, my home for the last decade, where I have played, managed, married and started a family.

The thing about football is that it's a living thing. It moves and changes, slowly but inexorably – and, over time, radically. Much of the recent change has gone hand in hand with the globalization that has touched most aspects of modern life. Mass culture is eroding national and geographic identities. Those children, who were all the same when faced with a football at the age of three, are, in many ways, remaining the same as they grow older.

Imagine going to six cities in five different continents – Bari (Italy), Bangkok (Thailand), Bloemfontein (South Africa), Buenos Aires (Argentina), Boston (United States) and Burnley (England): take one ten-year-old boy from each place and put them in the same room. Now imagine that language was not an issue (pretend there's a universal-translator machine like there is in *Star Trek* – work with me here!). What would the kids talk about? What would they have in common?

Chances are, they'd have plenty to talk about. Most

probably, they play the same games on the PlayStation, watch the same films on television and listen to the same music on the radio or their MP3 players. They've probably been driven around in the same cars and they would all be familiar with McDonald's (though the Italian boy's *mamma* might not have allowed him to eat there . . .). And they would all know who David Beckham is.

I think back to when I was ten. What could I have discussed with my foreign peers? Certainly a hell of a lot less than today's ten-year-olds. Maybe a bit about films or music, football, if it was a World Cup year. But that was it. Our common culture was far smaller than it is today. The world is shrinking – as we are often reminded.

Still, even when I was a child, a common thread linked me with my peers: we played our first football matches with friends, in streets, courtyards or parks, not in any organized setting. It's another stereotype, which goes right back to Pelé and his ball of rags in the *favelas* of Bauru, in the state of São Paulo, but it certainly holds true. Every professional today has a story about their first epic football battles. In fact, everyone who has played the game at any level, whether competitive or not, will probably find them familiar.

'We lived in tenements and there was what we called a back court where women put their washing,' says Sir Alex Ferguson. 'At each end you had two poles, which served as goals. Along the side, for maybe twenty odd yards, we had these dykes, which served as cellars for the shops nearby, and at the back there was a wall, so it was fully enclosed.'

If Sir Alex's matches were played in the shadow of the Govan shipyards, Marcello Lippi enjoyed rather more glamorous surroundings: 'From early May to late September we only played on the beach,' recalls the current Italy manager, who had the good fortune to grow up in Viareggio, on the Tuscan seaside. 'Then, when it got colder, we moved to the woods, where we played amongst the pine trees. Some pines served as goalposts, others were additional defenders you had to beat. Sometimes we wore shoes, sometimes we were barefoot. That's where you learn football, not in some boys' football school.'

Ray Wilkins has similar memories. 'Every single day after school we would meet up at the local park, which was just across the street from my house,' he says. 'And when school was out, we would meet at nine o'clock in the morning. Nobody was ever late. When it got dark, we'd simply move indoors. My brothers and I would play in the hallway, the front door was one goal, the kitchen door the other. Of course, when we played at home, we had to use a balloon . . . our mum wouldn't have appreciated it if we'd played with a proper football.'

Sven-Goran Eriksson may not have played at the level of Lippi, Wilkins or Sir Alex, but it was a similar story hundreds of miles away in Sweden: 'We had to wait for the snow to melt, of course,' he says. 'But as soon as it was gone, we were outside. And all we did was play football.'

The only thing different about my story was the scenery. There was a courtyard at the back of my house and we played there. There is little doubt in my mind that where you play as a child influences the type of player you become. My courtyard was a rectangle with garages on opposite sides and open ends. The sides were longer than the ends, but the garages served as convenient goals, so we played on a pitch that was wider than it was long. I was always a striker, of course, but because the pitch was so wide, I found myself covering the whole width of the front line, going out wide to receive the ball and delivering plenty of crosses into the box. That's the kind of striker I became, one that liked to roam the entire width of the pitch. Had our courtyard been long and narrow – who knows? I might have become more of a target man or a Romario-type, lying in wait to pick up scraps and used to moving in tight spaces.

I played there from September to May, but in the summer months we would move from the city of Cremona to our country home, where there was plenty of open space and, crucially, lots of grassy meadows. This totally changed my game. In Cremona, our courtyard was concrete, which meant that, naturally, I tried to stay on my feet: falling on concrete isn't much fun. Out in the country, though, when you could play on thick, luscious grass, it was a different story. My brother and I would spend hours practising overhead kicks, flying backheels and improbable headers. The ground was so soft that you wouldn't get hurt even if you landed on your head, as often happened. Again, it may seem simplistic, but it can't have been entirely coincidental that one of the things I was known for as a player was my aerial ability.

Environment plays a big part in how children develop their technical base, the skills in touch and control that remain with them for the rest of their lives.

'I grew up on a council estate in Rome and we played in an area between the buildings which was meant for people to hang their laundry out to dry,' says Paolo Di Canio. 'The ground was cement, there was rubble, there were steps and cracks in the pavement and you had to avoid the washing lines and the poles or you'd get decapitated. You had to learn quickly to control the ball in those circumstances, otherwise you'd just keep losing it.'

Most people I spoke to agree that this was a fundamental part of their development as footballers. 'Every summer we had a tournament in our back court,' recalls Sir Alex. 'We had the whole of Govan out. We had to have our own rules, because of the court. So you started by heading the ball and, after that, it was all one-touch football.'

I close my eyes and try to picture Sir Alex as a teenager, in shorts and a T-shirt, playing one-touch football with his mates in a narrow courtyard, surrounded by tenements under a (typically) grey Glasgow sky. I realize that the hours he spent out there were not so different from the three-on-three drills I did years later as a professional. It was training, even back then.

'It gave us a foundation where practice became our life,' says Sir Alex. 'You didn't know you were practising, you thought you were playing a game you loved.'

Changing Times: Victims of Affluence

That foundation built on the streets or in the parks is so important that, today, some coaches believe in integrating it in the training of professionals. Since he arrived at Chelsea, José Mourinho has revolutionized the training regimen by, among other things, replicating the street scenario. 'At Chelsea our academy works in that way,' he says. 'We don't develop aerobic capacity by running, we do it by playing three against three. Three on three is just like playing in the street: no goals, no stress. You have to give kids the same street conditions, which are to play, to practise, to try things without the stress. I think that's the way. The great players come from the street because the ball becomes part of their lives. They practise with it, they develop a street-football intelligence, which is essential. We need these same street conditions in our academy today. We are losing street football because of the way the world is going . . . and we have to get it back somehow.'

I know what he means when he talks about 'the way the world is going'. I look at myself, growing up in comfortable surroundings in a wealthy part of Italy, and I compare my childhood with my nephews'. When I was a boy, there was no Internet, no PlayStation, no VCR or DVD, all of which many kids today take for granted. There was television, of course (I'm not that old), but there were only two channels. Today there are several hundred. As a result, free time consisted mainly of one thing: playing with friends. And that usually meant football, at least for me.

After all, there were only so many things you could do. You could go for a bike ride, read a book, play board games . . . but not too much else. I could have played tennis or basketball, but that would have involved my parents or an older brother taking me to and from the courts. These days, I love golf, but I'm not sure I would have wanted to play it every day as a child (though my friend Massimo Mauro tells me he would much rather have become a professional golfer than a professional footballer – even though he is the only man to have played with Zico, Michel Platini and Diego Maradona!). For me, football was a natural – logical – choice.

Today, though, across almost all social classes, it's different. As Sir Alex says, 'Prosperity has brought more cars, more affluence, more attractions for younger people. So you have a barrier there for a kid growing up and wanting to be a footballer nowadays, as opposed to when I was young. All we had was football so all we did was play football.'

Of course, Sir Alex is several decades older than I am, and there is little question that, economic factors being equal, my generation had more options than his. But equally, today's kids have many more than I did. And, according to Ray Wilkins, the issue goes beyond that: 'It's not just the computer, though many kids today would rather stay indoors anyway,' he says. 'Crime is far higher than it was, at least in England. I would never send my kids out to play in the very same park I used to play in with my brothers. These days, there are too many freaks around.'

It's a similar story in Hertfordshire, where referee Graham Poll played football as a boy, before he got his whistle and cards. 'I go back to where I grew up, and the league where I used to play once had sixty teams. Now it has just ten,' he says. 'We have a football pitch and recreation ground only a hundred metres from my home and we never see any kids there. It's a different society in which we live. . . . Whether we're over-protective, whether the media makes us worry too much about our children and the risks of them being out on their own, I don't know . . . yet this is a suburban environment, it's very safe. Still, it's indicative of people all over the country. You just don't see kids out there.'

Traffic is another factor: a by-product of prosperity and economic development. Ciro Ferrara grew up in Naples, a city famous for its back alleys teeming with children. Today, when he goes home, he sees fewer kids out on the street: 'I don't think they've all become too rich to play in the streets, it's just that things have changed,' he says. 'With the cars and motorbikes zipping past, you can't play on the street in urban areas. They still play football, but in community centres and parks, where it's more organized. The downside, of course, is that it's less frequent.'

When Sir Alex revisits the epic one-touch football tournaments of his youth in Govan, he finds a bit of a footballing ghost town: 'When I go back, I don't see kids playing on the street. It just doesn't happen,' he says. 'Traffic is one reason. When I was a boy, you'd get the odd lorry supplying the local shop, but you'd never see a car. Nobody had one.'

Today, of course, cars are everywhere. In 2003 there were 29,895,982 on British roads and in Italy, 34,275,591. That's one car for every 1.69 people, counting children, the blind and people in prison!

It's hard to overstate how cars have changed our landscape, particularly outside cities. Not only has the intensity of traffic turned playing in the street into a dangerous activity, it has also redefined the way many live. The car, coupled with our desire for more living space, has led to urban sprawl. Go to any older village or market town and you'll see that the buildings in the centre are very close together. People used to live above the shops, often several generations in one household, packed together in tiny homes, because getting around was difficult so they needed to be near their shops and workplaces. The car virtually eliminated distance. People moved further away, which decreased population density almost everywhere but the inner cities. For kids, this had a major impact. Where once there might have been fifty families within walking distance, now there were half as many – and half as many children of your own age to play with. Which means more time spent indoors watching television or exploring cyberspace.

Of course, I'm now in my early forties, so maybe I'm a little out of touch with today's teens. So I asked Arturo Lupoli, the eighteen-year-old Italian striker at Arsenal, about his experience. Though he is originally from Naples, he grew up a few miles away from me.

'By the time I was ten or so, I didn't really play football with friends that much,' he says. 'There simply weren't too many opportunities. I did play football, but that was at the local community centre, at my local club and, after I signed with Parma, at the academy. I was driven to the first two and, when I joined Parma, they would send a mini-van to pick me up with the other kids.'

Richard Hughes, the Portsmouth midfielder, is a Scottish international, but he too grew up in Italy, before moving to Arsenal at the age of sixteen.

'I played a lot of football locally as a boy, but that was also because my dad coached our team, so I never had any problems getting to training,' he says. 'I grew up on the outskirts of Milan, near a large public park.'

All of these changes – technology, traffic, even crime – did not occur in a vacuum. They are a by-product of the more profound historical and socio-economic developments that swept Western Europe after the Second World War. Indeed, if you have kids and they ask, 'What's the point of studying history?' you may want to point out that recent political and economic events have changed football as much as any tactical innovation or amendment to the rules.

You Can't Fight the Flow of History

I'm not a historian, but I have read up a little on a few things. One of the most striking changes in Western Europe over the last forty-odd years has been the creation of a vast middle class, which has not only accumulated the material goods that were unavailable to all but the very rich just a couple of generations ago – refrigerators, cars and washing-machines – but has developed aspirations and ambitions that their grandparents could never have contemplated.

Take education, for example. Not too long ago, most people didn't finish high school, let alone earn a university degree. Now, in most cases, if someone wants a university degree – and is clever enough academically – it is within his or her grasp. How did this come about? Successive governments across Europe grasped the importance of education and invested heavily in it at school and university level. At the same time, the economy changed. I grew up in and around Cremona, a primarily agricultural area. The farms are still there, but now high-tech machinery does much of the work. Where a farm might have once employed thirty people, now it can be run by five or six. Elsewhere, agriculture has made way for industry, but over the last few decades, heavy industry and manufacturing have declined, sometimes sharply.

It's down, once again, to globalization, on a world and a local scale. The European Union's precursor, the Common Market, contributed to this, with the elimination of tariffs and trade barriers in Europe. Cheaper goods from elsewhere in the common market led to the decline of less competitive industries in other areas. And the process was repeated on a greater scale with the rise of the World Trade Organization and the industrialization of the developing world. Suddenly, European industries and manufacturers could no longer compete as other countries produced goods of similar quality at far lower prices – thanks to cheaper labour and the lack of trade unions. As a result, many industries, which had once guaranteed safe, stable and relatively well-paid jobs to people with skills but little formal education, simply shut up shop.

This obviously had a variety of knock-on effects. The very fabric of certain communities was torn apart and periods of recession, sometimes outright depression, followed. Yet this cloud had – depending on your viewpoint – a silver lining. It removed the 'safety net' that many had relied on, forcing the next generation to look for different jobs, mainly in the service sector, that sometimes required formal education. Gone were the days when young men could try to make a career of football in the knowledge that, if things didn't work out, they could always 'go down the pit' or work on the assembly line at Fiat. (Of course, their predecessors had it worse: Bill Foulkes, the Manchester United defender and 'Busby Babe', who survived the Munich air crash, worked in the coal mines while playing professionally for United and actually did a shift down the pit on the day he won his first England cap.)

Young men began to realize that the odds on earning a living as a professional footballer are incredibly slim and the sacrifices necessary even to attempt it are enormous. And if they didn't, their parents did. As José Mourinho remarks, 'If you come from a family with a good standard of living, you have parents who care about your education, you have stability in your life and, at fourteen, you get the chance to try to become a professional, it's not easy to take because your family knows how difficult it is to succeed. They will often try to dissuade you. But if, at fourteen, you have nothing to lose, it's a different story.'

Studying took priority over football in ways it never had before. Partly this was a necessity: for the uneducated, the respectable jobs in factories and mills had been replaced by midnight shifts at McDonald's and the local chippie. It was also because people began to feel they had too much to lose. 'Kids today have a billion things to think about,' says Marcello Lippi. 'Their lives are far more complicated than ours were. Of course they play a lot less football than we did. When I was sixteen I was registered for two different clubs and played two games in the same day. In the morning I'd play for a youth team, in the afternoon, using an alias, I'd play for an amateur team. What else was there for me to do? Now parents, and I can see why, don't want to raise kids who only know how to play football. They want more.'

Today we think that to want a better life than our parents had is the most natural thing in the world. But that wasn't always the case. In fact, for most of our history, there was almost no social mobility. You were born into a class and you stayed there. Nowadays we know that through hard work, natural ability and luck we can 'better ourselves'. But there's a downside. 'Kids today grow up with parents wanting them to get a better life than they had,' says Sir Alex. 'There's nothing wrong with that, I do it myself. But then you have a situation where, if the neighbour has a bike, your kid has to have a bike too, and if he has a computer, your kid has to have a computer. It leads to a situation where you're always trying to match others materially and bombarding your kids with distractions. And the result is that kids don't have time to themselves, to spend with their friends, just playing, practising, learning.'

It's that 'foundation', which both Mourinho and Sir Alex talk about: the skills that come not from the training ground but from endless summer afternoons playing four-a-side in the park, the back garden or the street. 'That foundation still exists in Brazil and in African countries,' says Sir Alex. 'When we talk about players with "natural" talent, we're talking about African and South American players. There's an obvious answer there in the sense that they are where we were fifty years ago. Kids have the opportunity to develop that foundation on their own.'

On this point, Mourinho is in total agreement, putting forward his own country as an example. 'Look, Portugal, by European standards, is a poor country,' he says. 'Yes, we have a nice quality of life, nice food and weather, but we don't have the opportunities you have in England. Now, I don't have the exact figures but, proportionally, there are many more kids who play football in Portugal compared to England. Everybody wants to play football in Portugal, like in Brazil or in Africa. It's the dream that can change your life, the hope for the future, because the standard of living doesn't allow for much else.'

The Class Divide in Football: An English Phenomenon?

The views of Mourinho and Sir Alex are quite depressing

if you take them to their logical conclusion. If playing in the streets gives you the fundamental skills to become a great footballer, and if becoming prosperous means fewer kids play in the streets, and we're all becoming more prosperous, doesn't it follow that we will produce fewer great footballers?

If this reasoning is correct, it would certainly appear so. And the only way to halt the slide is to improve the way we teach kids about football, somehow replicating the street in an organized setting – which is what Mourinho and others try to do at Academy level.

Yet thinking of this 'Prosperity as an enemy of talented footballers' argument led me to identify one of the most notable differences between England and Italy – indeed, perhaps between England and the rest of Europe. I thought about the many footballers and ex-footballers I had met, and it struck me that while in most of the world they come from all walks of life – some are the children of millionaire industrialists, high-powered lawyers, university professors – in England the vast majority are from working-class backgrounds. The exception, as always, are the kids of former athletes, guys like Frank Lampard, Jamie Redknapp or Michael Owen, whose fathers were professional footballers and who therefore grew up in a more comfortable (at least, financially) environment.

There is a long-held conventional wisdom about this, which aims to explain why the sons of CEOs and the aristocracy rarely become top sportsmen. There are two exceptions. The first, as I mentioned, are the children of successful athletes. They have two advantages over others. The first is often genetic. If Mum or Dad was an exceptional athlete their child might have inherited some of that co-ordination or athleticism. The second is that they were raised in a sporting environment. It's obviously not like it was in medieval times when the butcher's son would become a butcher, the farmer's child would farm the land and the thief's offspring continued his family's thieving tradition, but there is a proven statistical correlation, which applies across the board in all professions.

The other exception comes in those sports where there is what economists would call a high barrier of entry: the activities are expensive. Most race-car drivers begin at the age of six or seven in go-karts, which gets very pricey very quickly. It's a similar story for professional golfers (how many golf courses, with the odd exception in places like Scotland, are located near council estates?), showjumpers and sailors. The pool of people who have a chance of pursuing these sports is far smaller than it is in boxing, sprinting or, indeed, footballing.

So most professionals are drawn from lower-class back-grounds. The theory is that the sacrifices involved to become successful are too great for the privileged: first, they have too much to lose educationally and therefore are less likely to provide the kind of single-minded commitment required to succeed. And, because they have to prove themselves among so many, working-class kids are tough mentally and physically, which often makes the difference between success and failure.

It's an interesting theory, but I have serious doubts about it, not least because my own background was relatively privileged and I can think of several successful footballers who come from upper-middle-class back-grounds – Fernando Redondo, Oliver Bierhoff, Kaka and

Andrea Pirlo to name but a few. Are they merely the exceptions that confirm the rule? Or is there more to it than that?

The conclusion I reached was that while economic background plays a part, societal attitudes are just as important. This was where I came upon one of the first and most obvious differences between England and most other European countries. In England, football was traditionally a working-class sport; elsewhere it cut across social divides. 'In Italy and France I met footballers who were born poor and others who grew up wealthy,' says Marcel Desailly. 'The social extraction varies immensely. In England, there are no sons of doctors or lawyers or bankers. I think it's because football in Italy or France is seen differently. In those countries if a family has a son who is a professional footballer, it's something to be proud of. In England, if your son is a footballer . . . well, I won't go so far as to say that it's a reason to be ashamed, but for many it's a sign that the parents have somehow failed.'

Desailly's point is an interesting one. I did a bit of research and came up with just one example of non-working-class or middle-class professional footballers: Nicky Walker, who kept goal for Hearts in the 1990s, was the scion of the family which owned Walker's Shortbread. But that's it.

It may be that in England you're much more aware of class than we are on the continent. In Italy, we have marked regional accents, but generally they have nothing to do with social class. Someone from Palermo, for example, will speak in a certain way regardless of whether he lives in a castle or a council flat. The same applies for someone from Milan or Rome. In England, there are also strong regional accents, but there is also, for lack of a better word, a 'posh' accent, which tends to override the regional inflection. As soon as someone opens their mouth in England, you can make an informed guess about the level of education they received or the level of privilege they enjoyed. This is simply not the case elsewhere. Also, rugby and cricket have traditionally been the sports of the privileged in England, while football belonged to the working classes. In fact, until the 1990s, the upper classes in England had little interest in football, preferring cricket and rugby. There was probably a fair bit of snobbery as well, as if cricket and rugby were 'pure' sports, and football was common, even soiled. That's why we get phrases like 'That's just not cricket!' – to signify something that isn't quite on the level – or the saying that 'Rugby is a game for hooligans played by gentlemen, and football is a game for gentlemen played by hooligans'. Football was perceived as a rough-and-tumble working-class pursuit, not fit for a gentleman.

In fact, one aspect of football that was most distasteful to the privileged classes was the game's professionalism, which had been well established since the late nineteenth century. Rugby Union held on to its amateur status well into the 1990s with almost religious fervour, as if letting professionalism into the game was the equivalent of allowing money-lenders into the temple.

Cricket's relationship with professionalism is in some ways even more telling. Although some cricketers had been paid for a long time, there was always a sense that 'gentlemen' did not play for money. Indeed, for many years it was customary for captains to be amateurs, while the yeomen of the team, the fast bowlers, were professionals. In the 'Bodyline' series, it was the batsmen, the posh Douglas Jardine and Wally Hammond, who instructed the fast bowlers to bowl to the body. Thus, guys like Harold Larwood and Bill Voce, both former miners turned professional, were left the unenviable task of executing Jardine's instructions and becoming the villains, with all the controversy and acrimony that followed. As professionals, they had little choice: cricket was their livelihood. On the other hand, another bowler, Gubby Allen, an amateur who was equally upper-class, refused to bowl to the body. Until a few decades ago an annual game at Lord's between amateurs and professionals was known, none too subtly, as 'Gentlemen versus Players' – as if the latter could not be gentlemen.

These attitudes remain today among certain portions of the press and public opinion, which may explain why so much moralizing goes on in England when negative football stories surface. Whether it's a player signing a £100,000-a-week contract or misbehaving on tour or swearing at a referee, many are quick to compare football with rugby or cricket. This is usually followed by a resounding condemnation of football. This doesn't happen in Italy. We tend to be less moralistic about high wages and various forms of misbehaviour on or off the pitch – to be fair, footballers in Italy tend to be better behaved off the pitch (either that, or they simply don't get caught).

I suspect that, whatever their origins, these attitudes are what allowed English football to maintain a maximum wage well into the early 1960s of twenty pounds a week. In today's terms, that works out at just under £1,000 a week, or what some Premiership footballers earn today in less than two hours.

Of course, £50,000 a year is an excellent wage for most people in 'normal' jobs, but the difference is that a footballer's career is short – no more than ten or fifteen years. And, back in the 1960s, it was even shorter because medical facilities weren't what they are today. I'm always amazed to hear of former England players from the 1950s who died penniless, not because they blew their fortune on drink, gambling or bad investments but because they had been underpaid. In addition, the so-called retain-and-transfer system made them virtual servants to the clubs. At the end of their contracts, they could either be sacked or placed in a sort of limbo, where their wages were cut by 60 per cent and they remained the property of their club, unable to sign for another team without its consent. The irony – and injustice – of it is that these men were underpaid and taken advantage of at a time when stadiums were full, attendance was booming and the game was, by all accounts, healthy.

But there was another side-effect to all this: football, the working man's game, remained a game for the un-educated working classes. 'Footballers were treated by the powers-that-be the same way that factory-workers or miners were treated, which was very, very badly,' says Gordon Taylor, chief executive of the Professional Footballers' Association (PFA) – effectively the players' union. 'Beyond the obvious injustice, this situation meant that only the underprivileged classes came into football. It's logical, because anyone who might have had the opportunity to study or learn a trade knew they had a better future outside football. At best, football could offer them a few years of modest wages and that was it.'

This changed in 1962, when the PFA, led by Jimmy

Hill, forced the Football Association (FA) to abolish the maximum wage and the retain-and-transfer system. Freedom of contract, as we now know it, was still around thirty years away but at least out-of-contract players could move, for a fee set by a tribunal. 'The abolition of the maximum wage was absolutely crucial because it allowed people like me or Steve Coppell, young men who were by no means wealthy, but middle class rather than working class, to play football,' Taylor says. 'Had the maximum wage been in effect, our families would have sent us to university, they certainly would not have allowed us to play football.' The legacy of all this is that football in England remains a working-class sport, with all that this entails.

In the better public schools, where future leaders were produced, football is at best a marginal sport and at worst simply not played. All this, however, is changing and has been changing for some time, though we may not see the effects for another generation or so.

The introduction of the Premier League in 1992, coupled with the Bosman ruling a few years later, glamorized the game and gave it a new-found respectability. The Premiership gave football a bright new image and the kind of commercial set-up that appealed to the moneyed classes, the corporate world and women, a constituency of supporters that had long been ignored. The Bosman ruling led to a huge influx of foreigners (including yours truly), which added exoticism to the mix.

At the same time, things were changing on a wider, societal level. England is moving towards a less stratified society, with a large middle class and fewer people at either extreme. In the early 1950s, Giovanni Trapattoni, from the age of fourteen to eighteen, used to wake up at three a.m. to work in a bakery. After school, he played football all afternoon, then collapsed into bed at nine. I couldn't imagine doing that and I'm grateful that I never had to go through it. Today, even in deprived areas, there are football schools or academies, so kids who want to play can do so under the watchful eye of coaches, teachers, volunteers or parents. It's a positive development, because the kids are supervised. They reflect what they are taught so qualified, competent instructors are important. When you watch a bunch of eight-year-olds play football, you come to realize how much of their game is down to emulation. They copy what they are taught and what they see their heroes do on TV. Cultural differences are minimal: at most an Italian boy might imitate Francesco Totti's backheels, while his English counterpart does his best to replicate Alan Shearer's headers. 'Because of the way television presents football nowadays, footballers are heroes to kids,' says Sir Alex. 'They learn football through television and learn about their heroes. When I was a boy you'd see your heroes maybe once a year on television. Except for those kids who had the chance to watch their local team, that was the only contact they had, the odd game on TV and maybe stories and hearsay that was passed on. Today there is a much more direct identification with their heroes. It's basically continuous. They have much more clearly identified heroes they can strive to emulate. And I think that's good for football in many ways.'

Sir Alex is right. It *is* good for football – provided the role models are good ones. If they cheat and act like thugs, that's not so good. And that's why the other great influence, the supervising adults, is so important. As soon as you take children and put them in a grown-up context, everything changes. That's when, both consciously and unconsciously, the kids begin to absorb the adults' philosophy. And in that regard, between Italy and England there is a huge difference. It is where the footballing paths begin to diverge. This is where the kids cease being simply kids and become, at least in footballing terms, Italian kids and English kids.

Chapter Two

'You don't understand. I coulda had class. I coulda been a contender. I coulda been somebody . . .'
– Marlon Brando, as Terry Malloy in *On the Waterfront* (1954)

Early Pre-selection

I don't know if it's something that happens to all ex-footballers or if it's just me, but people seem to love to come up to me and tell me the footballing version of Brando's speech. They could have played professionally. They could have played internationally. They were the best footballer in a fifty-mile radius when they were ten or twelve or fourteen. Juventus or Manchester United or Real Madrid wanted them to come on trial. But then . . . it just didn't work out. And it had nothing to do with them.

'My mum wouldn't let me go on to a bigger club because it was two towns away and she didn't want me to take the bus.'

'The coach didn't like me. He had it in for me.'

'I hurt my knee and, back then, surgery wasn't an option.'

'The other boys were jealous of my ability and wouldn't pass me the ball.'

Or, my personal favourite: 'I liked girls too much to focus on football.'

Far be it for me to doubt the veracity of all these potential Maradonas but I suspect their excuses were just that: excuses. If you're good enough to play professionally, you're better than 99.9 per cent of the population. And that generally means you don't fall through the cracks – particularly not in this day and age. The obvious conclusion is that most of these folks simply weren't good enough.

However, the realization that someone isn't good enough only occurs once he enters 'organized football'. Before that, most kids dream of becoming professional. Reality sets in when adults enter the equation. And that's where everything changes.

It is also where Italy and England split. In Italy, youth coaching is about turning kids into the best possible footballers. In England, it's about using sport to understand values such as teamwork and sportsmanship. And it's about having fun.

Football does not exist in a vacuum and there are historical and social reasons for this. In England, until the early 1990s, the Football Association (FA) was dominated not by former professionals or club chairmen, but by teachers or representatives of local, often amateur football. These men – often disparagingly called the 'blazer brigade' – had their own priorities, which often had little to do with the higher end of the professional game: ethics, fair play, sportsmanship and healthy enjoyment. Winning was of secondary importance. After all, football was just a game.

In Italy, the FA is highly politicized. It is supposed to

serve the interests of football as a whole, Italy's 1,438,161 players and 16,993 clubs. Instead it's greatly influenced by the big Serie A teams, whose needs are regularly prioritized. And they, naturally, are more interested in an FA that produces good footballers rather than one that produces good *people*.

This is not to suggest that the Italian FA is some kind of giant football factory, spewing out left-backs and right-wingers, or that the English FA is naïve and unprofessional. Rather, their roots and priorities are different. The Italian FA's grassroots organization was perhaps traditionally a little too 'professional', while the English FA's professional department was perhaps a little too geared to the grassroots model. What works for Smallsbury Village FC does not always work for Manchester United. Equally, while it's true that what works for Milan may work for AS Castelpiccolo, it does not necessarily mean that AS Castelpiccolo or any other amateur side is better off following the example of Milan.

'In Italy, they are very good at teaching you how to play good football and how to be a much better footballer,' says Marcel Desailly. 'In England, they teach you the right values, but, in terms of technique and tactics, well . . . I could see it myself when I compared what the youth team players at Milan and Chelsea did. At Milan, they trained exactly the same way the first team did, down to the last detail. At Chelsea, they'd take two laps around the pitch, throw on yellow or blue bibs and off they'd go for a full-pitch scrimmage. Every single day.'

He's right: kids in Italy train the way professionals do. I went through it myself, both at my first club, Pizzighettone, and then when I moved to Cremonese at fourteen. In retrospect I think this is hugely important. A boy's first experience of organized football affects his vision of the game. And, for a kid in Italy, this means treating football as a job, something to be taken seriously – enjoyed, of course, but in a professional way.

The English boy's first experience of organized football is different, often in the context of a school team. In Italy, there is practically no football in schools but there are plenty of 'football schools'. For English kids football is an extension of school – the 'fun' part. Nobody is forcing the young Italian boys to join their local footall clubs, but, once there, they immediately adopt a 'professional' – some might say 'regimented' and quasi-military – attitude to it.

From a purely footballing standpoint, the set-up in Italy pays handsome dividends. There used to be a popularly held belief – put forward by the late Gianni Brera, a legendary football journalist – that Italian and, indeed, most Mediterranean footballers were quicker and more skilful than their northern European counterparts because physically they had to be smaller and not as strong. That might once have been the case, but no longer. In Italy we produce more than our fair share of big boys: Marco Materazzi, Francesco Toldo, Luca Toni, Dino Baggio, Paolo Maldini . . . the list goes on and on. In fact, there are so many similarities between Italy and England that it's eerie. If you compare the ten outfield players who started the opening game for England and for Italy at Euro 2004, you find that the ten Englishmen weighed an average of 75.6 kilograms, just 100 grams more than the 75.5 kilos the Italians weighed in at. One hundred grams is about the weight of half a prawn sandwich. In height, the

Italians were actually taller: 180 centimetres to the English 179.6 – less than a fifth of an inch difference.

Nature, Nurture and the Uncomfortable Genetic Taboo

So, there is virtually no physical difference between Italy and England. The differences that exist are the result of preparation. At least, that's what Tony Colbert, Arsenal's fitness coach, believes.

'Of course there are individual exceptions, but in general terms there are no particular genetic differences between English players and Italian players,' he says. 'However, there are athletic differences, due to the type of work done at an early age, I'd say starting at about eight. First of all, English players tend to be somewhat less co-ordinated than foreign players. It's something we notice right away in the exercise we do. Foreign players tend to be more supple, more agile. Having said that, English players have more endurance. They can run for ninety minutes, always at the same speed. They may lack the explosive acceleration to get to the ball first, but they maintain their pace throughout the game. Foreign players, on the other hand, are more used to accelerations and pauses. Their endurance is not as good but their quick burst of pace is better. I think this is a function of the work they do as kids. In England, traditionally, we always trained with the ball and often in scrimmages, eight versus eight or five-a-side. In that context, you're always running, always moving. In Italy, you do more specific work, stopping and starting, plus work aimed at improving the technical base of each player.'

Of the many people I spoke to while I was researching this book, Colbert stood out. With his trim build and moustache, he has an almost military bearing. But when he speaks, he is thoughtful and reflective, sounding more like a scientist or a professor than an old-school bootroom denizen. He is of a new breed in English football, which, until five or six years ago, was largely unknown: the fitness coach. His background is in athletics and he approaches the game from a fresh perspective.

Perhaps because of this, he is more prone to question things that, ordinarily, would be taken for granted. And when someone answers a question so completely, you can tell they've thought about the issue before. After I met him, I reflected on what he'd said. First, the genetic argument. We all grow up with certain stereotypes and myths that we take for granted, and tend to notice facts that support and reaffirm them. I suppose this is because it's subconsciously more comforting to find your beliefs proved correct than to admit you might have been wrong.

Here's a basic example. Many people still believe that cold weather or cold air causes the common cold. Even its name, 'cold' in English, '*raffreddore*' in Italian, implies that it's somehow a result of getting cold. But it's not true. There is no such thing as the common cold in Antarctica because it's caused by a virus. Yet the old wives' tale persists. People remember colds they caught in winter and forget about the summer ones.

So why do we associate the common cold with winter? Because there is a connection: in winter, people spend more time indoors, in close contact with each other, in places where there is little air circulation, and the viruses spread.

Back to football. In football, the genetic argument is awkward. Colbert denies that there are any significant genetic differences between Italians and Englishmen and that is easy enough for most of us to accept. If there are differences in athletic ability, they are a result – as Colbert says – of early training, social and cultural influences. We'll take a closer look at this later, but, in the meantime, there is another issue, which, these days, we tend to tiptoe around: race.

If you speak to some football people privately, including several I interviewed for this book, they'll say that black footballers tend to be more athletic than white ones. They'll point to the fact that, in general, they are faster, quicker and more powerful. Obviously, we're speaking in general terms here – John Terry is clearly more powerful than Shaun Wright-Philips and Michael Owen is quicker than David James – but there is a clear belief that black footballers are more athletic.

This idea is rarely discussed publicly in England, unlike Italy, where, in many ways, it is accepted as fact. I don't think it's hard to understand why: England is a far more diverse and multi-racial society than Italy and it's a sensitive issue because of the underlying implications. If blacks are naturally better athletes than whites, it's as if they have a God-given advantage, and this belittles their achievements: it implies that whites must have to work that much harder to compete with blacks. Or that blacks can afford to be lazy. This is close to ugly, long-held racial stereotypes and understandably makes people uncomfortable, particularly because of what some might see as the next logical step in this thinking: if blacks are more blessed in one department (athletic ability) surely they must be deficient in another (intelligence). Of course, this thinking is very far from the truth and highly dangerous. But there are differences between black and white players.

I thought back to my black teammates and the black players I have coached: in general terms, many tended to be more athletic – quicker, stronger, more co-ordinated. I looked beyond football: why are the best and most athletic basketball players black? Why are most of the top sprinters black? Or is this not so? Had I been infected by the stereotype?

I decided to do some reading and see if science could come to the rescue. And that was when things got really interesting. The first point is that, when we think of black versus white athletes the terms 'black' and 'white' are purely descriptive, referring only to skin colour. A more accurate – if wordy – term for black athletes would be 'of African descent'. Because that's the common link between Ronaldinho and Michael Jordan, Asafa Powell and Sol Campbell, or whatever contemporary black athlete you might think of. And, remarkably, not only are they all of African descent, they are, more specifically, of West African descent.

Because that's the point too many people seem to ignore. Most of the great athletes – footballers, sprinters, basketball players, or others in any sport that requires strength, quickness and co-ordination – of African descent can trace their ancestry to the same area of West Africa, countries such as Sierra Leone, Ghana, Liberia, Cameroon, Ivory Coast, Senegal and Nigeria. The rest of Africa has produced comparatively few, though countries like Kenya and Ethiopia, with their excellent tradition of long-distance runners, have provided a different kind of athlete. True, the North African countries and South Africa more than hold their own in football, but they are far wealthier and offer better coaching and infrastructure. In terms of the pool of athletic talent, West Africa stands alone.

Nowadays athletes of West African descent come from all over the globe, for one tragic reason. From the seventeenth to the nineteenth century, up to twenty million Africans were kidnapped and taken across the Atlantic Ocean as slaves. It was an African diaspora. Some went to work on the cotton plantations of the southern United States, others to the farms of Brazil and the sugar plantations of Jamaica – these men and women were the ancestors of Ronaldinho and Campbell, Jordan and Powell.

Far from being a racial argument, it's a geographic one. It's not blacks who are more athletic than whites. It's West Africans who are more athletic than Caucasians, Asians, East Africans, North Africans, just about anyone you care to name.

Except that's not entirely true either. The next question to which I wanted an answer was, *why* does West Africa produce 'better' athletes? Professor Kenneth Kidd, a Yale University geneticist, mapped African diversity as part of the Human Genome Project. His work inspired Malcolm Gladwell and Jon Entine, who, writing separately, have taken a totally different slant on the issue. They argue that West Africans aren't more athletic in absolute terms: they simply have a greater degree of variance in athletic ability. This means they produce proportionally more great athletes than Caucasians or Asians, but also more bad

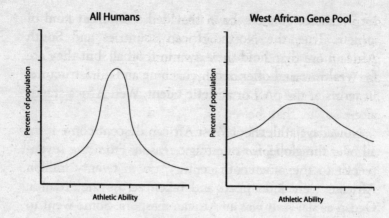

All Humans	West African Gene Pool
Percent of population	Percent of population
Athletic Ability	Athletic Ability

athletes and fewer athletes of average ability. Imagine that you could rate someone's athleticism on a scale of 1 to 5, with 5 being the best. Of 100 Caucasians, 70 per cent might rank as 3; 5 per cent as 5; 5 per cent as 1; and the remaining 20 per cent as 2 or 4. But, according to Gladwell and Entine, if you were to rate 100 people of West African descent, only 50 per cent would rank as 3; 10 per cent as 5; 10 per cent as 1; and the remaining 30 per cent as 2 or 4.

Now, when it comes to professional football, we see only the very best, in athletic terms, of a population. Today top-flight footballers are all top athletes (we have to be). So, it is lost on everyone that there may be more West Africans than Caucasians who are athletically inept because those people don't become professional athletes. The point is that, while those of West African descent as a whole are no better than other genetic groups, there are more great West African athletes than there are great athletes from other genetic groups.

Incidentally, one theory explains why there is greater variance in athletic ability among West Africans: they simply have more variety in their genes. Anthropologists agree that *Homo erectus*, the precursor to *Homo sapiens* (you and me) originated in Africa more than a million years ago. They disagree on what happened next (some believe *Homo erectus* left Africa and settled the rest of the world, others argue that he evolved into *Homo sapiens*, then branched out), but they are nearly unanimous in believing that the African *Homo erectus* must have carried the genes for *Homo sapiens*. In other words, all the genetic variants – the genes that make us tall or short, fast or slow, ugly or handsome – every possible combination, were present in *Homo erectus* in Africa a million years ago.

As man spread across the globe, some of those genetic traits were lost due to evolution and the necessity to adapt to different climates and conditions. But this didn't happen to West African Man. He maintained the same huge range of genetic variants because he didn't go anywhere and thus did not need to adapt much. Also, West African Man was largely isolated. To the north he had the Sahara desert, to the east, mountains, to the south and west, the Atlantic Ocean. Unlike North and East Africa, which were routinely invaded and today are ethnically diverse, West Africa was largely left alone, preserving its pool of wide-ranging genes.

It's an interesting theory.

But, of course, genetic or 'natural' ability is just one ingredient in the making of a top professional footballer, and, in broad terms, as Tony Colbert says, there is, in that regard, no difference between the English and the Italians. The athletic difference, as he suggests, is largely learned. And I can see why he believes foreign players to be more 'supple' and 'co-ordinated' than the English. I think of the great English defenders, such as John Terry or Sol Campbell, and neither looks as elegant to me as Paolo Maldini or Alessandro Nesta. There is a certain stiffness about them, a lack of fluidity in their movements and turns.

'We all noticed a certain rigidity in the English players, especially in training, when foreign coaches started to arrive in the Premiership,' says Marcel Desailly. 'They introduced exercises that were normal on the Continent but which the English had never seen and you could tell that, at times, it was awkward for them. I think this reflects the way the English have played historically and also the way the English footballers were raised. To them being strong and powerful was important. Co-ordination and balance weren't necessarily as important for the type of football they played.'

Colbert also attributes this to the training we do in Italy even as kids and I suspect he and Desailly are right. I remember doing the same drills over and over for hours – one-touch control, turn, shoot, left, right, over and over again. I must have done them tens of thousands of times. I enjoyed it and didn't really think about it, but, on reflection, I realize that my contemporaries in England probably never did them.

I think this improved our technique *and* our flexibility because it worked muscle groups in a certain way. It's the 'specific work' Colbert talked about, where the game is broken down into segments and they are worked on individually, whether it's quickness, control, vertical jump, whatever. It's a sharp contrast to the English way, where most of the work is done with the ball and where, as kids, most of the training consists of scrimmages. Obviously, if you're in a scrimmage or a practice match, you're constantly moving. This builds up the endurance Colbert talked about, though it doesn't necessarily improve quickness or reaction time.

It shouldn't be a surprise, then, that this is reflected in the way the game is played in England. The cliché is that the Premiership is a 'fast-paced' league played at a million miles an hour. In reality, what makes it 'fast-paced' is that there are no lulls; the speed is constant, but not particularly high. By contrast, Continental football, particularly Italian and Spanish, features more pauses – what Jorge Valdano calls 'time to think' – but also more periods of acceleration, when the pace suddenly picks up, often reaching levels beyond that of the English game. Valdano, ever the romantic (and not exactly a fan of English football – at least not aesthetically), famously compares it to a symphony: you need highs and lows, moments when the music slows, or even stops. This allows you to appreciate and savour the moment when it picks up again. It gives the player a chance to regain his breath and pick up his pace. Think of an English match as a five-mile race, while an Italian game is a series of sprints.

Skill or Commitment?

The pauses in the game also allow a player to display his technique. Think of Zinedine Zidane's famous *'ruleta'*, the step-over-and-turn move he uses to spin away from a defender and create space for himself. Most professional footballers, indeed, most footballers of any standard, can do it if they're in the back garden and nobody is near them. Doing it in traffic, in a game and at pace makes it difficult. And in England, where the movement is constant and often frenetic, it's much harder. As José Mourinho says, 'I don't agree that the English are less technical, it's just that it's different. It's more difficult when the defender is on top of you all the time. I worked in Spain for many years . . . When the defender is two metres away, anyone can control the ball nicely and pass it accurately.'

I see his point, but I'm not sure I agree. While I accept that times are changing, technique is and has been far more of a priority in Italy than it has been in England.

'The thing which struck me the most when I arrived at Milan was that technically the defenders were as good as I was and I was supposed to be the big foreign star, the skilful central midfielder!' says Ray Wilkins. 'I never thought I was bad on the ball, but at Milan I was made to look really bad in training on more than one occasion. We used to do this drill where you formed a circle, two players went inside and the guys on the perimeter had to pass the ball around, keeping it away from the two guys in the middle. When one of them managed to intercept the ball, you would change it around and someone else would go in the middle. Well, I was there with Mark Hateley and when the two of us were in the circle, it would only end when Mark would go and kick someone off the ball. It was the only way to end it. Otherwise, it would have gone on for ever, with the two of us, the two English lads, stuck in the middle.'

I suspect he's being modest. After all, he did win eighty-four caps for England, which means he couldn't have been a lead-footed donkey. In fact, having worked closely with him at Chelsea and Watford and seen him in training, I can say that his technique was 'exquisite' and 'terrific' – two of his favourite adjectives. Yet I believe that technique has traditionally been emphasized over other factors in Italy. Colbert shares my view: 'You are better than we are at identifying talented players and developing them,' he says. 'We are more oriented towards selecting those who can fight and run, even when they don't necessarily have the technical ability.'

Sir Alex Ferguson agrees, especially when it comes to English football's recent past: 'There was a period in English football when a lot of teams were just going for strength, height and that sort of thing,' he says. 'There were players who maybe couldn't pass the ball that well, but they had the skills which worked in that system. From 1983 to about 1993, when the Premier League started, there were many players like that.'

I don't think it's a coincidence that England's foot-balling heroes have traditionally included a disproportionate number of battlers rather than artists. Whenever I used to go to Elland Road and see the statue of Billy Bremner I was struck that Leeds United chose him as the embodiment of their legendary team of the early 1970s rather than the elegant Johnny Giles or the goal-scorer Peter Lorimer. Bremner was an inspirational captain, of course, and a giant in the history of his club. But I think it's fair to say that in England there has been greater appreciation of those who do the 'dirty work'.

By contrast, look at the great Inter Milan team of the 1960s. It won two European Cups under coach Helenio Herrera and was known as 'La Grande Inter'. Most of the adulation went to players such as the stylish Sandro Mazzola or the play-maker Luis Suarez or the elegant

Giacinto Facchetti, the attacking left-back who was the Maldini of his day. They were flashy, skilful players who looked and played like stars. The Billy Bremner of the team would probably have been the skipper, Armando Picchi, an outstanding defender, but hardly a poster boy. It's safe to say that if the two clubs, Inter and Leeds, swapped fans, there would be a statue of Giles or Lorimer outside Elland Road and Picchi would be hailed as the embodiment of 'La Grande Inter'.

The attitude of supporters and the media has much to do with this. In Italy, we demand results; in England, it's effort. The only times I've seen English fans turn on their club is when they believe the players aren't putting in the necessary effort. And when a team does badly, the English press don't question tactics or team selection, they talk about 'lack of heart and passion'. As in Italy, they'll blame the manager. But in Italy, the manager is blamed for his formation, his selection or the team's conditioning. In England, it's his fault if the players lack 'spirit'.

My Quadrilateral: the Elements of a Footballer

Today, clubs look everywhere for players. And, while there may be fewer kids actually playing, the sense is that it is more difficult for a potential professional to fall through the cracks.

'If you have a bit of ability, it's easier to be spotted,' says Lippi. 'I think we do a good job, especially in Italy. There are clubs all over the place and, with them, a parallel network of scouts. These guys don't miss anything. In that sense, we've improved tremendously in the last few years. It's very different from my day. As a teenager, I played with guys who were better than me, yet they never made it. Today I think it's harder for this to happen.'

Yet ability is only part of it. And scouting is by no means an exact science. You could probably represent a footballer graphically as some kind of quadrilateral. The base would be technical ability – by this, I mean all the basic ball skills such as controlling, passing, dribbling and shooting.

One of the sides would be athletic ability. This includes the obvious qualities of strength, stamina and pace, and those that are sometimes more difficult for the casual observer to notice, such as co-ordination, leaping ability and agility. Athleticism is not just about ticking boxes in various categories, it's about making distinctions between the different ways in which those qualities are applied to the game.

Take pace, for example. There are different kinds of pace over different distances and this is immensely relevant to the game. Some players are very fast over sixty yards but sluggish over five. For example, I was recently told the result of tests that Arsenal ran over sixty yards in the 2003–04 season. Guess who the three fastest Gunners were. OK, one's dead easy: Thierry Henry. No prizes there. You probably won't be surprised to hear that Jermaine Pennant was another. But it ought to astound you that the third Arsenal speedster was none other than Dennis Bergkamp.

Obviously Bergkamp is a phenomenal footballer, but few would list pace among his assets. That's because you would hardly ever see him going on a sixty-yard sprint during a match. Most of his runs are short, no more than ten yards. And over that distance he is not the quickest. Again, this makes sense, given his size and body type.

One of the quickest men I've played with was Gianfranco Zola. What we in Italy call 'explosive force' – quickness off the mark – he had in abundance. For a striker of Zola's characteristics, that 'explosive force' was far more important than his pace over sixty yards, because it enabled him to pounce on loose balls and accelerate away from defenders. Now, over sixty yards a number of players might beat Zola, including yours truly, if only because I have longer legs. Yet with Zola, it didn't really matter because he hardly ever had to make such a long run during a match.

But there's another twist when it comes to pace. It's what we called 'the Delta' when I was at Juventus, working with fitness guru Giampiero Ventrone. *Delta* is the triangle-shaped Greek symbol used in mathematics and physics to represent change. In footballing terms it signifies the drop in performance over time. For example, at Juventus we would do a drill where we were required to make, say, twenty twenty-yard sprints with forty-five-second intervals between each one. Naturally, if you're going at full pace, your first few sprints will be quicker than the last. It's only natural: fatigue builds over time. Obviously, as a player, you want to have a small Delta – that is, you want your twentieth sprint to be only slightly slower than the first. At Juventus, I played with Michele Padovano. He was quicker than me over twenty yards, but I had a better Delta. This meant that he would beat me in the first three or four sprints. Towards the end, however, by the fourteenth or fifteenth sprint, say, his performance dropped off and I started beating him.

In football, a good Delta can be vitally important, particularly for strikers and central defenders. You don't want their pace to drop off late in the game but to remain as constant as possible. I have to say that the Delta was one of my strengths. I might make fifteen runs against my marker during a game and, for the first few, I might get beaten to the ball. By the end, however, if my marker did not have a good Delta my repeated runs would wear him down and I would be beating him. This would allow me either to get to the ball first or at least to get open, forcing the other defenders to make an adjustment and clearing space for my teammates.

The second side of the quadrilateral is understanding the game, which is a combination of tactical knowledge, decision-making and intelligence. It's what Jorge Valdano calls 'knowing how to play football'. One of the things that make football such a wonderful game and, in many ways, a reflection of the world around it, is that this category covers so many different types of footballing intelligence.

There is the overused but distinct quality we call genius: the ability to envisage and conceptualize actions that are beyond the scope of an average footballer. Think of David Beckham scoring from sixty yards out against Wimbledon. Or Pelé dummying the Uruguayan goal-keeper in 1970. Or Gianfranco Zola's flying backheel against Norwich in the FA Cup. Those moments are special because of the creative spark behind them. They are the footballing equivalent of Leonardo da Vinci's *Mona Lisa* or Jimi Hendrix's psychedelic performance of the 'Stars and Stripes' at Woodstock. What sets them apart is not the technical side. Most professional footballers can run past a goalkeeper as Pelé did or hit the target from the half-way line as Beckham did. And while Zola's backheel was technically difficult, there are probably many strikers who could replicate what he did in training. By the same token, there are thousands of would-be Leonardos who could probably produce a reasonable copy of the *Mona Lisa*. And I would imagine that some studio musicians can perform a comparable rendition of Hendrix's 'Stars and Stripes'.

No, what makes them special is the spark that preceded each of these moments: the instinct to do something most of us would never even contemplate. And to do it at that particular time, in that particular context. That's genius. A good musician would have performed a different song in a different way at Woodstock. A good artist would have painted a more traditional portrait of the *Mona Lisa*. And, in the same way, a good footballer would have tried to take the ball past the Uruguay goalkeeper, or laid off the ball in midfield or tried to control it. Leonardo and Hendrix did what geniuses do: they innovated and did something nobody expected. In their own way, Pelé, Beckham and Zola did the same.

But if that's what we might call creative intelligence, there is another form of footballing intelligence which is just as important: analytical intelligence. If creative intelligence is the domain of artists, analytical intelligence is that of doctors and lawyers. It's the ability to assess and analyse a situation, then come up with the right reaction.

Imagine a trauma ward in a hospital. A patient is wheeled in, clearly in a critical condition. He is bleeding from several places, there is severe bruising on his neck and shoulders, his heart-rate is out of control and he is having trouble breathing. Would you know what to do? No. Neither would I. But a doctor would. In a short time he or she would have studied what was wrong and taken the necessary counter-measures, knowing that the slightest error could cost a human life. The doctor knows what to do thanks to a combination of experience, textbook know-how and intuition.

It's an exaggerated comparison, but a footballer is called upon to make comparable decisions during a match. He has to assess, analyse and decide in a split second. And the tools for doing this are not dissimilar to those that a doctor might use. He, too, would rely on the equivalent of textbook know-how (what his coaches have taught him), experience and intuition. To me, one of the best exemplars of footballing intelligence was Franco Baresi, the great Milan defender. I remember Paolo Di Canio writing in his autobiography that he was 'like a virtual footballer, [as if] he wasn't real, like there was a computer controlling him, shifting him around the pitch with mathematical precision'. I know what he means. Baresi's reading of the game was remarkable: he could see a situation develop and accurately predict how it would unfold.

Another player like that was Ian Rush. I know that he had a disappointing time in Italy (although his year at Juventus was nowhere near as disastrous as some people have made out), but he was one of those players who might have popped out of a footballing textbook. His runs and movement as a striker were exceptional. No movement was wasted, everything had a purpose. And his ability to read the game, to anticipate where the ball and the opponents would go made him a joy to watch.

You cannot divorce this kind of intelligence from the

team context: you can't think in terms of what *you* are going to do, you have to consider the impact it will have on the other twenty-one players on the pitch, all of whom are, presumably, thinking footballers too. This adds an extra layer of complexity. In the space of a few milliseconds, your mind has to process not just where the ball is and where it's going, but also where the other players will go, *and* figure out the best way to react. I know it's a cliché, but when you stop to think about how much information you have to process in a fraction of a second, you realize what an amazing machine the human brain is.

Those are the base and sides of the quadrilateral. At the top is the truly intangible quality, the one I'll call 'balls'. It's difficult to describe, but you know when a player has it. The English also call it 'bottle'. It's confidence in your own ability. It's self-belief. It's willingness to work hard. And perhaps, most of all, it's the ability to bounce back from setbacks. Because in football, defeat and failure are your constant companions. You learn at an early age that you cannot always win. Sometimes it's your fault, sometimes it's factors beyond your control, but the simple truth is that you will get your butt kicked. And you will need the mental strength to lift yourself back up.

It's very difficult to assess a player in this department until you work with him, whether as a coach or as a teammate. There are things you only discover on the pitch. For example, there are players who 'hide' in crucial moments. They don't want to take responsibility so they won't show for a pass or they won't make a run, fearing what might happen if they receive the ball and make a mistake. And there are others who play to the crowd. If it's an ill-tempered game, they'll make a bad tackle and get themselves booked or sent off, thinking that the fans will say, 'Look at him, he wants to win so bad, he gets himself sent off!' I hope most supporters aren't fooled by players like that, but often it's tough to work out what's happening unless you're in the thick of it.

I think you could probably plot every single footballer, past or present, on the x and y axes of a graph, using this quadrilateral. Have a go. Take a little break. Grab a pen and some paper and think of your favourite footballers. Then rate them in each category. Because technique is more important, rate them out of twenty in that department, and use a one-to-ten scale for athleticism, for intelligence and 'balls'.

Now draw an x and y axis (for those who weren't paying attention in geometry class this is basically a cross). Now plot the players on the graph. If your guy has a 14 rating in technique, mark off 14 centimetres on the positive y axis (the line rising from the centre of the cross). Then mark the athleticism rating on the positive x axis (the line extending to the right of the centre of the cross). Repeat the process with the other two categories (marking the intelligence score on the line extending to the left of the centre point and the 'balls' score on the line descending from the centre point), then connect the dots. This should produce a kite-like quadrilateral. There is your player, graphically represented. And, if I'm right, I think you'll find that the bigger the quadrilateral, the better the player. (See page 423 for some examples of this.)

To be a top-flight player, with few exceptions, you need all four sides to be of a certain length. This is not to suggest that they are all equally important. In the modern game, particularly in Italy and England, maybe less so in

South America, athleticism is an absolute prerequisite. I know people joke about guys like Teddy Sheringham and Sinisa Mihailovic, saying they are slow. In England, the running joke is that 'They didn't lose their pace because they never had it.' Well, that's not true. They aren't as quick as they once were: Mihailovic is thirty-seven and Sheringham forty. But while neither was ever a potential Olympic sprinter, both were, and are, very athletic players.

'Balls' is a different issue. I can see how, if someone is athletic, skilful and understands the game, he may be able to get by, at least for a while, even though he is lacking in that department – I'm not going to name names because each case is different and, frankly, I'd be guessing. The other three factors are external: they can be more or less objectively tracked. But the 'balls' category is different. At most you can make an educated guess about how much or how little a player has in this area. But you are not in the player's mind so you cannot be sure. Still, if you think back to any footballer who enjoyed several great seasons and then – after a period out through injury, or after a change of manager, or perhaps because of something in their personal life – slowly faded away, you'll know what I'm talking about.

What happens to those players who come up short (literally) in one or more of the four categories? Generally they end up in the lower leagues. Most lack technique. Italy's Serie C and England's Leagues One and Two are full of guys who are superb athletes and very strong mentally, both in terms of 'balls' and understanding the game, but technically weak. They're the role players, the 'water-carriers', the guys with plenty of heart but not much skill, who will run themselves into the ground.

Somewhat rarer are the players who have the other qualities but are wanting athletically. For them, those qualities have to be so much bigger to make up for what they lack in pace, agility and/or strength. I think of Swansea's Lee Trundle, a gifted player, but a guy whose physical limitations mean he will probably never play top-flight football.

In the past, there were probably more players like him but, as we know, athleticism has become a key component of modern football. If you're not quick, if you can't last ninety minutes or if you constantly get knocked off the ball, you can't play at the highest level, no matter the size of your footballing brain or how skilful you are on the ball.

Some people see this as a shame. Certainly, in Spain and South America they lament the fact that the physical aspect of football has become so important. They see themselves as purists, and argue that technique and creativity should be the foundation on which football is built, while athleticism should complement but never stifle them. In England, this is less of an issue because in the past athleticism was always a key ingredient, often at the expense of technique. But in Italy and other Latin countries it is a more recent phenomenon.

I remember reading an interview with Pep Guardiola, the former Barcelona midfielder, in which he said there would be no place for him in the modern game: 'If I were a twenty-year-old at Barcelona today, I would never make it as a professional. At best I'd be playing in the third division,' he said. 'What can you do? I am not quick, I never had the stamina to run for ninety minutes like central midfielders have to do today. I am not good in the air, I am not physically strong . . . All I could do is pass the ball fairly well . . .'

While I have tried to forget about Guardiola (after all, he was pulling the strings for the Barcelona side that beat my Sampdoria in the 1992 European Cup final at Wembley), I do remember a thing or two – especially that, in his prime, he was one of the most influential midfielders in the world. While he is no doubt exaggerating his athletic deficiencies, I know what he means. He had a superb football brain and the skills to execute, but he was neither strong, quick nor mobile. And I can see how today's scouts or youth coaches might look at him and conclude that, unless they could graft his brain and feet on to another player, there would be no room for him at the top. Partly, this is a result of the way football has gone: the pace of the game has increased, as have the physical demands. When you don't have the ball, all eleven men have to defend – you can't have 'passengers'.

There is a third category of player, those who have 'balls' as well as all the athletic and technical skills but are found wanting in terms of understanding the game. They don't grasp tactics or teamwork, either because they view themselves as 'anarchists', putting themselves ahead of the team, or simply because they're not very clever. I am not talking about guys like Edmundo, Paul Gascoigne or George Best. Their careers may have been cut short, but if they were mentally deficient they would never have made it to the top in the first place. I'm talking about guys you've never heard of, the ones who were simply shut out in their teens when it became clear they'd never make it. Ask most professionals and they'll be able to name one or two guys they played with as kids who fell by the wayside because they couldn't handle the mental aspect. Those cases are further evidence to me that football is played first and foremost with your brain, and the heart comes a close second. Without a big heart, you won't get through the tough moments. But without a brain to channel what your heart tells you, you won't get anywhere.

Chapter Three

Little Soldiers Following Orders: How I Did It

To some degree we can list the attributes of a successful footballer: technical, tactical, athletic and temperamental. The trick is to identify a child's potential and help him reach it. This is where, in many ways, Italian and English football truly diverge. On the one hand, you want to begin working with kids at an early age, so that you can instil in them the correct habits. On the other, if you're not careful, you will regiment them and lose the 'street football' quality that everyone seems to agree is so important.

'You have to get the practice ethic into the kids as early as you can,' says Sir Alex. 'It helps that some clubs are dealing with kids as young as seven. They are trying to create a foundation through basic technical skills and practice. You have to have that first. It's like if someone gives you a bag of tools and there are only a few tools in it. Even if you are a trained electrician or plumber, but you only have one hammer and a few screws in your toolbag, there isn't much you can do. What we at United believe in is getting kids who have a full bag of tools before they come to us at sixteen. Then it's up to the coaches to put the football part into it, the tactics and all that.'

Sir Alex believes that young children should be given the full range of tools – physical and technical – with the exception of the tactical, results-oriented aspects of the game, which will come later. You can teach a twelve-year-old to pass, control and shoot the ball, while also teaching him how to improve his stamina, flexibility and quickness. There are specific drills you can do that replicate the qualities that emerge in 'street football'. I suppose it's the difference between IVF treatment and making babies in the old-fashioned way. In the latter, it happens naturally and without supervision, in the former it takes place in a lab, under very controlled circumstances.

Juventus boss Fabio Capello agrees that the tactical aspects of the game should be kept well away from pre-teens: 'I was in charge of Milan's youth set-up for six years, so I think I know what the Italian approach to kids is,' he says. 'They go to these "football schools", which are cropping up all over the place. Originally they used to take you from the age of twelve, now they've got eight-year-olds. I have big reservations about the methods of many of them. At eight or even twelve, you should be focusing on two things: having fun and improving your technique. The other aspects can come later. What's the point of trying to build up the fitness of a ten-year-old if his body is still growing? And what's the point of cluttering his mind with tactical notions and formations? All you're doing is stifling his ability to express himself.'

Sadly, Capello's view is all too often ignored in Italy. Young kids are taught to win by any means. And in England, Sir Alex's vision of teenagers who join academies with 'all the tools' is similarly quite rare.

I think back to my own youth and weigh up my

experience against the words of Capello and Sir Alex. I started playing organized football at thirteen, when I joined Pizzighettone, a semi-professional club that ran some youth teams. Before that, I played at my local 'oratorio', one of the Catholic community centres that are dotted all over Italy.

At the oratorio, Don Angelo, a football-loving priest, supervised our games. He wasn't a coach, just a man who loved the game, with the special gift of knowing how to relate to kids and sort out the squabbles. Come to think of it, he was the only adult I worked with as a boy to whom teaching values was more important than teaching football.

I remember one day when he was refereeing a game and a player on the opposing team passed the ball back to the goalkeeper, who slipped and fell over. All he could do was lie on the ground and watch the ball roll past him into the back of the net. I was ten and I suppose I had an undeveloped sense of right and wrong, but it seemed unfair that the goal should stand. The next time the ball was in our area, I handled it blatantly, trying intentionally to give away a penalty. It was my way of levelling things.

Don Angelo saw it rather differently. He rushed over, picked up the ball and began to lecture me. I can still see his finger wagging in my face. 'No! We don't do things like that!' he said. 'I know why you did it. You didn't think the previous goal should stand and you wanted to even things up. You think this is sportsmanship? This isn't sportsmanship. Sportsmanship is accepting what happens on the pitch, whether it's to your advantage or disadvantage . . .'

To this day, it's probably the only 'life lesson' I was explicitly taught on a football pitch (apart from the ones

I picked up indirectly). Don Angelo illustrated how, in life, when things happen that are beyond your control, you have to accept them and move on. You can't right a wrong by committing another wrong. It's not the most profound message, but it stuck with me all these years because such moments were rare. Most of the time, the only guidance we received had to do with things like marking opponents and springing the offside trap.

It was at Pizzighettone that I had my first real coaching experience. I was thirteen and most kids, even back then, entered organized football at an earlier age. Indeed, while I was joining my first 'real' club just down the road from my home, my good friend Roberto Mancini was moving two hundred miles from his native Jesi, on the Adriatic coast, to Bologna. The club had scouted him at an early age (he always was a bit of an *enfant prodige*) and signed him up.

My first coach was Franco Cistriani, a true footballing purist, an aesthete who revered talent and technique above all else. It probably had a lot to do with the fact that he taught literature at the local college and thus had a deep love of the arts. He spent his mornings teaching his students to appreciate the beauty of great literature and his afternoons teaching his young players to create beauty in football. He was the kind of figure you don't seem to find in youth football now, particularly in Italy, let alone professional football: he epitomized the saying 'It's not about winning or losing, it's about how you play the game.' And he wanted us to play good football above all else. Indeed, I think the result really didn't matter to him. What mattered was passing, movement, control . . . all the technical elements that constituted his idea of aesthetic football.

As my first proper football coach he had a profound influence on me. Until then, playing with friends at the *oratorio* or in the courtyard by my house, I had always felt free to try things, to experiment. I was unafraid to fail, not because I didn't care about success – I have always been competitive – but because I wanted to find new ways to win. In fact, perhaps this was why I became a well-rounded player, who was fairly useful at most things rather than being outstanding in one area and wanting in others. I was never the fastest, the strongest, or the most skilful but I could do most things reasonably well and I was eager to test myself. Not coincidentally I played a variety of positions, from central midfield to winger to striker.

Had my first experience of organized football been with a different coach, one who didn't encourage technique and good football but instead put results above all else, I might have become a different player – I might even have been turned off the game entirely. Cistriani allowed me to develop in my own way, within his vision of football, which I believe was the right one, particularly for kids. Had he been obsessed with winning, he might have made me focus on my strengths, rather than work on my weaknesses. Or he might have taught me to play safe, do just enough to succeed, to pace myself, conserve energy . . . all of which play an important part in football but which, frankly, have no place in a thirteen-year-old's world.

Although I scored a fair few goals, my career at Pizzighettone was brief. This was because the local chapter of the Italian FA ruled that I was ineligible for my age group. No, it's not what you think – I wasn't a brawny thirteen-year-old running around in the under-nines. In fact, I was too young . . . by nine days. You see, I was born on 9 July and, according to the Italian footballing bureaucracy, the cut-off date for each age group is 30 June. I should have been playing in a younger age group, but since there was no younger age group, I was put in the next youngest. Which – as it turned out – was illegal.

Some people think Italians are easy-going and have a relaxed attitude towards rules and regulations. Whatever the case may be in other areas, it certainly does not apply to football. I was told I was ineligible to play for Pizzighettone. I stuck around, training with the club but not allowed to play, even though I could obviously hold my own. I begged and pleaded, but the local chapter of the Italian FA were inflexible. Not only could I not play, I could not move to another club. Not until the season was over. After a whole year on the sidelines, I moved to Cremonese.

From a footballing perspective, the move made sense. The man in charge of the academy at Cremonese was Guido Settembrino, a legendary figure in Italian youth football. It was he who had discovered Franco Baresi and his brother Beppe a few years earlier. In fact – if you'll pardon a brief digression – the Baresi brothers' experience shows just how difficult the task of scouting and youth development can be. Four years earlier, in 1974, Settembrino had taken them to Inter for a trial. Franco was fourteen, Beppe sixteen. In one of the most bone-headed moves ever, Inter took Beppe but rejected Franco, suggesting that he was too small and weak ever to become a professional footballer. You probably know what happened next. Franco Baresi went across the street to AC

Milan and captained the club for nearly twenty years, shattering records and establishing himself as one of the greatest defenders in the history of the game. It's easy now to deride Inter for failing to spot Franco Baresi's potential. To me, however, it's simply a reminder of how tough judging kids can be.

Anyway, as I embarked on my first season with Settembrino, Franco Baresi was winning his first Serie A total with Milan at just eighteen. It was evident to all of us that we were working with a special coach. And it's a good thing we realized that, because if we hadn't we might not have put up with his drill-sergeant ways. Settembrino was an old-school disciplinarian – he would not have looked out of place alongside Lou Gosset Jr in *An Officer and a Gentleman*.

We were kids and yet he treated us like, well, soldiers. Discipline was essential. If your shoes were untied, if your jersey wasn't tucked in, if you were late for training, if you didn't pay attention . . . All those things were grounds for a fine. And the fines weren't symbolic: it was a thousand lire each time, which was around fifty pence – quite a lot of money to a fourteen-year-old kid in 1978.

But the fines weren't just for things like sloppiness and tardiness. No, he fined us if we misplaced a pass or mis-controlled a ball. It may have seemed harsh, but it forced us to remain concentrated and disciplined. He wasn't try-ing to turn hyperactive fourteen-year-olds into soldiers: rather, he prepared us for the life of a professional footballer, at least in Italy. Which, then as now, is about discipline, on and off the pitch. And it was a case of sink or swim. I saw some players, several of whom were very gifted, drop out as soon as he cracked the whip. They just wanted to play football: rules and regulations didn't suit them.

Others thrived in Settembrino's hands. I saw kids who blossomed, thanks to the structure, because Settembrino's rules made us feel part of a group, a unit. They wiped out differences: everyone was treated the same. And they made us feel special, giving us a confidence and a toughness we would carry with us for the rest of our footballing lives. Indeed, every time we stepped on to the pitch we took with us a self-belief and a faith in each other that bordered on swaggering.

Settembrino's 'boot-camp' complemented my previous experience with Cistriani. The structure and work ethic I learned from Settembrino dovetailed nicely with the freedom and technique emphasized at Pizzighettone. I do wonder sometimes what might have happened if the timeline had been reversed and I'd started out under Settembrino's regime. Would I have stuck it? Would I have become a different type of player? By the time I joined Settembrino I had developed enough on my own that his regimen did not stifle my identity as a footballer, but instead strengthened my self-belief. I am not sure this would have been so if I had only ever worked with coaches like him.

My next coach in many ways completed me, because he represented the middle ground between Cistriani and Settembrino. Emiliano Mondonico is now a veteran Serie A manager, with over twenty-five years' experience. Back then, however, he was a recently retired thirty-two-year-old striker, fresh from the Italian FA's coaching academy at Coverciano. When Cremonese's manager was sacked, Settembrino took charge of the first team and Mondonico came in to coach the kids.

In many ways it was an emotional return. Mondonico was something of a local hero in Cremona. It was there that he started his career and it was there that he returned. He was a favourite of the president, Domenico Luzzara, a man who had suffered a deep personal tragedy when his son died in a car accident and, perhaps as a result, Luzzara became a father figure to Mondonico.

As a player, Mondonico had been the ultimate free spirit, a man for whom the phrase 'mercurial talent' could have been coined. He came of age at the time of flower-power and counter-culture, and his football reflected that. He was hugely gifted but also extremely strong-willed and undisciplined. Today you might call him a 'flawed genius', but back then he was known as Cavallo Pazzo – Crazy Horse. A player of his talent should have had a long and successful international career, but he never played for his country and mostly bounced around the middle-tier sides before he returned to Cremonese. His critics said he preferred to be a big fish in a small pond rather than test himself at the highest level. Whatever the truth, he did not seem to care what others thought.

You may reckon that a guy like that was not the best candidate to be teaching children about the game, but towards the end of his career he had realized why he had under-achieved as a footballer. He came to understand his shortcomings. And, I suppose, he wanted to give something back to the game by ensuring that the next generation did not repeat his mistakes.

He was an artist on the pitch and thus had a genuine appreciation of entertainment, technique and creativity, the whole aesthetic side of the game. But it was important to him to instil in us the values that perhaps he had lacked as a player, which prevented him reaching the top. He emphasized the importance of discipline, tactics, organization – everything that had been antithetical to him as a footballer but as a coach he embraced.

Even though we were a well-drilled and organized side, Mondonico allowed me to follow my instincts and attempt the odd bit of skill or flair, whether it was an overhead kick or a thirty-yard volley. I guess this was a legacy of the old Mondonico, the footballing genius who always preferred the difficult or intricate over the tap-in.

Teaching Skills, Not Values

I was fortunate to work with all those men, Don Angelo, Cistriani, Settembrino and Mondonico. They gave me an excellent footballing education and they weren't merely expert coaches: they were good men and great role models. Still, it strikes me that very little of my football education had anything to do with teaching – or even discussing – values such as sportsmanship or fairness. We hardly broached the concept of football as a 'game', as something to celebrate. It was as if there was a basic assumption that we were there to win, otherwise there was no point. Everything we did followed from that.

Which brings me to one of the biggest and most obvious topics: the issue of diving, cheating, simulation, gamesmanship, doing something to get an edge. It's a seminal difference between England and Italy, much more complex than it appears, and attitudes to it have been evolving in both countries. One thing I want to make clear is that, when I was growing up, I was *never* encouraged to fall over at the slightest contact or, worse, take a dive when there was no contact at all. Perhaps others are taught to do this, I don't know, but it was never taught or encouraged at the clubs for which I played.

Yet I picked things up in subtle ways. Mondonico, for example, was a free spirit, but he wanted to win too. He used to join in our five-a-sides and squad scrimmages and, typically, as coaches often do, he refereed while he played. Invariably, if his team was losing or the score was tied at the end of training, he would fall over in the box and award himself a penalty. It happened countless times. Sometimes he did it lightheartedly, at others he was brutally serious. They say actions speak louder than words and, to me, these incidents were eloquent. Regardless of whether he was smiling when he awarded himself the penalty or whether he pretended he had really been fouled, the message was the same: he hated to lose and was prepared to do whatever it took to win. We all saw it and took it on board. And in that sense, it was part of our footballing education.

Back then, many did not view such tricks for what they are: cheating. They were seen as clever or, as we say in Italy, 'furbo'. 'Fare il furbo' – 'being clever' – has negative connotations, but it's an accepted part of the game, something which cannot be eradicated. It just happens. When an opponent won a penalty against us by diving or making a meal of slight contact, the attitude among players and coaches wasn't to condemn him for cheating but to point the finger at our own defenders for allowing it to happen. 'He was clever!' we were told. 'He tricked you and he tricked the referee. Next time, you boys at the back have to be more careful. Don't give him the chance to do something like that again!' We were engaging in footballing realpolitik. Bad things happen; it's up to you not to allow it.

Consider this analogy. You park your expensive car in a dangerous part of town and leave it unlocked, with the keys in the ignition. It gets stolen. Who's to blame? The thief who took your car or you for having given him the opportunity to steal it? Ethically, of course, the thief is to blame. You should be able to leave your property unattended without having to worry about it. You have done nothing wrong. Yet in the real world, it doesn't work that way. Sure, the thief is to blame. But try going to the local police station to report your car stolen and tell them you left it unattended in a dodgy neighbourhood with the keys in plain sight. If they're polite, they'll wait until you've left before exploding into laughter. And if they're not, they'll laugh in your face. The assumption is that someone will *always* be willing to steal your car if you give them the opportunity. If you put yourself into a situation where you can be harmed, well, you'll get no more sympathy than the limbless man who used to juggle chainsaws.

Of course, when it comes to the real world, the English are no more naïve than the Italians. They don't run unnecessary risks: they don't juggle chainsaws and, if they park in dubious areas, they don't leave their keys in the car. Yet the Italians take the 'real world' with them on to the pitch at youth level, while in England there seems to be – at least where the kids are concerned – a greater sense that the 'game' is just that: a game. It's a game where kids have fun and – directly or indirectly – learn a thing or two about sporting values.

In Italy, the game is 'real' even among ten-year-olds.

And because it's real, the rewards go to the winners, not necessarily to the nice guys or those who play by the rules. It mirrors life: those at the top are generally winners but not always paragons of virtue. English kids – traditionally – have been spared that little life lesson, the notion that you can get to the top by cheating as long as you don't get caught. Italians, however, are taught that many succeed by cheating, which is why they have to be careful not to be cheated themselves.

I suppose each system has its merits, though I know which one I prefer. The Italian system teaches kids to protect themselves. The English system doesn't accept cheating as inevitable, but condemns it as something to be eradicated. In that sense, English football strives for Utopia, while Italian football is rooted in realism – which is one step away from cynicism.

Diving was another weapon in the strikers' arsenal. In fact, it was a necessary weapon. Away from the penalty box, we would be kicked, elbowed and shoved with impunity, but in and around the area the balance of power shifted back to the striker who, whether by fair means or foul, could win a penalty or – and this was the acme of cleverness – get his opponent sent off.

It's not much of an example of sportsmanship. In fact, it ignores sportsmanship, placing the end-product, the result, above everything else. I think this attitude stems from the people who coach youth football in Italy. Too many don't do it for the satisfaction of teaching kids (they probably don't see themselves as teachers), they do it because they are personally ambitious. They want to win trophies and championships, perhaps move up the coaching ranks to professional football. They measure their worth as coaches by the league table at the end of the season. It's not that they don't care about the personal development of the kids, they just don't view it as part of their job. In their experience, values are something the kids should learn from their parents, not from a football coach. Their job is not pedagogical. It is to do one thing and do it well: teach the kids to be good footballers.

'In Italy at youth level you learn to be clever and tactically savvy,' says Marcello Lippi. 'You play on Saturday and spend the whole week preparing for that one game. We are obsessed with results. It's not like that in other countries. Elsewhere, they worry about playing and improving. Results are secondary.'

Of course, there is a flipside. Because we care more about the results than we do about the football, we are good at winning. Our emphasis on tactics makes us tough to beat at any level, and our teams are usually well disciplined and organized. 'We Italians are Latins, but we're a certain type of Latin, more like the Argentines than, say, the Spanish, French or Brazilian,' says Lippi. 'We're tough, but we're also technically gifted. But, most of all, we are the most tactically evolved nation in the world. We have a versatility that nobody else comes close to, anywhere in the world.'

You only have to look at the results in youth competition to see that Lippi is right. Italy have won five of the last ten European Under-21 championships. (And, back in 1986, we were beaten finalists, but I don't really like to think about it too much since I was on that team, which lost to Spain on penalties. Contrast that with England, who have failed to reach even the semi-finals in the last twenty years. It's a similar story at Under-19 level.

In the last ten European Championships, Italy have reached the final three times, England just once, in 2005.

Youth competitions are great, but there is a downside. Richard Hughes, who played in Atalanta's youth ranks until he was seventeen before moving to Arsenal in 1996, highlights the knock-on effect of Italy's results-driven attitude to the youth game.

'In Italy, when I started and was coached by my dad, it was all about having fun,' he says. 'Then I joined Atalanta when I was ten and things began to change year after year. By the time I left, I really did not enjoy my football any more. What drove the point home was my final year. I remember working really hard in training all week, spending every free moment on football and then, come Saturday, I would never play, because there were guys who were a year older than me and I was told that my chance would come. And it struck me that it was like a job, but one which gave me no real satisfaction. It was only after moving to Arsenal that I started to love football again.'

José Mourinho, as always, doesn't mince his words when assessing the way young footballers are formed in England: 'I felt when I arrived at Chelsea that the way we look to the formation [of young players] was not the correct way,' he says. 'And I guess Chelsea is no different from other clubs. When you look to the youth football in England you don't find many talented players. You look to United, Arsenal, Liverpool and the good young players are more from abroad. You have to go abroad because there is not a lot of talent here.'

Of course, the results aren't lost on the English FA, which has tried, to its credit, to take steps to improve them. There has been a shift away from the pedagogical aspects of youth football towards emulating the professionals. 'In the last few years things have been changing,' says Andy Cale, head of player development at the FA. 'We had always believed in the philosophy that the best way to teach kids was through values and personal development. As a philosophy, it's undoubtedly correct, but the nature of football is such that, above all, you want to win. And this is also because the structure of youth football in this country has changed. Now many clubs have academies, and they invest a lot of money to maintain them, which means that certain clubs emphasize the importance of winning, even at youth level.'

English youth football was given a thorough makeover in the mid-1990s and now we are starting to see the effects. The teaching-oriented sporting approach of the past has been slowly phased out in favour of a more professional way of doing things.

'In England, they always had more fair play and that's great,' says Marcel Desailly. 'But they also had more flaws, more phobias, probably because most English players come from uneducated lower-class backgrounds. They aren't as conscious of the importance of what they're doing. True, on the pitch they'll run their heart out and respect their opponent. But off the pitch they don't seem to realize that, even as a teenager, their behaviour will impact on their future. And so they behave the way they do. The Italian youngster is already a professional. He's serious, well prepared, he pays attention to what he eats and drinks . . .'

And that is pretty much the crux of the matter. In England, the traditional attitude towards youth football was ideal for the 99.9 per cent of young footballers who never turn professional, but for those who wanted to make a living out of the sport, it was wrong – and the FA set out to turn things round.

Poor Predictor of Future Performance: Youth Football

It's impossible to talk about football in England without looking at Charles Hughes, the man behind what the rest of the world thinks of when they think of 'English football'. He is a controversial figure because many of his ideas, particularly in tactical terms (for example, that one should never need more than three passes to shoot on goal, which inevitably led to the long-ball game), have largely been discredited.

Hughes was a firm believer in the notion that gifted young players should train with players of equal ability. Thus, he set up the original Centres of Excellence, dotted around the country with the main one at Lilleshall, a sort of super-lab for the best and brightest. It was there that the likes of Steven Gerrard, Michael Owen and Sol Campbell learned their trade. The concept, in some ways, was similar to the sports academies in Eastern Europe, which yielded tremendous results. Yet there were a few fundamental problems.

'Hughes did many great things, but in his philosophy there was no room for ex-players,' says John Barnwell, chairman of the League Managers' Association. 'For him, coaches had to be teachers. Now, obviously, there aren't many ex-footballers who go on to become schoolteachers. And so, as a result, you had people who never played the game working with kids. There was lots of theory and not much practice. That's why we felt the FA had to change.'

Given the influence of schoolteachers it's not surprising that youth football in England was more values- than results-driven, with all that that implies. The amateur set-up worked for amateur athletes. And while kids are obviously not professionals, when you're dealing with the best and brightest, you're dealing with future professionals. You simply can't treat them as you would 'normal' kids – or not if you want to create solid professionals. The seminal change came in 1996, with Howard Wilkinson's 'White Paper'. Wilkinson, too, gets stick sometimes for being too 'old school', yet his White Paper was revolutionary in bringing English youth football up to speed with the rest of Europe: Lilleshall was closed and the regional centres were replaced with academies run directly by the clubs with FA supervision. Some take kids as young as seven and the FA keeps a close eye on them, with periodic inspections and a long list of mandatory standards and prerequisites. The idea is to create an environment to instil in kids the technical and behavioural skills that will serve them well once they become professionals.

The changes were not only motivated by the belief that they would produce better players. As so often happens, a number of other factors made this possible. Without them, it's unlikely that Wilkinson would have had the power to push through his restructuring.

'They realized that the old system was, first of all, very expensive to run,' explains Andy Cale, 'and, with Lilleshall, some kids did not want to go, or their parents did not want them to move so far away for two years. And then there is the fact that with the new system the clubs are more involved in the development of the player . . . or, at least, they can see him up close.' This last factor is very important. Clubs cannot sign fourteen-year-olds on a permanent contract. But they prefer to have them around, partly to oversee their development and partly to create a bond with the individual so that when he's old enough he'll sign professional terms. This creates a closer identification between young player and club, which engenders professionalism.

'When I was growing up, nobody taught me how to be a professional,' says Ray Wilkins. 'And even as an adult, although I was playing for the biggest, most important club in England, Manchester United, I only learned what it means to be a professional after I moved to Milan at the age of twenty-seven. That's where academies can really make a difference, teaching the importance of things such as diet, for example. When I was a young player at Chelsea, our pre-match meal was a big T-bone steak and a whole loaf of bread. That's unthinkable today.

'And when I think of my time at Milan, the players all looked like bankers or lawyers, even the youth-team players,' he adds. 'They were all very serious. They lived for football, it was their job and they paid attention to every detail. England was the opposite. And I will admit that I didn't behave professionally either. If we were playing on a Saturday, I'd have no qualms about going out on Friday night, for example. And our attitude to alcohol, of course, was totally different. I'll never forget how, in my first few months at Milan, there were always half-full bottles of wine left on the table at the end of a meal. In England that would have been unthinkable . . .

You don't leave alcohol, you drink it to the last drop.'

The FA's changes in youth development are still very much a work-in-progress. One of the problems is that, increasingly, youth academies are judged by results in the short-term as much as they are by the type of adult players they produce. Also, two parallel shifts are taking place. The first, of course, is from the pedagogical/sporting model to the more professional/organized model. The other is a shift in style, from the physical, direct game championed by Charles Hughes to a more technical approach, based on a short-passing game. 'For years, at every age level, we would play the biggest and strongest kids because it suited our playing style,' says Cale. 'But then we realized that they weren't improving technically and, as they got older, they found themselves playing against opponents who were just as big and strong but were far better on the ball. So for a while we focused on the boys who were technically gifted, without worrying about size. The problem is that, at that age, there is a huge difference in size between the kids. And they might have been technical but against boys who were twice as big there wasn't much they could do. So they'd suffer heavy defeats, which did their confidence no good. So, we've tried to find a middle ground, identifying kids who had size and the potential to improve technique. And, at the same time, we looked for gifted kids who we believed would fill out and grow in terms of size and strength.'

Cale makes an excellent point. At youth level, particularly the twelve-to-sixteen age group, there is a tremendous trade-off between size, strength and athleticism on one hand and technique on the other. The simple truth is that results in those age groups are often meaningless in terms of predicting future success as a footballer.

Ever heard of Ghana's Daniel Addo? How about Oman's Mohamed Kathiri? No? Scotland's James Will? Didn't think so. Or, if you have, you know a heck of a lot about football. Those three guys were voted player of the tournament at the FIFA Under-17 World Championship in 1995, 1993 and 1989 respectively. Now they should all be in the prime of their career, but I think it's safe to say none has lived up to the promise he showed at sixteen.

It's only when I look at the last three winners that I recognize the names. Landon Donovan, winner in 1999, played in the 2002 World Cup and is probably the best United States player. France's Florent Sinama Pongolle, who won in 2001, is on Liverpool's books and, while he hasn't been a regular, could yet establish himself. And, of course, the 2003 winner looks like a budding superstar: it's Arsenal's Cesc Fabregas.

I can't help but notice, too, how few youngsters go on to establish themselves as top-drawer players. I've looked over the winning teams' squad lists and searched for familiar names. In 1997 Brazil featured Matuzalem and Ronaldinho; two years later they were led by Adriano. What about all the others? I did a bit of research on the 2001 winners, France. Those boys are all around twenty-one now and should be breaking into top-flight sides. Yet of the eighteen-strong French squad, only nine players are with top-division teams, and, of those, only five or six are regulars. The most famous, as of 2005–06, are probably Sinama Pongolle, Lyon's Jeremie Berthod, Antony Le Tallec, on loan at Sunderland, and Mourad Meghni, on loan at Sochaux.

This suggests that results alone can be misleading when related to kids who are still growing. For every Cesc Fabregas, there are plenty of James Willses. If this is true worldwide it's especially so in England, where the physical nature of the game traditionally penalized the more gifted kids. 'Traditionally we were aggressive and physical, while others were technically better,' says David Platt, former coach of the English Under-21 side. 'The other countries noticed and started getting more physical. We realized this too, and tried to get more technical. The problem is that it's far easier to teach kids how to be physical than it is to teach them technique. And that's why it will take time for us to reach the level of other nations.'

It's encouraging for English football that there is a definite will to change and improve after a long period of isolationism, where many believed there was little to be learned from other countries. People are starting to look not only to Europe but all over the world. 'Now that football is a global phenomenon, we can't just think in terms of our continent,' says Barnwell. 'For example, we focus on Europe, particularly on France and Clairefontaine, and we don't pay much attention to what they do in South America. And yet the South Americans have had enormous success, probably more than the Europeans. Why? Because they looked to Europe and incorporated European ideas into their own footballing culture.'

He's right. There's always more to learn. And people are trying new and different things. Think of Simon Clifford, owner of non-league Garforth Town. His football schools around the country have adopted Brazilian training techniques, which, he believes, improve elements such as touch and control. It can only be positive for the English game. One thing I've learned in my two and a half years of research is that diversity – of playing styles, training techniques, tactical systems – is at the heart of footballing success. And the FA's academy system, which is largely decentralized, will hopefully allow it to surface.

There is no understating how important the academy system may be to English football: for better or worse it represented a seminal change, one that is slowly undoing the old order. England is becoming more like the rest of Europe, which not everyone sees as positive. 'Now that we have academies, too many players feel they've already made it at a young age,' says Wilkins. 'When I was their age I would be cleaning the boots of the first-team. They were my role models, and I tried to learn from them as much as I could. Today you don't see that kind of respect from the young players. They think everything is owed to them. And I don't like that.'

Maybe Wilkins is just being a grumpy old pro. But perhaps he has a point. There is no question that the new generation of English footballers – from Michael Owen to Frank Lampard, David Beckham to Steven Gerrard – are real athletes who, in terms of professionalism, are equal to their counterparts in Italy and elsewhere. The risk, as Wilkins points out, is that they have not only learned foreign virtues, such as professionalism, they have picked up a few foreign vices along the way.

It's the Wind, Stupid! (Not the Cold . . .)

During the course of my research I took advantage of the

opportunity to compare views with many of the greatest coaches in football today. And one of the things I realized was that you can build the greatest youth academy and have the best scouts fill it with the best players. You can get the best coaches, schooled in the best training methods and, if you're really powerful, you can also make sure your pupils have the best influences outside football. You can isolate your academy, so that they think only of football and are blissfully unaware of distractions such as alcohol, money or sex. But there is one thing that nobody – not even José Mourinho – can control: the weather.

There is no escaping that. If you want to train seriously, you have to do it outdoors, which means you are at the mercy of the climate. Anything other than a temperate day – say, twelve to twenty degrees with clear skies and no more than a light breeze – will affect your work. An old stereotype maintains that players from warmer climates are naturally more technically gifted because they spend more time outdoors, playing with the ball. It's often used to explain Australia's dominance over England in rugby. 'It's all about the climate,' says Fabio Capello. 'I had a long discussion about it when I went to Scotland to see Andy Roxburgh. I worked with a Scottish youth side and had them do the same drills I would do in Italy. I realized that, between the wind, the rain, the cold, there was no way they could do it. How can you possibly teach somebody anything in those conditions? To me, it's pretty obvious and it explains why Brazilians are more technical than Europeans and, in Italy, the further south you go the more technical they are. You train better in good weather and the only way to become good is to train!'

I don't entirely accept this north/south divide of talent.

Even within Italy, while it's true that the likes of Gianfranco Zola (Sardinia), Francesco Totti (Rome) and Antonio Cassano (Puglia) were raised in the south, it's equally true that Alessandro Del Piero (Padova), Roberto Baggio (Vicenza) and Gianni Rivera (Alessandria) are from the north, and they're no less gifted or creative. When I look at England, for every talented 'southerner' like Glenn Hoddle I can think of several gifted 'northerners', like Wayne Rooney or Paul Gascoigne. Holland is a northern country and yet the Dutch may be one of the most technically gifted nations in the world, both in terms of skill and creativity. The average temperatures in Holland are not very different from England's, so why do they produce such different footballers?

I grew up in Cremona, in the north of Italy, which can be very cold and foggy in winter. Indeed, in Italy we talk about the 'famous London fog', a literary and journalistic stereotype. Well, I saw much more fog in and around my hometown than I ever saw in London. And, when I come to think of it, I remember just as many bitterly cold days in Turin as I do in England. I don't like stereotypes and clichés, especially when there is an opportunity to find the truth. Is southern England really colder and wetter than northern Italy, where I come from? I commissioned a bit of research. And what I discovered may shatter a few myths.

I looked at three English cities (London, Birmingham and Manchester) and three Italian cities (Milan, Turin and Rome) and evaluated data on average temperature, wind speed, rainfall and hours of sunshine per month. More than two-thirds of the population of each country lives within 150 miles of one of these cities, so they seemed like good samples.

The average annual temperature in the three English cities was 10°C, compared to 13.7°C in Italy. Not an enormous difference, but a noteworthy one, right? Not really. If you discount the summer months, which in footballing terms are largely irrelevant as it's the off-season, the gap narrows considerably. From September to May the average temperature in London was 9°C, which is marginally lower than in Milan (9.9°C) or Turin (9.7°C). In fact, in the three English cities, the mean for the non-summer months, 8.2°C, is only a few degrees lower than in the three Italian ones, 10.8°C. And in January and February, Milan and Turin are not merely colder than London, but colder than Manchester and Birmingham too. So, there's the temperature argument debunked.

What about rainfall? It's always raining in England, isn't it? At least, that's what we believe in Italy.

Well, we're wrong. The three English cities receive an average of 671 millimetres of precipitation. The three Italian cities had – wait for it – *867 millimetres*! That's right! It rains more in Italy – or, at least, in our sample cities. In fact, according to the data, London and Birmingham both had less rain than Rome, and Milan was far wetter than Manchester. Go figure. I guess the British Tourist Board will want access to my research.

Still, when I was going through the data I did get frustrated. The research showed clearly that there was no substantial difference in temperature and it rained more in Turin than in London. So why did it *feel* colder in London? The answer came when I looked at wind speeds. The average monthly wind speed in the three English cities was 15.3 kilometres per hour, compared to 10.3 kilometres per hour in the Italian cities. That meant that in England the wind blew some 50 per cent harder than it did in Italy. A substantial difference indeed! And if we exclude the non-footballing summer months, the gap increases. The average in Manchester, Birmingham and London is 15.6 kilometres per hour while in Milan, Turin and Rome it's just 10.1 kilometres per hour.

When I uncovered this data, I felt vindicated: it supports what I had suspected for a long time – that wind, more than any other climatic factor, influences the development of a footballer. It seems basic, it seems simplistic, but it is an absolutely *huge* factor. And it's not just something that affects young players: it has an impact on how a team trains and, therefore, how it plays, even at professional level.

Arsène Wenger shares my view on this: 'One of the first things I had to get accustomed to as soon as I arrived in England was the weather,' says the Arsenal boss. 'And I don't mean the temperature or the rain but, most of all, the wind. The wind ruins everything. It forces you to do only one type of exercise. It forces you to work on either speed or continuous movement. It's very rare that you get the chance to sit calmly and work on technique or on tactics. You have to keep the players moving, otherwise they get cold. And this is something which begins way back when they are children.'

The wind affects everything. You can be the most technical footballer in the world – you can be Zidane and Maradona rolled into one – but if a fierce wind is blowing, you won't be able to do any meaningful work with the ball in the air, whether it's volleying practice, heading or keepy-uppy. Even any kind of passing over ten or twenty feet becomes pointless when it's windy. And it's not just down to the way the wind affects the flight of the ball. No. As Wenger points out, the wind makes everything feel colder. You don't want to do a shooting drill or individual ballwork in which players spend lots of time standing around. You want to keep them moving so that their muscles stay loose and they're warm, which means doing drills at pace or running scrimmages. That isn't a bad thing, but it does mean it's harder to work on individual technique.

'If you want to work on technique, you need to have the right conditions to do so,' says Ray Wilkins. 'Almost all my memories of training I did as a boy are associated with intense cold and a fierce wind. I don't know why, but I don't remember any sunny training sessions, though, obviously, there would have been some. It's something I see now as a coach. When it's windy, everything changes. If you want to coach, you need to communicate, and to communicate something to a player, you need to calculate where the wind is coming from and make sure it's behind you, otherwise he won't hear a thing. It's obvious that, in those conditions, it's a lot easier and maybe more logical too, to hand out bibs, stick two cones on the pitch and play an eight-a-side.'

Wilkins's point also illlustrates why it's tougher to do tactical work in England. I have clear memories of standing on a training pitch in Italy as the coaches explained what they wanted us to do tactically in excruciating detail. We would play for about thirty seconds, then everything would stop and they would explain it again if somebody made a mistake or didn't make a crisp enough run. All of this, of course, was in addition to the time we spent in front of the blackboard.

This type of tactical work gave us a solid base in terms of movement and reading the game. It enabled us to learn a variety of tactical systems, both how to implement them and how to react when our opponents adopted a certain formation. In England the wind makes it impossible to replicate that kind of work.

Does it explain why, generally, Italian players have better individual technique than their English counterparts and why in Italy we spend much more time on tactics? No. Or, rather, not on its own. But it's certainly a factor, with the cultural, social and historic factors we looked at.

There is a danger, I think, in putting too much weight on a single factor. For example, the wind makes conditions colder, which explains why English football is usually played at a faster pace than the Italian game. Fine. But how do you explain the directness of English football? In windy conditions, does it make sense to launch high balls into the box? Is Route One football logical when you don't know which way the wind will take the ball? I would think not. I would have thought that, in windy conditions, you'd want to keep the ball on the deck.

The point is that we often mistake cause and effect. We look for links and explanations that, sometimes, aren't there, such as temperature and rainfall. Wind conditions are another issue. More than any other climatic factor, they determine what kind of players are produced and their characteristics, both technical and tactical.

Chapter Four

Two Boxers

Imagine two amateur boxers, each aspiring to turn professional one day. Boxer A is aggressive and direct. His stance isn't dictated by the need to defend himself; rather, it's a point of attack. He keeps his gloves low or wide or forward, depending on how he plans to land his next blow. Because that's what it's all about: pummelling the opponent. And if he gets hit too, so be it. The ability to withstand punishment is, after all, a mark of pride. It's about being the last man standing and giving everything you have. Otherwise, what fun is it? What's the point of doing it at less than full throttle?

Boxer B sees it as a question of survival. For him, too, it's about being the last man standing, which is precisely why he wants to make sure he's covered and his guard is high at all times. He knows that, as long as he is on his feet and has the necessary energy, he has a chance to deliver the knockout blow. That's why he's patient. He's in no rush to win. Staying alive is enough for him. In the meantime, he waits for the right moment: the opponent's mistake, the one glimpse of daylight that affords him the chance to land his blow. He knows all about *yin* and *yang*, about strike and counterstrike, about using the opponent's force to his advantage.

Boxer A is fearless. His sport may one day become his livelihood, but he knows that defeat is part of the game and he has learned to accept it. As long as he gives everything he has in the ring, he can live with defeat, because he knows that most likely he will fight again. And, even if he doesn't, well, it's only a sport. He doesn't worry about his opponent or what he's going to do. Why should he? His opponent, like him, is just another fighter. And if he's stronger than his adversary, he will win.

Boxer B is congenitally insecure. The fear of defeat keeps him up at night. It terrifies him. He simply cannot contemplate it. He has worked so hard to become a boxer that he can't afford to slip up and see his dream of turning professional slip away. Boxing is survival, and to survive you need every edge you can find. Boxer B studies his opponent maniacally, pushes himself to the edge in training, constantly second-guessing himself. Is his strategy sound? Is he training hard enough? Does his opponent have something up his sleeve? He plays out every possible scenario before he steps into the ring. The fight is often won before the timekeeper's bell, and if he's smarter than his adversary, he will win.

If you've read this far, you've probably figured out which boxer represents English and which Italian football. I don't know enough about boxing to say whether Italian and English boxers have the same mentality as us footballers. But I do think the boxers I described reflect what the traditional Italian and English footballer would be like if they stepped into the ring. That fundamental difference in mentality manifests itself in many different ways. One of the most important aspects can be summed up in one sentence: 'To the Italian footballer, football is a job: to the English footballer, it's a game.'

'In the Italian psyche there is a certain type of nervous tension, a stupid nervous tension, which is instilled into young footballers from an early age,' says Fabio Capello. 'And the result is that, when they are on the pitch, they would rather be somewhere else. To them it's a job. It's not fun, not a game. When I was at Real Madrid, training would end and everyone would stay and eat, get a massage, go to the gym together . . . in Italy, they'll stay as long as they have to and then they'll go. We don't have this joy inside us. It's almost as if they don't like being footballers.'

José Mourinho sees it in the same way. 'You go see the Italian Under-16 team and you can see a little Maldini running around the pitch, never smiling, just tackling and being strong and disciplined,' he says. 'No tricks, no nutmegs, he just plays to win. If he has to cheat, he cheats. If he has to kick the ball into the crowd, he kicks the ball into the crowd. If the manager has to put in a defender in the last minute, he does it. You have to win, you are taught to win. Here in England, on the other hand, there is much more emotion. This is part of their culture, this is what they want. They want to play. But, in other countries, we want to win. That's the difference.'

It follows on directly from the basic conception of football: whether it's a 'job' or a 'game'. If it's a job, the objective is simply to get the result, which is winning. It doesn't matter how it's achieved. If it's a game, the objective is to compete, to strive, to give 100 per cent effort. Not coincidentally, as anybody who has played in both countries will confirm, in England you can be a mediocre footballer, but if you run yourself into the ground and chase everything, you will always be applauded. And, if you are wonderfully skilled, but shirk the tackle and like to 'conserve energy', which is a nice way to say you're lazy, you will be criticized in England, no matter how many goals you score.

'I think here you are put under pressure if you don't fight and work hard,' says Mourinho. 'In other countries, you are criticized if you don't perform. Here a striker is criticized if he doesn't chase his opponents, in other countries he gets criticized if he doesn't score. It's about philosophy, it's about attitude, it's about what is important to the people watching.

'In Italy, if you pay five million for a striker and he scores one goal all season and that's from a penalty, he can't walk the streets . . . "Go home, you're rubbish," all that . . .' he adds. 'Here, Mateja Kezman is applauded. Here they can forgive you if you show attitude, commitment and what they think is respect for football.'

It's not just about winning, it's about competing. And if the English fan suspects you're not competing, he will turn on you. Again, without getting too philosophical, it strikes right at the heart of the game-versus-job argument. English fans want to see a game, Italian fans want to see a result. You can't have a game without maximum effort, so, if that is lacking, the English will criticize. Equally, Italian fans would argue that you can't have a result without thinking about every detail. And that's why they'll criticize both lack of results and what they perceive to be lack of attention to detail or, in a word, professionalism. Because, in Italy, it's a profession.

This has wide-ranging implications, both good and bad, for both. And, as with so many other aspects of the game, the situation is changing. While generalizing is difficult and risky – there are, obviously, plenty of exceptions to every rule – there is little question to me that this is where we should start when we look at the game in either country.

'I think Italian players have a bigger respect for the profession,' says Sir Alex. 'They also enter a system that is very professional, which has a certain discipline. And it has been that way in Italy for thirty or forty years. Clubs elsewhere are now starting to copy the Italians in that sense.'

That Sir Alex refers to it as 'the profession' rather than 'the game' makes it clear where he stands.

Football Intelligence

'Until a few years ago, the typical English footballer did not apply himself much in training,' says Tony Colbert, Arsenal's fitness coach. 'He was convinced that the training you did from Monday to Wednesday was entirely irrelevant. Only on Thursday did he really begin to work, maybe because he wanted to impress the manager ahead of the weekend. It's changing now because the new generations are beginning to understand the importance of working hard in training and the old guard is starting to disappear.'

In Italy, every training session – indeed, every moment spent at the training ground – is equally important. It's drilled into us from an early age and we believe it. To us, the notion that if you train well you will perform well on match-day is so obvious that it's automatic. We don't contemplate short-cuts, we do as we are told. And because most Italian professionals have been raised in that environment, we simply repeat what we have been taught.

In England, even at a successful club like Chelsea, it's a different story. Don't take my word for it, ask José Mourinho. 'If I don't tell the players that it's compulsory to stretch after training, they'll finish the session with shooting practice or kickabouts,' he says. 'Why? Because shooting is what puts the ball into the net and putting the ball into the net is what matters. I have players, and I'm talking about some of my very best players, who think they can play ninety minutes at maximum effort one day and, the next day, play another ninety minutes just as hard.'

Which brings us right back to the crux of the matter: game versus job. Mourinho's players love their football. They would play all day every day if they could. There is in that a purity – an innocence – which, in many ways, we don't have in Italy. Yet it can cause players to neglect the basic elements of being a footballer, such as training, discipline and, perhaps most of all, the mental side of the game. 'I keep telling my players, "You have to think the game, you have to control your emotions, it's not just about scoring goals,"' says Mourinho. 'But they play with their heart, while we [in Portugal and Italy], we play with our brains. Their game is all about heart, ours is all about brains. Football played only with the brain is not beautiful. But football played only with the heart is not successful.

'[At the end of the 2003–04] season, when I was still at Porto, I came to London to watch Chelsea play Monaco in the Champions' League semi-final,' he adds. 'At the time, there was a lot of speculation that I might be the next Chelsea manager. I ran into Gus Poyet, who knows me well from Spain, and he said to me, "If you come here, you will have a big problem. You want to think football, but they [the English players] do not want to think football." I never forgot his words because when I started pre-season training a few months later, that is exactly what I felt. Fortunately, I had some great allies in some of the foreign players like Claude Makelele, a man who knows and understands the thinking side and who knows that to be a better team you have to work every day of the week and think football.'

Mourinho may have felt he had a mountain to climb in terms of getting his team to 'think football' but he managed to bring Chelsea round to his way of thinking. And it's a credit to his players that they embraced his ideas and, ultimately, were successful. Of course, he is not the only foreign manager to have come to England and successfully implemented his ideas. Arsène Wenger and Rafa Benitez are two obvious examples.

Other foreign managers who had been successful elsewhere faced a difficult time in England, from Jozef Venglos at Aston Villa, back in the early 1990s, to Christian Gross at Tottenham and Egil Olsen at Wimbledon. Perhaps their methods weren't suited to the English game, or their clubs were in turmoil at the time, or they made crucial errors. But I think one reason is probably that the players weren't receptive to their methods, and that they failed to win them over. It was not that the players ignored their foreign managers' instructions, it's that they did not fully understand or believe in the work they were doing. Like many things, football training is more effective when you grasp why you are doing it and how it affects you. It's the difference between fully participating and going through the motions. In other words, it's not what you do, it's how you do it.

'I think, above all, it's a question of intelligence,' says Tony Colbert. 'Not preparation, but intelligence. The intelligent player learns from his mistakes, the less intelligent player makes the same errors day after day. Maybe in the past training in England was based mostly on brutality, not on intelligence, and players who had potential to improve weren't given the opportunity.' Colbert isn't suggesting that the players who worked with Venglos, Gross and Olsen were 'less intelligent', rather that their formation as footballers was perhaps not based on personal improvement. As Mourinho might say, they weren't taught to 'think football'. And when faced with a manager who demanded precisely that, they struggled because they were asked to do something they had never been asked to do before.

Arsenal are perhaps the most obvious case of this. Before Wenger's arrival, their game, under George Graham, was very different. It was what we in Italy would call 'typically English', albeit with a counter-attacking twist. The central defenders were essentially destroyers, whose main job was to clear the ball without worrying too much where it went. The midfielders often watched as the clearances flew over their heads: their main task was to win the ball back. The wide men ran straight down the touchline, like a wing in rugby. There were plenty of long balls and crosses, often from deep positions. It was traditional and predictable, but also effective. And, in the words of a famous Arsenal fan, it was also awful to watch. 'Really, Arsenal were terrible,' says Nick Hornby, interviewed in David Winner's book *Those Feet: A Sensual History of English Football*. 'It was as bad as it has ever been, I think, just before George [Graham] got sacked. The one triumph was the 1994 Cupwinners' Cup in Copenhagen and it was hilarious. I think Kevin Campbell was in midfield, with Ian Selley and Ray Parlour, who was still drinking at the time. And we were playing Parma who had [Tomas] Brolin, [Tino] Asprilla and [Gianfranco] Zola. Arsenal had one shot – the Alan Smith goal – and then it was the Alamo for the rest of the game.'

Actually, Hornby is wrong about the midfield: Parlour wasn't there, but Paul Merson, who was also drinking then, was. Whatever your views on that team – whether you share Hornby's assessment or whether you like Graham's football – it's hard to argue that it was anything but radically different from what was to follow and Wenger's fluid game.

'If you were a wide midfielder, that's all you did, you stayed out on the wing and ran up and down, up and down,' says David Platt, who joined Arsenal just after Graham's departure. 'You never came inside, you never created space for the full-back. There was a tactical rigidity, which might have worked sometimes but when it didn't work there were no alternatives.'

Wenger arrived amid general scepticism. He had made a name for himself at Monaco in the late 1980s and early 1990s, then spent two years working in Japan, in relative obscurity. That was why one newspaper famously greeted his appointment with the headline 'Arsène Who?'. Throw in the fact that, at the time, there were few overseas managers in the English game and a certain mistrust of foreigners prevailed, and you begin to see what an uphill climb Wenger faced. There were serious doubts about him, as he freely admits. 'When I arrived, I immediately noticed that there were eight players over the age of thirty,' he says. 'For a new manager, so many veterans are like a ticking time bomb. There was a risk that they would reject me and my methods. After all, they weren't just veterans, they were successful veterans, who had won titles and trophies under George Graham, following his methods. They had the backing of the press and the supporters. It would have been very easy for them to shut me out. The easiest thing for me to do as a new manager would have been to get rid of them. But I couldn't get rid of eight players in one go. Especially since, let's face it, I was coming from Japan and nobody knew me. And also I did not think it was right to get rid of players just because they were veterans. They were English and they were used to a different way of doing things.

'I tried a different approach,' he goes on. 'I tried to convince them that if they followed my methods I could prolong their careers. I admit it. The economic aspect was important as well. Many of them earned a quarter of a million pounds a year, and they were veterans at a very important club, guys who had played for their country and who had won trophies, both domestically and in Europe. I am proud that they listened to what I had to say and trusted me. I think it's thanks to this and their hard work that many of them played until the age of thirty-seven or thirty-eight. And they were able to sign big contracts, which was only fair given what they had achieved.'

Indeed, guys like Tony Adams, Steve Bould, Martin Keown, Nigel Winterburn and Lee Dixon always gave Arsène Wenger credit for prolonging their footballing lives. Winterburn played until he was thirty-nine. Dixon, Bould and Keown retired at thirty-eight. Adams hung up his boots at thirty-five, but that was largely through injury.

But Wenger's contribution goes well beyond lengthening their careers. He revolutionized the way they viewed the game. They became more professional in the way they trained; they paid more attention to diet and fitness. They learned a whole new concept of football, which was often more complex and mentally demanding than the one they had known.

'Ultimately, it's all about intelligence and, in that sense, we were fortunate at Arsenal,' says Colbert. 'Guys like Lee Dixon are English to the bone. They were used to doing things a certain way, but they had the intelligence and the mental openness to trust Wenger and follow his way. They are proof that, while it's true that football prepares you in a certain way, you can always change. But only if you have that basic intelligence.'

I thought about this. I know that many like to joke about footballers and their intelligence. I don't think we're any more or less clever than any other cross-section of people . . . except rocket scientists maybe. But the point is that intelligence encompasses many different aspects and one of these is the ability to know when to follow orders and when to use your own judgement.

'There is a story I like to tell,' says Wenger. 'In Japan, if you, as a manager, tell the players to sprint at high speed into a brick wall, they will do it unquestioningly. Then, when they crack their heads open and fall to the ground, they look at you and feel completely betrayed. They trust their manager and can't believe he would do anything to hurt them. The English player, in some ways, is like the Japanese. He'll run at full speed into the brick wall, crash into it, get up, dust himself off and do it again. He won't feel betrayed by his manager, indeed, he won't even think about it. He won't ask himself the point of running into the wall, why it makes sense to do so. He'll just get on with it.

'Now, the French player, like the Italian, will react differently when you tell him to run into the wall,' Wenger concludes. 'He'll look at you and say, "Sure, we'll run into the wall, but why don't you show us first how it's done?" You see, the thing is that they only trust the manager to a certain point. You have to prove to them that what you are doing is useful. They have to believe in what they are doing.'

Dealing with Authority

It's easy to say that Wenger is reflecting national stereotypes and, in some ways, I suppose he is. But stereotypes often have a basis in truth. And, broadly speaking, the French and the Italians are far more chaotic and argumentative than the English or the Japanese. I don't like to use terms like 'the English' or 'the Italians' because it can be dangerous to generalize about entire peoples, particularly in this day and age. But it's undeniable that there are national characteristics which go beyond football.

Anyone who has seen a queue at a bus stop will have no trouble in telling you that people in Manchester queue differently from those in Milan.

And this brings me to one of the most obvious differences. There is a far greater respect for authority in England, whether it be the police, the 'do not litter' signs or the manager of a football team. This does not mean that English people are necessarily better behaved than Italians, just that they have a different sense of respect.

I should probably clarify what I mean by respect. Respect does not mean fear. Nor does respect necessarily engender obedience. It implies an understanding and an appreciation of authority, even when you choose to defy it. In Italy we tend not to differentiate between the individual and his role. So if a person, for example, hates the police or politicians of a certain party, he will also hate them as individuals: he won't just hate what they represent or believe. It's the opposite of 'hate the sin, not the sinner'. In Italy, we tend to hate both – or, worse, we hate some sinners and love others to the point at which we happily overlook their sins, as long as they are on our side.

In England the situation is different. There is a greater respect for an individual charged with authority. Even when public officials are criticized – often as harshly as in Italy – there is a degree of restraint. People may have said the most awful things about Margaret Thatcher or Tony Blair and their policies, but it rarely seeped into the personal, into the private, the way it does in Italy. Arsène Wenger feels that English footballers have a greater respect than Italians for their managers and are more likely to follow orders because they feel a natural bond with their boss. That bond is probably also nurtured by the fact that, in England, clubs are slow to sack managers. In Italy, chairmen are far more trigger-happy. Wenger maintains that the English player lives up to the militaristic metaphor whereby he is going into battle and the manager isn't some general hiding in camp, but leading the troops from the trenches. 'Here in England, you often hear someone say, "Do a job for the manager,"' says Wenger. 'Or you'll hear a manager explain that the lads lost because they didn't follow him, or the press question the players' commitment to the manager. It is taken as automatic that there must be a special bond there. Whenever something goes wrong, you rally round the manager to defend him. Whenever things are going right, the players give credit to the manager. This does not happen in other countries.'

Indeed, I can think of an even more obvious example: the way people react to substitutions. Obviously, no player enjoys being taken off the pitch, but in Italy we are often quick to express our displeasure. You'll see a player ignore his manager as he walks off, or even have a go at him, kick a water-bottle, or go straight down into the tunnel. And it's not just the hot-heads who react in this way. One of the enduring images of the Italy side at the 1994 World Cup comes from the Italy–Norway match in the group stage. We lost our opener against the Republic of Ireland, thanks to Ray Houghton's long-range effort, and could not afford another slip-up. After just twenty minutes our goalkeeper, Gianluca Pagliuca, was given a red card for handling the ball just outside the penalty area. It was probably a bit harsh but, according to the laws of the game, the referee had no choice. In such a situation, you have to get your reserve goalkeeper on to the pitch and it's customary to take off an attacking player. I don't think a single person, except the Italy coach, Arrigo Sacchi, could have imagined what came next. Sacchi chose to take off Roberto Baggio, Italy's star player, which took everyone by surprise, including Baggio. As he saw his number called, the cameras clearly captured him turning to a teammate and saying, 'My goodness, this guy's gone mad!' His reaction was bemusement, but ultimately quite innocent when compared to some of the things we've witnessed in Italy from players in similar circumstances. In England, you rarely see a player vent his anger at being substituted, and, when it does happen, it's hardly ever an English or British player. They simply don't question the manager's judgement, in public or in private.

But Italian players can be very different. When I was managing Chelsea, I had to take off Gianfranco Zola, who was hardly a hot-head, at Stamford Bridge. He was far from happy. He did not make a scene – it's not in his nature to do so – but he did walk out on the club. He walked straight into the dressing room, showered, got dressed and went home.

As manager, I couldn't stand for this, because it showed lack of respect for the group. Thankfully, Zola, a professional and a team player, was probably the first to realize it. The next day, at training, he immediately apologized to everybody. I'm sure he still felt that he was unfairly substituted, but he was big enough to understand that you don't walk out on your teammates.

In fact, come to think of it, I too behaved in that way. It was at Juventus, with Marcello Lippi in charge. We were playing away to Cremonese, my old club, and we were losing 3–2 and he took me off the pitch with seven or eight minutes to go. We eventually equalized in the final minute. I was furious. I still had the sense to give him five as I came off the pitch, but I immediately went down to the dressing room and vented my anger. I kicked the lockers, smacked a few of the benches around and then got changed and left. Later I apologized. The point is that I believe few people would describe Zola, Baggio or me as excitable or hot-headed – we are not like my friend Paolo Di Canio, for example. Yet we all fell victim to this, we all readily challenged authority in a very public way.

Wenger mentions the 2003–04 season, when Claudio Ranieri, the Chelsea manager, was often attacked and criticized by the press. For most of the season, rumours of his departure gathered steam until, by the spring, everybody knew that, come what may, he would not be back the following year. Yet throughout the season most Chelsea players, particularly the English ones such as John Terry and Frank Lampard, defended him to the hilt, praising him at every opportunity.

Now, I don't doubt that Ranieri was an important influence on their careers and they had a special relationship with him. But I do think that Wenger is right: such things happen in England far more frequently than elsewhere. In Italy you certainly would not see such open, wholehearted support for an embattled coach. It's not because we're horrible or ungrateful: it's just that we weigh our words a little differently. If a manager is under pressure, he probably isn't entirely free of blame. As a player in Italy, if your manager is in the firing line and you are asked about him, you have to be careful what you say. Obviously, you can't criticize him directly, because that would land you in trouble. But neither can you say everything is wonderful, the gaffer's doing a fabulous job and the players are all behind him, as you might in England.

Why? There are several reasons. First, if the team is doing poorly and you say something like that, people will assume you are either a liar or stupid. And in Italian football it's not good to be seen as either. Second, even if you genuinely believe the boss is blameless, you probably don't want to be too closely associated with him because, if the team is under fire, the president may sack him and you don't want to be seen as the 'old boss's guy' when a new manager comes in.

These are the kind of mental acrobatics many of us go through in Italy – quite the opposite of England. But then the English are off to war, blindly trusting their leader, while the Italians aren't quite so sure . . .

'Look, it's in the blood of the English. It's the almost military attitude with which they approach everything,' says Wenger. 'They do as they're told, they follow orders, they do not question authority and they never give up, not even when they are three goals down and there are two minutes to go. I don't think it's a coincidence. Every time there is a war, the English almost always win. The Italians on the other hand . . .'

There was no need for Wenger to finish the sentence. I knew where he was going with it. And, admittedly, he has a point. As a nation, we are far less warlike than the English – not to mention the Germans – so our record in war is not quite as good as our record in football. The football-as-war analogy is popular in some coaching circles but in my opinion it is flawed. Football is a collaborative effort, it's the synthesis of the individual and the collective: it's not about blindly following orders.

The words of Jorge Valdano come to mind: 'Who do you think is better at thinking, processing information and making decisions? The brain of one manager? Or the brains of eleven footballers on the pitch, striving towards a common goal?'

The trick, of course, is knowing when to question and when to obey, when to let your concerns and personality come to the fore and when to blend in and be a cog in the machine. That's from the players' perspective. The manager needs to know how much expression and dissent to allow, from whom to allow it (because, despite what some coaches try to do, you can't treat all players the same), and when and how to allow it. Because chain-of-command obedience is a double-edged sword. It may have worked in the trenches during the First World War and it may have helped Wenger when he first arrived at Highbury, but, sooner or later, it has to evolve into something else or it becomes negative.

The Italian University and the English Elementary School

With this in mind, I looked up my old friend Giovanni Vaglini. Giovanni was an assistant fitness coach at Juventus, and when I took over at Watford I asked him to join me. I felt it was important to give players a more scientific and structured fitness preparation and Giovanni, who had studied all aspects of fitness at the highest level, seemed the ideal man for the job. On top of everything else, he was also hard-working, enthusiastic – and perceptive.

'The English were undoubtedly obedient and attentive to everything I asked,' he says. 'In England, nobody, not a single player, ever said no to me or even did a single exercise at less than 100 per cent. That was undoubtedly good. What was less gratifying was that nobody had the courage or humility to ask me anything about any of the fitness exercises we were doing. They had no interest in establishing any kind of dialogue with me or trying to understand what I did.

'It wasn't just me,' he goes on. 'There were older players, experienced ones, and I noticed the younger ones had no interest in getting close to them either. They were there to do a job and they did it. It was like punching a time card. For someone like me, who came from a club like Juventus, it was quite a shock. It was like going back to elementary school after having worked at university.'

Because football was a 'game' to the English players, training was something they tolerated, a necessary evil they had to endure if they were to get into the starting eleven on Saturday. Vaglini's words may sound harsh, but I think his analogy is accurate. The rapport with your professors at university comes close to the rapport you have with your peers. You are not as far removed from your teachers as you were at school: you seek out dialogue, you build a relationship. And you question: you question the professor, you question the texts, you question all of academia. At elementary school, your teacher is a giant (literally as well as figuratively), all-seeing and all-powerful. You don't really want to be there, at least not in the lessons, which are often boring. You do the work to keep the teacher happy, but you don't concern yourself with why you're studying what you're studying.

And when the bell goes and the lesson is over, you can't wait to get out.

Vaglini worked in what is now the Championship. But the experience of Sven-Goran Eriksson, working with the finest footballers England has to offer, was not dissimilar: 'Well, I've only worked with the very best, so I don't know exactly what is going on at club level,' he says. 'But the sense of sacrifice and work ethic of the English is simply unbelievable, extraordinary. There is never any kind of discussion. They hear a command and they get on with it. In Italy, no, they are all ready to argue. Why are we doing this? Shouldn't we be doing that? Maybe it's a Latin thing . . .'

The tendency to criticize and analyse every command can obviously be negative if it leads to indiscipline or delays decision-making. Then again it can also be an opportunity for dialogue, for introspection, a chance to evaluate and question methods.

'An expert athlete, one who knows how to train, will understand his body better than anybody else,' says Vaglini. 'And at that point, if you know yourself and your body, well, it seems obvious to me that you'll want to have a good and open dialogue with your fitness coach. If you understand a certain exercise, if you know how your body and that exercise work, well, you're going to apply yourself better and train better and you'll be the first to benefit. To me, this is obvious. And it's equally obvious to me that if all you do is follow orders you're going to lose out.'

The constant questioning of authority is thus potentially valuable but also potentially dangerous. And, uncannily, it reflects once again the broad national stereotypes: 'In England they are convinced that they are the masters of football,' says Lippi. 'Football is XYZ and there is one proper way of doing it. And so they do the same things over and over again, whether it's what they have been told to do or what they've figured out for themselves. Once they pick a path they don't deviate.

'In Italy, our minds work rather differently. We always believe there is a better way and we spend most of our time criticizing the status quo. Our brains are livelier, more capable of critical thinking. And that's why we're more progressive, more open to change, to dialogue. If we see something isn't working, we'll try something different. And this applies to everything, from the players to the managers to the tactics. I actually think our mentality is beneficial, even though you can pay a high price for it.'

I can see Lippi's argument. In fact, the importance of critical analysis, dialogue and open discussion throughout the chain of command is regularly emphasized in management bestsellers. Obviously, you want a subordinate to believe in and understand what you are doing. And yet the people in the trenches or 'on the shop floor' know the situation best: they can come up with practical solutions to improve productivity. That much is a staple of MBA programmes and leadership seminars.

If you can think critically and discuss issues freely with your superiors you will have a much clearer view of the 'big picture', you'll feel appreciated, you'll see the importance of your own work and how it relates to that of others and the company – or football club – as a whole. I believe that, in that area, we in Italy are somewhat ahead. Because we are encouraged to think critically, we have a clearer view of the 'big picture', which, among other things, makes us far more receptive to ideas on tactics and formations. In Italy, footballers revel in tactical talk but in England it's greeted with the same enthusiasm as a trip to the dentist.

'There is no question that the Italian footballer is stimulated by talk of various systems and the movement of players on the pitch,' says David Platt. 'On the other hand, these things are of little interest to the English players. I notice it every time I talk to my players about tactics. After about twenty minutes I realize that I've lost them, their eyes glaze over, you can tell they're thinking of something else. If I don't do a single tactical session over the course of an entire week the English player either wouldn't notice or would notice and wouldn't care. But the thought of spending a whole week without any kind of tactical work would terrify the Italian. To him, tactics are an essential part of the game. And if he hasn't prepared tactically, he doesn't feel prepared on the pitch. And that scares him and makes him very uncomfortable because for the Italian players football is first and foremost a job. The game aspect of it is a distant second.'

Again! In England it's a game, in Italy it's a job. It's something on which most of the people I spoke to seemed to agree.

'We, and I include Portugal with Italy, forget to teach the other side of football, the one which is also beautiful, the one which says it's a game,' says Mourinho. 'Here in England they teach that, but they forget to teach the other things you learn in Italy or Portugal: hydration, what to eat, the way you behave, the way you train, the way you stretch.' He may be exaggerating, but he's not far off.

Wenger is on the same wavelength: 'In Italy, football is no longer a sport, it's a job, an industry. You have lost something, you are too severe, the players don't enjoy themselves any more. It's rare to see an Italian player smiling in training or on the pitch. He is totally focused and concentrated and he can't think of anything else. In England, they laugh, they have fun and they still give a hundred per cent. You only need to look at the environment in the dressing room before a match. In Italy or France they are tense, they are fully concentrated on the game, they are thinking about what they need to do. In England, it's like a discothèque. There is music, fun, chaos . . .'

Rational Latins, Irrational Anglo-Saxons . . .

I think of Wenger's words and my mind sails back to the dressing rooms I've been in: at Cremonese, at Sampdoria, at Juventus, at Chelsea, and with the Italian national team. There is little question that he is right. At the Italian clubs there was always dead silence: it was like being in church or a library. Everybody was wholly concentrated and you could have cut the tension in the air with a knife. It was totally serious, totally joyless. In England, on the other hand, it was often like a mobile disco, with pounding music, laughter and jokes. The players are fully relaxed and, at the same time, fired up.

And that really doesn't make sense. Isn't Italy supposed to be the country of the sun, of creative, fun-loving people, relaxed attitudes and full-on passion? Isn't England supposed to be a dark, dour, rainy place filled with stiff, joyless, business-like people, the nation of shopkeepers and repressed passion? Are these stereotypes complete rubbish?

Wenger thinks so. 'Of the two, Latin culture is easily more rational. It is more open to analysis and self-examination than English culture,' he says. 'And there is a good reason for this. If you think about it, the culture of a country is dictated by what they learn in school. We in France have Descartes. His rationalism is the basis for all of French thought and culture. In Italy you have Machiavelli, who is also about being rational and calculating. Here in England, maybe because they are an island, they are more warlike, more passionate. They view it like an old-style duel, a fight to the death, come what may. When an Englishman goes into war, that's it, he either comes back triumphant or he comes back dead. But the Italian or the Frenchman is not like that. He will calculate, he will think about things, he will do what he needs to do to protect his own interests.'

Sometimes giving up is rational: sometimes it's best to walk away, and live to fight another day. I always wonder what really goes through a person's mind when, say, they are 3–0 down and score a goal. You always see them rush to pick the ball up in the back of the net and sprint to the half-way line to restart the game, in hopes of staging a dramatic comeback. I ask this because I wonder if it's rational to restart the game quickly. True, you give yourself more time to score another goal. But you give the opposition more time to score another goal too. And, surely, in terms of damage limitation, losing 3–1 is better than losing 4–1.

That thought crossed my mind one day at the San Siro, when I was with Sampdoria. We were facing Milan at a time when they were just about invincible. That afternoon the situation was rather bleak as we were losing 4–0 and were down to ten men with just six minutes to go. Suddenly I received the ball in a good position after a mistake by the Milan defence. I saw an opening, and blasted the ball into the back of the net, making it 4–1. As I have always done (and probably have been conditioned to do), I rushed to collect the ball from the back of the net and raced back to midfield, all the while shouting encouragement to my teammates.

And as I did this, a horrible thought slipped into my mind: Why am I doing this? What's the point? I bet no team in the history of football has come back from being four–one down with six minutes to go . . . So why bother? Shouldn't I be slowing down and taking my time? After all, why give them more time to score a fifth?

That is rational thinking. It is *not* the way an English player would think. He would believe in some kind of miracle, while the Italian would focus on damage limitation. Which, as a strategy, probably seemed reasonable just two minutes after my goal when Demetrio Albertini scored for Milan, making it 5–1 and rounding off our humiliation. It was as if I was being punished for being irrational, for not realizing that my goal had been a lucky one, that it did not entitle me to believe I could defy logic. And, indeed, my arrogance and insolence in rushing back to midfield, was somehow punished by the football gods.

It's about playing the percentages. It's about doing a risk-benefit analysis – what are the risks of hurrying back to restart play? Do they outweigh the benefits of scoring a second goal to make it 4–2? How do they compare to the risk that the opponent will score again, turning it into a 5–1 scoreline? And I should point out that when we talk about risk we're talking almost exclusively about the media's and the fans' reaction. From the manager's standpoint a loss is a loss. But when it comes to the newspapers, television, and the fan on the street or at the supermarket, it's a different story. To them, 5–1 is a humiliation worse than 4–1. It is not just another loss.

And that's why we play the percentages. Wenger maintains that it's natural for the French or the Italians to do so. And, in a startling development, Sir Alex Ferguson agrees with him: 'I think that in Italy when a game goes to two–nil you tend to think that the side which is losing comes to accept the fact that it won't happen for them that day,' he says. 'So they'll sit back, conserve energy, live to fight another day. It's very pragmatic that way. In England that never happens. We always try to come back. We don't have that rational way of thinking you have in France and Italy. It's not our way. Machiavelli . . . That's rational, that's Italian. Christ! He could think!'

One of the reasons I admire both Arsène Wenger and Sir Alex is their ability to step back and view the game in its wider context. When you do this, sometimes you get a little ahead of yourself, a little pretentious, you search for meaning where none is present. But here I think they're on to something. If you look at the protagonists of the traditional English literary canon – whether it's Beowulf or King Lear – they are great heroes or tragic figures who see the world in terms of black and white. The rational characters in those stories are devious, like Lear's elder daughters, who plot against him. Even Hamlet, who appears clever in setting up a play to expose his father's murderer, is driven by madness and anger.

Contrast this with Descartes, whose belief in reason and rationality was so strong that he decided to prove God's existence. Or Dante: when he ventured into hell and purgatory, he took a guide with him, Virgil, to explain things along the way and keep him out of danger – which was far more rational than setting off to poke around down there on his own. And when Dante got to heaven, he was bright enough to ditch Virgil and saunter in accompanied by the beautiful Beatrice – an even more rational move.

Machiavelli famously argued that 'the end justifies the means', which marked him out as the epitome of cynicism and amorality. He wrote his masterpiece *The Prince* as a sort of how-to manual on grabbing and maintaining power. He was careful not to pass judgement on the ethics or morality of a certain action, but approached it from a purely practical point of view. What do you have to do to keep power? He concluded that there were some situations in which killing or imprisoning your opponent was the smartest and safest thing to do. In other situations, though, he insisted that it was best to be kind and generous. His point was that if you have a goal you pursue it by any means necessary, and everything you do is geared towards it.

How does that apply to football?

Well, if you're 0–3 down and there are ten minutes to go, Machiavelli might have argued that it's best to walk off the pitch and give up. Rationally, the odds of coming back from a three-goal deficit are tiny. Unless it's a final, it makes more sense to conserve your energy, avoid the risk of injury and focus on the next match.

How would Machiavelli feel about cheating? Diving to

win a penalty or, better yet, Diego Maradona's 'Hand of God' goal? He would not have a problem with it, provided you weren't caught. After all, he made a distinction between 'good cruelty' ('cruelty' being his by-word for misbehaviour) and 'bad cruelty'. Good cruelty is not only something you get away with: it's something you do once, and when it's done, you never have to do it again and it allows you to be safe and victorious. Bad cruelty is something that doesn't complete the job, that engenders more uncertainty and, ultimately, leads to more cruelty.

I would imagine then that Machiavelli would have commended a successful dive to win a penalty if it is decisive and the player gets away with it. He would also have pointed out, however, that diving to win a penalty – like the extreme 'cruelty' described in *The Prince* – is something to be done rarely, but with full conviction. If you think about it, it makes sense. If a player dives too often, his opponents will begin to loathe him and, as Machiavelli pointed out, 'It is better to be feared than loved, but it is better to be loved than hated.' Furthermore, that player will develop a reputation as someone who dives and cheats. This will not only hurt his image, it may make match officials wary of him and more reluctant to grant penalties. Then, of course, there is the simple fact that a player who dives and gets caught, these days, is supposed to get a booking and that can be damaging. So, Machiavelli's capsule message on cheating is this: only do it when the reward far outweighs the risk, when you are confident you will not be caught and, above all, do not do it often. Which all seems very rational to me.

There is a fine line between cynicism and realism and Machiavelli would probably have said that he was only being realistic. It is evident that he was a cynic in the most literal sense of the word. He wrote: 'Because this is to be asserted in general of men: that they are ungrateful, fickle, false, cowardly, covetous, and as long as you succeed they are yours entirely; they will offer you their blood, property, life and children, as is said above, when the need is far distant; but when it approaches they turn against you.' This kind of thinking is rather distasteful to me, but it reminds me of the Italian and, indeed, the Latin mind-set: we often tend to think the worst of people. Giulio Andreotti, one of our most prominent post-war politicians, once said: '*A pensare male si fa peccato, ma spesso ci si azzecca.* (Thinking bad thoughts of someone is a sin, but often it's spot on.)' This attitude means that you are always on the defensive. The unknown is a threat. The known and non-threatening can become dangerous. Things can always go wrong. And that is perhaps why, historically, we've looked to shut up shop, defend leads and kill off games. We don't want to take chances, even against weaker sides. It's in our nature that, if we're 2–0 up, we play the percentages and risk as little as possible. Letting a two-goal lead slip in Italy is perhaps a greater sin than losing 6–0: it means that, mentally, you got it wrong. And that is unforgivable because the mental side is some-thing you can control – certainly more than the physical or technical. Or, at least, that is the perception. In reality, second-guessing is easy and offers up no real answers. Think of the 2005 Champions' League final. The media, particularly in Italy, speculated endlessly about what went wrong as Milan began the second half with a 3–0 lead in a game they were dominating, then allowed Liverpool to get back to 3–3. 'When something goes wrong, in Italy the natural tendency is to criticize, never to help or offer some kind of alternative solution,' says Capello. 'We Italians are over-critical and arrogant, all of us. We're convinced we all know more than the next guy.'

And so many were convinced they knew better than poor Ancelotti. But Milan's trauma that night – some people called it the 'Istanbul effect' – probably lingered over the team far longer than any other defeat. And I am convinced that this had a lot to do with the belief that the worst humiliation is to give up a lead. In the World Cup or European Championships no Italy side has ever taken a two-goal lead, then lost or even drawn the game. It just doesn't happen. And that was why Istanbul was so hard for Milan fans to bear and so hard to explain for neutrals. It's in our nature to look for answers even when perhaps there aren't any, even when – as was maybe the case in Istanbul – it's just the randomness of football working its magic.

Remember our two boxers? If Boxer A, the English boxer, dominated his opponent for twelve rounds, then got caught by an unexpected knockout blow, he would be gutted by the defeat but he would accept it, as long as he felt he had given 100 per cent in the ring. If the same happened to Boxer B, the Italian, it would be a disaster. There would be all sorts of recrimination and the match would replay endlessly in his head. He would feel it was a match he had lost, rather than one that his opponent won. To an Italian athlete, the biggest crime of all is having the upper hand and letting it slip away.

Yet there is another train of thought, parallel and, in many ways, complementary to Machiavellian rationalism: it's a kind of basic humanitarianism, a belief that, all things being equal, helping others is better than hurting them. It is distinctly Italian and linked to a strong sense of solidarity with those less fortunate, a hallmark of Italian thinking since the Second World War. The two forces that most shaped the Italian political and social landscape between 1945 and 1990 were the Roman Catholic Church and the Communist Party, both of which preach helping one another and working towards the 'common good'.

In football this rears its head in a rather unfortunate way, particularly in Serie B where, late in the season, if a team has nothing left to play for, it will too often throw matches if its opponents need points. When the fixture list is drawn up in the summer, the coach and general manager will get together, study the last six games and say something like, 'Against so-and-so, we're OK. If they need points, we'll give them points, and if we need them, they'll help us out . . .'

If both clubs need points, or if neither needs points, they'll go at it and face off fair and square. But if one has no incentive and the other is desperate, all too often the outcome will be scripted. This is so common that late in the season many bookmakers won't accept bets on such matches. It is taken as read that this will occur. In fact, it is seen as rude and churlish not to give your opponent the points if you don't need them. It's as if you're gratuitously condemning them. Which is a crime in a country that still believes, 'There, but for the grace of God, go I', and that next year the shoe might be on the other foot.

In England, things could not be more different. On the last day of the 2004–05 season, none of the relegation issues had been decided and four clubs went into it in danger of going down: Norwich (33 points), Crystal Palace (32 points), Southampton (32 points) and West Bromwich Albion (31 points). These were the fixtures of those four clubs:

Fulham v Norwich
Charlton Athletic v Crystal Palace
Southampton v Manchester United
West Brom v Portsmouth

An Italian would have looked at the table and immediately predicted the outcome. Norwich would win at Fulham, since the latter had nothing left to play for. Palace would win all three points at Charlton, as the Addicks had no incentive to do well. Southampton would beat United, no question about it – Sir Alex's men had already secured third place and a spot in the Champions' League. As for West Brom, of course they would win against a Portsmouth side, which, somehow, had avoided relegation. Four teams in desperate need of points and four wins, meaning Norwich would stay up. It was so obvious.

It was also so wrong. Of the four threatened teams, only West Brom took all three points. Norwich and Southampton lost, while Palace were condemned when Charlton equalized eight minutes from time. Such a scenario, to an Italian mind, is not rational. Fulham had nothing to gain by beating Norwich. Nothing at all. And, in fact, they had something to lose: had they allowed Norwich to win, they would have been owed a favour in future. Now they had nothing. Next time the two teams met, no matter the circumstances, Norwich would be merciless.

That kind of thinking is not part of the English game. Maybe it's too rational. Or maybe it's the wrong kind of rationality. I quickly learned how things worked in the Premiership. On the last day of the 1997–98 season, I was playing for Chelsea and we were hosting Bolton at Stamford Bridge. We had nothing left to play for, they had a slim one-point lead over Everton and were desperately trying to avoid relegation.

When I broke the ice, seventeen minutes from the end, the ground fell silent. Chelsea supporters wanted Everton to go down and, because of this, both sets of spectators cheered as one. They wanted Bolton to equalize, maybe even beat us, since, at the time, Everton were winning 1–0 against Coventry (they would eventually draw, 1–1). I could feel the tension in the air and see the despair and fear in the eyes of the Bolton players. Yet there was no talk of us throwing the game. It was the furthest thing from anyone's mind. The mere suggestion would have been greeted with horror. And so, as the minutes ticked away, far from Bolton levelling the score, Jody Morris scored for Chelsea, making it 2–0. At the final whistle, the Bolton players and their fans were in tears. Had they been Italian, those tears would have been tears of rage and we would have been the bad guys for not gifting them the result they needed.

In an Italian setting, what I did was far from rational. It was foolish, selfish and mean-spirited. In an English setting it was a display of sportsmanship.

The Manager

Chapter Five

A Job Anyone Can Do?

They're probably the most criticized people in the world of football. When their team wins, they have to share the credit; when it loses, it's their fault. Managers occupy a unique place in the football galaxy. First of all, there are relatively few, which means they are easily outnumbered by players and the press, not to mention supporters. Indeed, there are more referees and club officials than managers, which makes the 'hot seat' a lonely place. Not only are they few in number, they are also seen as privileged, which further adds to their isolation. The privilege stems from the fact that the rest of the football world – club officials, the press, fans, players – is generally convinced that they, too, could do a job in management, given the chance. This puts managers on an entirely different plane from footballers.

Only a fool or a madman (or possibly another professional footballer) would believe he can play football better than Thierry Henry or Alessandro Nesta. Henry and Nesta are simply different from the average person. They are superb athletes blessed with technique and skill. They even look different.

Managers are another matter: anyone can imagine

themselves as a manager. In fact, most of us could impersonate one, at least outwardly, because a manager's traits are mental, not physical. In Italy we like to say that we have sixty million national-team coaches. And indeed many people honestly believe that they could be a better manager than, say, Gerard Houllier or Alberto Zaccheroni. That's because the skills of a Houllier or a Zaccheroni are hidden from view, like much of the work they do.

You can judge the work of a footballer – without any kind of mediation – because you can see what he does with your own eyes on the pitch. A manager's work is once removed: you only see the reflection of his work on the pitch. And that reflection is channelled through eleven men. I suppose it's the difference between seeing a beautiful woman in person and seeing a portrait of her. In person, you have a full grasp of her beauty, perhaps even her temperament and personality. With a portrait, it's a different matter. A skilled artist may make her appear more beautiful than she really is, just as great players can make a manager appear better than he really is, but a poor artist may make her appear ugly, lifeless, flat. In either case, the end product is not the woman, it's a representation of her and, as such, it will be more or less distorted from reality.

This analogy sums up some of the issues with managers and the way they are perceived. They are judged by their 'results', but it's difficult, if not impossible, to assess correctly how well a manager does his job because, first, he does it away from the public eye, and because many external factors influence a team's results – the one measurable aspect of his job.

Because most observers can't actually see what a manager does and because his achievements can be explained away by other factors – great players, a solid club – people tend to assume that the job is relatively simple, that just about anyone could do it. The man on the street – assuming he is sane – knows he can't be the starting centre-forward for Milan or Manchester United because Andriy Shevchenko and Ruud Van Nistelrooy are better players than he is. Is it so ridiculous for him to think that he could do a better job than the managers of those two clubs, Carlo Ancelotti and Sir Alex Ferguson?

In many people's minds, the answer is 'No.' Managers are 'fortunate' because they do a job that just about anyone who loves football could do. That's why they are always under such scrutiny. This is true in both England and Italy, although the scrutiny manifests itself in different ways.

In Italy, coaching is seen as a profession that, like all skilled trades, requires study and, often, an apprenticeship. This may seem to contradict what I've just said, that Italians are convinced anybody can do the job of manager, but it's not necessarily so. Italians accept that you have to study and go through a process to become a football coach, just as you will to become a lawyer, doctor or priest. But there isn't the same deference towards the manager's job, perhaps because many feel they could have taken that very same path.

In England, on the other hand, it seems that many view the ability to manage or coach as innate: it's not something that can be learned, either through an apprenticeship in the lower divisions or, indeed, at a coaching course. 'We believe that a baker or a butcher can easily go and manage Manchester United,' says John Barnwell, head of the English League Managers Association. 'Coaching badges are a new phenomenon and many in English football are against them.'

The opposite is true in Italy: the Coverciano coaching school opened in 1958 and coaching badges have been mandatory ever since. Nearly five decades of history have enabled Coverciano to evolve, constantly refining its curriculum and developing as close to an academic setting as you're likely to get in football. I don't believe it's co-incidence that in the last decade Coverciano graduates have taken charge of some of the biggest club sides in Europe as well as various important national teams. Giovanni Trapattoni won league titles at Bayern and Benfica, Fabio Capello did the same at Real Madrid. Claudio Ranieri finished second in the Premiership with Chelsea and won the Copa del Rey with Valencia. Nevio Scala won a title in Ukraine with Shaktar Donetsk and has coached the likes of Besiktas, Spartak Moscow and Borussia Dortmund. Walter Zenga won the Romanian title with Steaua Bucharest (OK, he was sacked with three matches to go and the team in first place ... close enough) and also coached Red Star Belgrade. In terms of sheer numbers that's quite a record.

In contrast, I can count four British coaches who won silverware abroad in the last decade: Sir Bobby Robson won two league titles at Porto and a Cupwinners' Cup at Barcelona; Graeme Souness won the Turkish Cup at Galatasaray; Roy Hodgson won the Danish League at FC Copenhagen; and Stuart Baxter won a league and a cup at AIK Solna in Sweden.

The same holds true domestically: there seem to be more Italian managers in high-level positions in Serie A than British bosses in the Premiership. At the start of the 2004–05 season, there was only one true foreign manager in Serie A, Rudi Voeller at Roma. Zdenek Zeman of Lecce is not Italian either, of course, but he has lived and worked in Italy for most of his life and is a graduate of Coverciano so it makes sense to consider him Italian.

In England, at the start of that season, four of the twenty sides had non-British managers: José Mourinho at Chelsea, Arsène Wenger at Arsenal, Rafa Benitez at Liverpool, and Jacques Santini at Tottenham. By the end of the season, there was another, Alain Perrin at Portsmouth, while Santini had been replaced by another foreigner, Martin Jol. Strictly speaking, David O'Leary at Aston Villa is also non-British but we can't consider him foreign since he has worked and played in England for most of his life.

The point here is clear. There must be a reason why there are so many foreign managers in the Premiership, and why three of the top five Premiership sides chose a foreigner to lead them.

It's not as if Italian clubs are xenophobic or unwilling to give jobs to foreign managers. Between 1995 and 2005, Milan (Fatih Terim and Oscar Tabarez), Inter (Hector Cuper, Mircea Lucescu, Luis Suarez and Roy Hodgson), Roma (Zeman, Carlos Bianchi, Nils Liedholm, Rudi Voeller) and Lazio (Sven-Goran Eriksson, Zeman) have all had foreign managers. (Only Juventus has remained resolutely 'Italian'.) But if you compare Italy's five most successful clubs – Roma, Lazio, Juventus, Inter and Milan – against England's – Manchester United, Arsenal,

Liverpool, Chelsea and Newcastle – in the same period, the difference is staggering. The foreign managers in Italy were in charge for a total of 12.5 seasons, or 25 per cent of the time. In England, it was twenty-six seasons, or 52 per cent. Note that I'm not counting Scottish managers as 'foreign'. I'm not making a political statement: I just don't think that in this respect there is much of a difference, especially since many top Scottish coaches (such as Graeme Souness, Kenny Dalglish and George Graham) spent much of their playing career south of the border. But if I did make a distinction between English and Scottish managers, the figures would be even more staggering: Glenn Hoddle, Kevin Keegan, Sir Bobby Robson and Roy Evans are the only Englishmen to have taken charge of a top five club in the past decade. Between them, they lasted just eleven seasons, which means that, over the last ten years, non-Englishmen have been running the top five English clubs for 78 per cent of the time.

The numbers support a fact that, in my opinion, is undeniable: Italy produces more top coaches than England. Why? I imagined it would have something to do with the paths undertaken to become manager and where they diverge.

Where Do Coaches Come From?

By and large, the road to becoming a manager is similar in both countries. The vast majority of coaches are former professionals who played at a very high level. There are exceptions, of course, such as Arrigo Sacchi and Alberto Malesani in Italy or Lawrie McMenemy and Ron Atkinson in England, but most successful coaches from both countries seem to have the same basic background: they played at the highest level and went into coaching after their retirement.

Notice that I said 'successful coaches *from* both countries' not '*in* both countries'. There is a reason for this. There are examples, particularly in England, of foreign coaches who were not outstanding top-flight footballers but nevertheless went on to become excellent managers.

Rafa Benitez came through the ranks at Real Madrid but then, for most of his career, played the equivalent of third-division football in Spain before retiring at twenty-six and going into coaching. José Mourinho did not play top-flight football at all: he went straight into coaching and scouting. Arsène Wenger only turned professional at the age of twenty-eight, having spent most of his career in amateur football. He was a marginal player and, three years later, a full-time coach. Sven-Goran Eriksson, the England manager, didn't have much of a footballing career either.

It's a debate that has engulfed Mourinho: 'Over the last three years I felt a lot of pressure to take a stand on this issue, to argue that having been a top player is not necessary because, obviously, I am a very successful manager but was not a very great player,' he says. 'I felt pressure to lend my face and my reputation to this argument. But in reality, I can't do that, because I don't believe it. I believe that to be on the pitch as a player can be very important, but it is not compulsory. It is a bit like studying or going to university. It does not mean that you will be a success, but it does give you an advantage.'

This does not mean, however, that just anyone can be a great manager. No, according to Mourinho, you still need the all-important ability to 'think football'. 'There are great players who do not think football,' he says, 'and they do not become good managers. Then there are people who think football even though they were not good players, and they can make it. But you have to be in football to be thinking football. For me, I was an assistant for twelve years at top clubs with top players. When you have that role, it's a different relationship, you are totally immersed in football. I lived with them, I worked with them, I slept with them. It was just like being a player, only I did not go on the pitch. That helped me think football. You need this, if you are not a player. You can't just take a coaching course at twenty-four and become a top manager at thirty. You need to have some relation to the game.'

He's right: you *do* need an intimate knowledge of the game, and most acquire it through being a player. Not everyone, after all, becomes a paid scout as a teenager and starts coaching in his early twenties, like Mourinho.

Still, there are some, especially in the old guard, who respectfully disagree. 'Look, if you were a good player you can teach things others cannot,' says Capello, who, of course, was an outstanding player in the 1970s and scored a legendary goal for Italy at Wembley. 'There are elements of technique, of timing, of co-ordination which I don't think you can understand if you never played the game at a certain level. And because you don't understand them, because you don't have them inside you, you can't teach them to others.'

As someone who played at a high level, I can see where

Capello is coming from. I was fortunate to work with some very talented players as a manager, but I was never awed by them. Even though perhaps they could do some things that I could not, I still felt I fully understood what they were doing, partly because my technique as a player was quite good and partly because I played alongside some outstanding footballers in my career. So I agree with Capello: it is an advantage to have played at the highest level. It is not the kind of thing you can pick up, as Mourinho picked up so many other things 'living and sleeping with players'. It is something which is inside you.

And yet it is not a prerequisite. Far from it. It is simply another tool, another string for one's bow. Put it this way. Having been a great player gives you an enormous advantage over ordinary players or those who have never played at all. But that is all. Imagine that it's a race. Someone who has never played professionally, like Mourinho, might be on foot, Claudio Ranieri, who was a good, but not world-class footballer, might be on a skate-board, and Fabio Capello, an outstanding player, has a shiny bicycle. Capello has an advantage, but he still has to get on that bike and pedal his butt off to beat the other guys.

What they all share is the process that begins when you stop being a player and start thinking in terms of being a coach. According to Wenger, it's quite a journey: 'You have to learn to forget. Not forget your experiences as a player, but forget the way you processed the inputs and stimuli you received as a player. When you are a player, your mental energies are all turned inward. They are entirely focused internally on yourself as an individual. It is there that you find your most important mental inputs.

How do I feel? How can I improve? What do I need to do?

'As a manager your inputs are all external. What a manager thinks or feels is only relevant as a function of these external inputs. And those inputs are different because they are based on others. How are the players? How is the team playing? How are the opponents playing? All of a sudden you have to be more perceptive and less self-analytical. It's not an easy thing to learn. It's a psychological process which is totally different and not everyone is capable of doing it.'

Indeed, when I made the transition to player-manager the inputs around me multiplied. All of a sudden I was concerned with how the right-back was training or how the reserve goalkeeper felt about high balls into the box. I had spent much of my career getting to know my body intimately, familiarizing myself with it so that I could know exactly when something was wrong or needed to be tweaked. But once I had crossed the line into management, my own inputs became insignificant compared to those of the players. I like to think I was able to negotiate that changeover, but Wenger is right: it is not for everyone.

In any case, the point of the above exercise was to show that the background of Italian and English coaches is not dissimilar. Generally, they tend to be former professionals and a fair proportion are former internationals. One of the main differences, however, lies not so much in the type of people who become managers but at what stage of their career they do so. And here the differences are massive.

Simply put, in England managers reach the top flight at a much earlier age and with far less experience than they do in Italy (with some exceptions), where you only get a shot at the big-time after a long apprenticeship. It shocks most international observers that English clubs can even consider a player-manager.

Thrown In at the Deep End

In February 1998, when I was still a full-time player, I became player-manager of Chelsea. At the time, somebody suggested it was like 'giving an eighteen-year-old the keys to a Ferrari' and, in many ways, it was. While Chelsea back then did not have Roman Abramovich's billions, we had invested lots of money and assembled a very good squad. Furthermore, I was told that I would have more money to spend in the next few seasons.

When I look back, I still find it amazing. True, I was an experienced player and I had worked with some outstanding managers and coaches. I had an interest in management and as a player I had studied the tactical and fitness aspects of the game. Yet in many areas I was little more than a novice. In Italy it seemed crazy to many that a club which had invested so much would entrust everything to a thirty-three-year-old who had no managerial experience and was still a full-time player. Then again, at Chelsea it had become a habit: I was the third player-manager after Ruud Gullit and Glenn Hoddle. Since then, Stuart Pearce at Nottingham Forest, Stuart McCall at Bradford City and even my old friend and teammate Attilo Lombardo at Crystal Palace have had spells in charge as player-manager. Unsurprisingly, none of us lasted long. In many cases player-manager appointments are precipitated by a crisis or, possibly, reflect lack of vision on the part of the club – because, almost always, it's a bad idea, plain and simple. McCall, Pearce and Lombardo all took charge of their club when things were going poorly, and it's no coincidence that all three were relegated. Each team was struggling, the owners obviously did not feel like hiring another manager or, perhaps, could not find someone willing to take on the job, so they simply promoted from within, choosing – always – a figure beloved by the club. That way, the club buys time with the fans, who will not turn on one of their heroes. This kind of thing still goes on in the lower leagues.

'Many club chairmen go with player-managers because they are already contracted as players . . . It's buy one, get one free,' says Barnwell. 'Obviously, sometimes it works, but it's not a serious solution. A professional who is still playing full-time is unlikely to have the necessary skills to do the job. And yet many clubs do it when things are not going well, saving themselves [a manager's] wages.'

I soon realized that it was going to be hard to play at a standard with which I was satisfied while I was coaching and managing the club. I played my last match the following season and, instead, focused on coaching. I also brought in Ray Wilkins to help me (alongside Graham Rix, who was already there) and told the club that I would leave player contracts and transfers to the managing director, Colin Hutchinson. As I saw it I had far too much work already. I'm not sure how others manage, I just know that I could not do it.

The player-manager is becoming extinct in top-flight football and it's probably a good thing. I say this although my stint was rather successful: in the two and a half seasons I was player-manager, we won five trophies – and, indeed, Gullit and Hoddle had done well before me. In this day and age though, we would be the exception, not the rule. It is simply too much to ask of a player at that age, with no experience and no coaching course behind him.

Having said that, England still has a predilection to take on young managers, before they have accumulated much experience. Consider the following facts. At the start of the 2004–05 season, nineteen of the twenty Serie A managers were either Italian or were formed, in footballing terms, in Italy. (Without wishing to offend anyone, for these purposes I consider Zeman Italian and O'Leary British.) Of those, only two, Fabio Capello at Juventus and Inter's Roberto Mancini, had no experience outside the top flight. In England, there were sixteen British or British-formed managers, of whom nearly a third – O'Leary at Villa, Sir Bobby Robson at Newcastle, Chris Coleman at Fulham, Steve McClaren at Middlesbrough and Graeme Souness at Blackburn Rovers – had no significant managerial experience outside the top flight.

Even more surprising is the different level of experience between Italian and English managers. An average Italian Serie A manager had spent seven seasons in lower-league football, while his English counterpart had spent less than half as much time, 3.4 years, outside the Premiership. This is a staggering statistic: it shows that English top-flight clubs place little importance on experience, and on coming up through the ranks.

Apparently it's a recent development. 'It wasn't always like this,' says Barnwell. 'I started at Peterborough in the old Third Division. Around that time, Ron Atkinson, who would go on to manage Manchester United, was in non-league football, just like David Pleat, who would go on to Tottenham – he was at Nuneaton Borough. And, of course, Jim Smith. He was at Colchester before working for twenty years in the top flight. Brian Clough, before winning two European Cups at Nottingham Forest, was down at Hartlepool, in the Fourth Division. All of us learned the job in the lower leagues. But today club chairmen are blinded by the big names. Today if they see a player with fifty caps they'll immediately give him a top job. That's what happened to John Barnes at Celtic. He failed and, of course, not everybody fails, but those who succeed are obviously the exception to the rule.'

It is difficult for me to grasp why a club would so happily entrust their team to someone without experience (although in my case it worked out . . .). In Italy the term 'gavetta' means the years a would-be manager has to put in before he gets the job – his apprenticeship, if you like. Sure, the odd coach, like Capello or Giovanni Trapattoni, might never have worked outside the big-time, but most come up the hard way, from the bottom of the pyramid.

If you start further down and work your way up, the experience you gain is invaluable. You face a variety of situations and learn how to deal with them, often making mistakes. That was partly why I took the job at Watford: I wanted to measure myself in a different reality, one where I lacked the advantages I'd had at Chelsea when I walked into a top side that was on its way up. I felt Watford would present a series of challenges that would make me a better coach and help prepare me for my next job. I suspect many, particularly in England, saw it as a step down, a job in which there was little to be gained and the risks far outweighed the rewards. To me, though, real-world experience is essential. And I would have thought that, given the difficulties young British managers face in establishing themselves at top clubs, English football should focus on looking for guys who are a bit longer in the tooth and, perhaps, have spent more time building up their skills.

Ray Wilkins explains: 'Once upon a time clubs would look for managers who came through the ranks of the football pyramid, but today there is such a huge gulf between the Premier League and the rest of English football that it's difficult to do so. I mean, there's an abyss in every sense. Clubs are reluctant to take a guy from the Championship because the Premiership is full of stars, millionaire footballers with big personalities and big egos, and it's difficult to find someone in lower-league football who is capable of handling those kinds of players.'

To some degree, I can see how that might apply to the jump to, say, Manchester United or Liverpool, but surely the leap from a promotion contender in the Championship to a bottom-half Premiership club is not that great? After all, it ought to be a natural progression. Nobody expects a manager to go from League One to Arsenal or Chelsea, but they can work their way up. In England, though, this doesn't happen, and the game is worse off for it.

'But that's the culture of English football and it has always been that way,' says Andy Cale, of the FA. 'Clubs have always gone for famous ex-players who were seen as winners. In the last ten years some chairmen have become a bit more clever, but it's obvious that it will take time. In the meantime, however, this attitude in choosing managers has had disastrous effects. Just look at the number of sackings each year.'

Indeed. (And I've put together some interesting statistics on that issue, to which we will come later.) But I think it is clear to see that giving jobs to inexperienced managers has damaged the English game.

These seven years that the average Italian boss has spent outside Serie A are of crucial importance: they've given him a chance to grow, learn, develop in the equivalent of a long, fruitful apprenticeship. In England, on the other hand, too many managers fall into big jobs in the top-flight, either because of their reputation as players or because clubs simply don't think experience is that important.

What Did You Learn at School?

Compounding the issue of inexperience in England is the lack of a long-established coaching course, as there is in Italy at Coverciano: without its licence, you are not allowed to coach in Serie A or B. In England, the coaching courses are newer and attitudes towards formal education are far different.

'Our approach is both exploratory and pedagogic,' says Franco Ferrari, dean at Coverciano. 'Coaches come to us with some kind of imprint already there, usually what they learned as players. We view a big part of our role as illustrating the alternatives. We want them to be, as much as possible, comfortable with any kind of system so that they can pick the one that they believe suits them best.'

Like most coaching courses, there are modules on fitness, psychology, technique, nutrition, tactics and other aspects of working at the highest level. A recently retired footballer learns that he is now on the 'other side of the barricade' – it's almost a coming-of-age ritual. You begin to comprehend fully the various things to which you were subjected as a player. 'My very first course was back in 1975,' says Marcello Lippi. 'Within two weeks I began to view everything differently. Things as varied as sports medicine and equipment, they began to make sense to me. I started to understand why as players you were asked to do certain things. It was an eye-opener because it encouraged me to question and evaluate all the things we take for granted in football.'

But the learning is not just something which takes place in the class setting. At Coverciano interaction between students is not just encouraged, it is an integral part of the experience. Somehow one can't help but open up to one's colleagues. 'That's what I found truly important about Coverciano, the exchange of ideas between myself and my colleagues,' says Lippi. 'We would talk about everything – psychology, tactics, training methods. It was a constant evolution which helped me out tremendously. The more I think about it, what I hold dear is not just the course in itself, it was the atmosphere around it, that challenging, thought-provoking environment.'

In that sense, Coverciano is an academic environment, not dissimilar to a traditional university, another meeting point for young minds filled with intellectual curiosity. Some are bright, some less so, but they all share an enthusiasm for what they do and the belief that they can be the best or, at least, make a serious difference. Like any university, Coverciano is also a breeding ground for the radical, the smug and the self-assured. And, probably, that is part of the secret of its success.

'Coverciano does not give you truths, it gives you

possibilities,' says Lippi, 'and it has to be that way, because if there is one thing I've realized in many years of football it's that managers, particularly young ones, are extremely arrogant. They are convinced that they have nothing to learn, that they have the footballing truth in their grasp. But if you take them and you put them in a place like Coverciano there is a totally different spirit. They are surrounded by others like them and they'll want to take each other on, to explore each other's beliefs. It is like being back at school.'

In England, coaching badges have been around for many years, but coaching courses have only recently become formalized. It was only after considerable pressure from UEFA that licences became mandatory in the Premiership. Typically, this was met with resistance. I don't know if conservatism is a characteristic of footballers or of England (or, indeed, of English footballers) but there was a lot of opposition. It was the usual complaints from veterans:

- We never needed one before, why do we need one now?
- What's the point? If you're a bad manager, a coaching badge won't turn you into a good one.
- We won the World Cup without it, why do we need it now?

These attitudes are so prevalent that even the League Managers' Association can do little, as John Barnwell explains: 'In the summer of 2003 we had a big meeting and we were all in agreement. It was decided that every Premier League manager had to either have a coaching badge or be enrolled in a course to get one. Well, a few weeks into the season Leeds sack their manager and bring in Eddie Gray, a veteran of the club and favourite with the fans. Now, Eddie Gray didn't have the required qualifications. Eight years earlier he had enrolled in one of our coaching courses, but he didn't complete it.

'We tried to speak up, but we did not get far. Leeds simply announced that Gray was an interim manager and that was that: he did not have to abide by the rules. Now, I know that Leeds were in financial difficulty and that Eddie Gray is a legend in Leeds and he loves the club so he probably didn't ask for a big wage . . . but still. We had all pledged to abide by a certain rule, that managers had to have licences, and then, all of a sudden, Leeds do what they want, as if the rules no longer matter. I am not having a go at them, it just seems that certain attitudes will never go away. We are working to change that, but it takes time.'

Indeed it does. Some people simply point to the past, citing Sir Bobby Robson or Matt Busby: 'If they didn't need a badge, why do I?'

That argument is foolish for many reasons, not least because football has changed tremendously. But that two of the greatest managers British football has ever produced were short of a coaching badge certainly does not negate the notion that it can help a manager's development: 'I had my full coaching badge when I was twenty-four,' says Sir Alex Ferguson. 'To me it's the most important thing. It's quite right that you should have your full badge to coach. In my case, I became a full-time professional at twenty-two and I immediately said to myself that if I was going to commit myself full-time to this game, I had to learn as much as I could. So I did the course and I went every year for a refresher course. In fact, the year I got married I did not go on my honeymoon. I went on a refresher course.'

I believe that a well-run coaching course can be invaluable in the development of a manager and I am glad that one of the greatest ever, Sir Alex, shares my view on its importance. (But I cannot recommend skipping your honeymoon as he did. I know my wife would never have let me get away with it . . .)

I am surprised by the opposition and general distrust of the coaching course that I find in England. It is seen as a chore, like standing in line to get a passport so that you can travel abroad. Too often, the coaching badge is viewed as merely a box you need to tick. Because of this, the English coaching course is not all it should be. The old adage of getting out what you put in holds true: people see it as an ordeal so they get little out of it.

'European countries have always been ahead of us in terms of preparation,' says Barnwell. 'We never had the benefit of managers who were prepared properly. We have always been convinced that a great player can hang up his boots, sit on that bench and become a great manager straight away.' From the head of the English League Managers' Association, that's quite an indictment. Certainly Barnwell speaks freely and candidly, which I admire. He is not afraid to point out the deficiencies in English managers, the people he represents.

Wenger, too, speaks plainly: 'The English are behind because they do not have an academic approach to football,' he says. 'In France we've had a coaching licence and a coaching course for years. I took my first course when I was twenty-five. Even when I was a young player I knew I wanted to coach and realized I had a lot to learn. In England, if you were a good player the road is all downhill.'

So another common thread links Sir Alex and Wenger: both men did coaching courses in their early twenties, when they were still immersed in their playing careers. 'When I was a player at Dunfermline I would sit down for lunch and say, "OK, the salt is the central defender, the pepper is the right back, the brown sauce is the striker . . ." and I would plan football tactics and situations,' says Sir Alex.

To me, it seems obvious that if you love the game so much, if you are so passionate about it that you think about it in every spare moment, you would want to talk about it in an academic setting, such as a coaching course. If the thinking side of football is so important to you, as it clearly was and is to Wenger and Sir Alex, surely you would want to compare notes and ideas with your peers? And yet, because a coaching course is not ingrained in English footballing tradition, it is greeted with scepticism, if not outright hostility.

'It's true, our managers, with some exceptions, are blinkered,' says Tony Colbert. 'They all think the same way and rarely see things from another point of view. But that's the way we English are. We mistrust all things foreign, beginning with the euro. After all, we're an island nation. I myself, despite being English, come from outside the football world, my background is sports science so I, too, was met with scepticism. I met managers who said, "This is how we've always done things, so we're not going to change." Others said, "Well, we know this method works, why try something else?" Very few of them even wondered if it was possible to do things differently or if, by doing things differently, somehow they might improve things.'

The irony in this is that, for all its outward traditionalism, English football has, on occasion, been very progressive in adopting new ideas and concepts. The English league was among the first in the world to award three points for a win, and one of the first to introduce play-offs for promotion to the top flight. Countless English attitudes appear immutable but, in fact, are relatively recent developments – such as the practice of throwing recently retired players in at the deep end of coaching. There is a perception around the world that this is just the English way of doing things, but twenty to thirty years ago it was easier for a schoolteacher to become a manager than an ex-player.

'In the past the Football Association insisted that to coach you had to be a qualified teacher,' says Gordon Taylor. 'We at the PFA led the battle against it. We were convinced – and we still are today – that those who played football at the highest level are best suited to teaching the game, as long as they themselves have the proper instruction, of course.

'The Football Association viewed things differently – this was the time of Charles Hughes, after all – and that's part of the reason why their courses were not very good. They were full of people who had never played the game at a high level. For ex-players it was virtually impossible to participate. For them it would mean becoming qualified teachers at the end of their careers and only afterward could they begin to coach.'

I can't imagine there were many ex-players who, at thirty-five, hung up their boots and cracked open the books to become qualified schoolteachers just so that they could get into coaching. It seems like an absurd barrier of entry, designed to protect those who were already in the system (the schoolteachers) while keeping out those on the outside (the ex-players). It reminds me of some of those laws they introduced in the south of the United States after slavery was abolished, laws which stipulated that one could only vote if one's grandfather had voted. Clearly, if slavery had just been abolished not too many freed slaves had grandparents who voted, which essentially meant the whole thing was a sham.

As it happened, according to Taylor, there was a silver lining to the FA's intransigence. Because it was virtually impossible for players to get into the FA's coaching courses, unless they were qualified schoolteachers, there was mounting pressure for an alternative. The PFA stepped in, setting up its own courses, which were run by ex-pros. It quickly turned into an ideological battle, with Charles Hughes and the FA on one hand and the PFA and the players on the other.

That Man Again . . . Charles Hughes's Legacy

Hughes was one of the most influential figures in the English game throughout the 1960s and 1970s. He was the FA's technical director and his *Football Association Coaching Book of Soccer Tactics and Skills* neatly codifies a certain vision of the game; it's close to the stereotype of English 'Route One' football. Hughes was an advocate of direct play and famously suggested in 1989 that 'Brazil has the least likely chance of winning the World Cup in the future' unless they 'eradicate and change their views'. In his view, Brazilian football was not direct enough, an opinion seemingly countered by the fact that the Selecao won two of the four World Cups held since his famous pronouncement and reached the final in another.

In Hughes's defence, his view of the game was based on his statistical analysis of matches and, in particular, a study of the areas of the pitch from which goals were scored. A team's objective thus became to get the ball into those areas as frequently as possible. He called the areas the POMO – Positions of Maximum Opportunity – and they became the focus of all play. Get the ball into the POMO enough times and you're sure to outscore the opposition. Equally, the game became fiercely territorial. Like a rugby match, it was about gaining ground on the opponent, because the closer you got to his goal, the closer you got to POMO. He had succeeded in reducing football to a mathematical formula . . . or so he thought.

'He believed in things which today might seem absurd,' says Taylor. 'For example, he said that Brazil would be a far stronger side if they passed the ball less. Or that one should never pass the ball more than three times before shooting on goal. And you always had to hit the ball long because it increased the possibility of winning a throw-in or a free kick and thus gaining ground. Every movement, both in defence and in attack, was based on statistics and percentages.'

There was a very definite logic to Hughes's approach. For example, if half of all goals are scored from set-pieces, it means that this is the most 'efficient' way of scoring. In a typical game only a fraction of the time is taken up with set-pieces yet they provide 50 per cent of the score. So Hughes figured that if a team increased the number of set-pieces awarded to them, it would increase the number of goals they scored. It was pure mathematics and probability.

And how do you earn more set-pieces? By winning penalties, corners, free kicks and throw-ins. The way to do that is to play with a direct, up-tempo style. Penalties and free kicks result when an opposing player fouls one of your men. Fouls, usually mistimed tackles, occur when two players from opposite teams come into contact with each other. How do you increase the number of fouls, and thereby set-pieces? You run at the opposition as much as possible. A similar argument relates to the winning of corner kicks and throw-ins. More often than not they result when the opposition is under pressure. And the way to put them under pressure is to be as direct as possible, to hurry them up, to bombard them with crosses and long balls. This was Hughes's thinking. It was all about creating the circumstances for something positive to happen, whether it was winning a free kick or reaching POMO. And everything had to be done at pace because the idea was to reach POMO as often as possible. After all, the statistics had told him that, say, teams score 20 per cent of the time when they have the ball centrally and just outside the box. Hughes reckoned that if, in the course of a game, a team reached that area five times they would score one goal. But if they reached that same POMO area ten times they would score two goals. Hence the direct, long-ball game.

The possession game favoured by countries such as Brazil, Holland and others seemed anathema to him. To Hughes, knocking the ball about did not serve any purpose. It did not put the opposition under pressure and thus did not force them to make errors. It did not lead to set-pieces. And, most of all, it wasted precious time, time that could be spent getting the ball forward as quickly and directly as possible.

The problem with this thinking is that although it may work on a blackboard, when it is put into practice other factors come to the fore, which are obvious to those who have played football at any level.

'Hughes believed keeping possession was useless because when you were keeping the ball you weren't shooting on goal or reaching POMO or winning set-pieces,' says Taylor. 'Well, that's fine if both teams are thinking like that. But if you employ Hughes's tactics while the opposition plays possession football, well, you've got a problem. You find yourself continually giving the ball away and not getting it back. And that forces you to spend an enormous amount of energy because, as anyone who has kicked a football knows, winning the ball back is extremely tiring. You may run around furiously for two or three minutes before you win it back. And then, if you play Hughes's brand of football, you'll kick it long and just lose it again and find yourself chasing again. Over ninety minutes that can destroy a team. In fact, keeping possession is a way for a team to get a breather.'

Hughes's brand of football worked when both sides employed it. Or, rather, when both teams play 'long ball', the one who plays it 'the most' tends to win. If neither side values possession it's clear that the team which gets the ball forward most quickly or most often will emerge victorious. But if one team can play possession football – or vary its playing style – it will have the upper hand. I don't think it's a coincidence that in Hughes's heyday, the

1970s and early 1980s, English football produced two exceptional sides – the legendary Liverpool teams and Brian Clough's Nottingham Forest – which had a very different approach.

The Liverpool teams, which won four European Cups, have acquired almost mythical status in footballing lore. Growing up, I had seen them play on television and remember that they were truly special. I knew less about Nottingham Forest, winners of the European Cup in 1978–79 and 1979–80, so I spent a weekend watching old videos of Clough's side, and realized that this team in many ways had escaped the English footballing stereotypes.

Forest's 4–4–2 was a modern, flexible formation. The strikers were both comfortable on the ball, and while they were good in the air, it was more a result of timing their leaps than their size and strength. Their movement was good too: rather than simply waiting for the ball, they often retreated to help out the midfield, thereby creating space for teammates to run into.

The midfield was busy and hard-working – you can tell that the two central midfielders were the main ball-winners, given the task of dictating the spacing between defence and midfield as well as midfield and attack. In that sense, it was traditionally British. What was less traditional was the play on the flanks, particularly on the right, where there was a very physical winger and an attacking full-back, like Viv Anderson, who would come forward regularly with overlapping runs.

Beyond that, what made Forest different from Hughesian football was the way they defended. When the other side had possession, the team retreated into their own half, waiting for the opposition, goading them to come forward, like a cobra ready to strike. They did not press them high up the pitch, as Hughes might have wanted, but instead forced them to come out of their shell. The result was twofold. On the one hand, it funnelled the opposition towards the two central midfielders who were good at clogging up the space and making it difficult for the other team. At the same time, it freed space behind the opposition's back four, which Forest were good at attacking. As soon as they won the ball they came forward with a direct but intelligent counter-attack. I make this point about Forest to show how even though in those years much of the rest of the world may have regarded English football as tactically naïve and unsophisticated, some teams were playing different, modern football. Liverpool and Forest were exceptions but they proved that there was a different way of doing things and that it could be successful. Unfortunately for English football, not enough people took notice until several years later.

'We at the PFA, together with the players, published a pamphlet in the early 1990s where we were very harsh with the FA,' says Taylor. 'We pointed out to them that, even though England invented football, even though we have more professional clubs than any other country, more registered footballers than any other European nation, more spectators than any other nation, in reality England had always underachieved. In fact, in 1974 and 1978 we did not even qualify for the World Cup! This should have been a sign that, instead of admiring ourselves and our glorious history, the time had come for a change, and for us to finally improve ourselves.'

His views are echoed by David Platt: 'We always tend

to isolate ourselves, to cut ourselves off,' he says. 'It really bothers me that so many of us are still convinced that we're the best at everything. There were people with me at the FA who are convinced that our coaching course is the best in the world, yet until very recently all our courses were based on Charles Hughes's teachings. To get your badge you had to recite his principles from memory like a parrot. Now things are changing but it's difficult to rid yourself of the arrogance and the dogma that for many years was part of our DNA.'

Unlike the Coverciano course – which generally enjoyed the support of public opinion, the footballing establishment and the players – the English coaching course struggled to get off the ground. First, there was the ideological battle between Hughes and the 'progressives', both in terms of tactical principles and in terms of whether the course should be made more accessible to former players rather than just schoolteachers. And then there was the need to convince aspiring managers that the course was worthwhile, which was far from simple in a country where badges, licences and even identity cards are viewed with scepticism.

When, like me, you come from the outside into English football, you are often surprised that you take some things for granted and others do not. The importance of a coaching course was one. When I reflect on what Platt and Taylor said – that there was an ingrained arrogance and a reluctance to change in English football – I found myself wondering the same about Italy: are we equally convinced that our way of doing things is the best?

On some issues we are, particularly when it comes to organization, fitness work and training facilities and methods. On others, such as stadiums, merchandising, governance . . . well, we'd have to be mad to think we're the best. On tactics and coaching, we have a lot to be proud of, perhaps because we do not believe that there is one 'correct' way of doing things. Indeed, Coverciano teaches us that there are many different tactical systems and formations, each of which has its merits and drawbacks.

I took the UEFA Pro licence at Coverciano and the UEFA B licence with the English FA. I found that the English course tries to emulate Coverciano but for the time being lacks the history of debating and academic discourse of the course in Italy.

'I didn't learn much at the coaching course,' says Platt. 'Sure, they'll teach you a few things here and there but I learned little that was new to me. I think it's because we're not yet ready for that kind of dialogue and debate. We're just not used to it. Each of us sits there, pretends to listen to the others, then goes off and does his own thing. There is no discussion. It's too comfortable. I would want a course which is "uncomfortable", which forces people to ask themselves basic questions, then find answers. I would want a course which pushes you intellectually. But maybe we're not ready to be forced to think.'

The good news for English football is that enough people now see the importance of a proper coaching course, one that is not just a formality but a true learning experience. 'A good course gives you a wider vision of the game, a more solid base,' says Barnwell. 'Without it, managers simply put into practice what they learned as players because that was all they knew. If they were lucky enough to work under a good manager they'd know that manager's system inside and out. That's the best-case scenario. And yet football is constantly evolving. You have got to stay up to date. Those who have always done things a certain way and don't know any alternatives rarely know how to reinvent themselves or react to a sport which is changing.'

Ultimately, I think the role of a good coaching course is not dissimilar to that of any good school. To me a good school teaches you the basic facts, the cultural tools that you will need to go through life. But it also teaches you from multiple perspectives and, where there is debate, illustrates the various viewpoints with their pros and cons. A good school does not teach you *what* to think, it teaches you *how* to think. Coverciano is already a long way towards that goal. The English course remains behind but it is now on the right track.

Part of the difficulty English football has had in recent years in producing top managers capable of successfully running the biggest clubs in Europe stems largely from the two factors we have discussed: the coaching course is still a 'work-in-progress', not a serious academic endeavour, and clubs tend to rush young managers through the process, handing out top-flight jobs often without taking into account whether or not their new boss has enough experience. The old process of working your way up the ranks has been largely abandoned in favour of 'fast-tracking'.

'When I go back through my notes and read about the training sessions I ran two years ago, well, they are very different from the ones I run today,' says Mourinho. 'Why? Because you have to keep changing and learning. You have to keep analysing your methodology. That comes from having a good base but also from building the experience. Nobody can teach you that when you're a player. When you're a player, you don't care about those things. You don't have the mentality to learn. You must go and be a coach or manager. It is important to have a good knowledge, but you also need the experience.'

That's why a change in attitude on this issue, coupled with a strengthening in the breadth and style of the FA coaching courses would help to produce a breed of successful English managers capable of meeting the challenges of Premiership football. It's important that the English game gets this right because, in the Premiership, a manager is not just a coach, he is responsible for many other aspects of the game, including scouting and transfers. Putting somebody, however smart, in charge of budgets worth tens of millions of pounds while asking him, at the same time, to manage a club is not just risky, it's foolish. Like giving an eighteen-year-old the keys to the Ferrari.

Chapter Six

A 2500-year-old Strategy

Have you ever tried to explain tactics in football to somebody who has no clue about the game?

It's not the easiest thing to do. Deconstruct tactics, and you find that basically it's a way to minimize a team's weaknesses while maximizing its strengths. That is what it boils down to. The concept is simple: it's about gaining an advantage over your opponent and it has been around for thousands of years.

Sun Tzu, a Chinese military historian who lived nearly five centuries before the birth of Christ, neatly summarized a number of the same concepts in his book *The Art of War*. It's about military strategy, of course, but many of the ideas are valid and can be applied in the present. *The Art of War* is regularly assigned in the dog-eat-dog world of MBA courses, and Luiz Felipe Scolari, who coached Brazil to the 2002 World Cup, gave a copy to each of his players and ordered them to read it. Some of the players, such as Cafu, the captain, have said reading that book gave them the tactical understanding to win the World Cup. (On this point, I'm not so sure. I would have thought that a team with Ronaldo, Rivaldo and Ronaldinho wouldn't need millennia-old advice . . . but I'll take Cafu's word for it.)

Proponents of Sun Tzu argue that his principles can be applied in any confrontation, negotiation or even something as mundane as a football match. And, in fact, his tenets are at the heart of what we call tactics and gamesmanship.

Consider the following pearls of wisdom.

1. All warfare is based on deception. Hence, when able to attack, we must seem unable. When using our forces, we must seem inactive. When we are near, we must make the enemy believe we are far away. When far away, we must make him believe we are near. Feign disorder and crush him.

In Italy this is basic stuff. And I don't mean deception in terms of diving and tricking the referee into granting a penalty. It's the dummy run, it's the movement of a striker into space, it's a full-back advancing to help his team gain a man advantage in midfield. It's about making yourself seem weaker than you are, lulling your opponent into a false sense of security, then striking without mercy. This kind of thing is at the heart of what we call tactics. If it did not exist, the stronger team would always win.

As an aside, the idea of appearing weaker than you are is useful in many situations, but there are occasions when you need to do the opposite. It makes sense to appear weaker if your opponent already believes you are weaker or if he believes you are level in strength. But if he already thinks you're stronger, make him believe you're even stronger than you are. Like the blowfish who makes himself big to scare his predators, it can be a good way to demoralize your opponent before even going into battle.

> 2. The general who wins a battle makes many calculations in his temple before the battle is fought. The general who loses a battle makes but few calculations beforehand. Thus do many calculations lead to victory, and few calculations lead to defeat . . . even more when there is no calculation at all! It is by attention to this point that I can foresee who is likely to win or lose.

This one seems obvious. The better prepared you are, the better off you will be. And this is common to England and Italy. Yet I think it goes beyond that. When Sun Tzu talks about 'calculations' he means figuring out every possible scenario and conjuring up a course of action for every possibility. If the opponent attacks on the flank, what do I do? If he retreats, what do I do? If he splits his force, what do I do? The idea is to have an answer for everything. Effectively, you are playing the match (or fighting the battle) beforehand in your mind, examining every possible permutation and finding a way to deal with it. Many say that battles are won or lost before you step on to the field. He who thinks through every detail beforehand and has an answer for every situation is bound to win.

This is where another factor comes into play, one in which, I think, Italian football is ahead of the English game: research. In football terms, it means scouting.

You can have the finest tactical mind going through every possible scenario in 'calculations' before the match, but if he's working with poor or incomplete information, it won't help much. If he believes Adriano prefers his right foot or that Michael Owen is not particularly fast, then his calculations and his game plan will be fundamentally flawed. This is where the scouting comes in. How much do you know about your opponent? And how much does he know about you? Your game plan will only be as good as the information available to you.

I should point out, however, that Sun Tzu and I are not in complete agreement on this point, although I think it's important because it's how many managers, especially Italian ones, approach the game. Over-analysis is risky and we've seen numerous Italian teams who are guilty of it. They become so detail-oriented that they lose sight of the big picture. They burden themselves with so many calculations and instructions that they become preoccupied with what to do next rather than with the task at hand, which is playing football and winning the game.

> 3. Tactics are like water, for water, in its natural course, runs away from high places and hastens downwards. Water shapes its course according to the nature of the ground over which it flows. The soldier works out his victory in relation to the foe whom he is facing. Therefore, just as water retains no constant shape, so in warfare there are no constant conditions. He who can modify his tactics in relation to his opponent and thereby succeed in winning may be called a heaven-born captain.

So, Sun Tzu advises us to plan an approach based on the opponent's qualities and characteristics. This is a hallmark of Italian football. We worry about our opponents end-lessly and try to make adjustments accordingly. We pride ourselves on being 'tactically flexible', which means we will adjust and counter whatever moves he makes. We try to be 'chameleon-like', both as a way of protecting ourselves against an opponent's changing tactics and keeping him off-balance and unsettled.

Tactical flexibility is not necessarily negative or defensive, though it is often associated with being reactive, rather than proactive. The basic assumption is that the weak are reactive, while the strong are proactive. How many times have we heard managers say, 'Well, we're not going to worry about the other team, we're just going to go out and play our game'? I've probably said it myself. It's a sign of strength: the idea is to impose your game on the opponents, not react to what they do. There is little concern for the opponent and even less attempt at making adjustments to counter what he does. When a manager changes formations in Italy, he is seen as looking for solutions. A manager whose team is comfortable in a number of tactical schemes and formations is considered a good tactician, whose team is sophisticated and modern. In England, if a manager changes things round, he is confused, a 'tinkerer', or he 'doesn't know what his best team is'. The idea of varying formations or personnel based on your opponent seems, in every sense of the word, to be foreign. This is where Sun Tzu is least 'English' and most 'Italian'.

4. The good fighters of old first put themselves beyond the possibility of defeat and then waited for an opportunity of defeating the enemy. To secure ourselves against defeat lies in our own hands, but the opportunity of defeating the enemy is provided by the enemy himself. Thus the good

fighter is able to secure himself against defeat, but cannot make certain of defeating the enemy.

This might as well be the recipe for 'Catenaccio', the famous (some might say infamous) system developed in Italy in the 1960s. It sums up the basic truisms of a safety-first approach. Defending is – generally – easier than attacking because it does not require the same level of creativity or technique, whether in war or football. Scoring a goal is tougher than defending, if only because a striker has to beat a defender and a goalkeeper and put the ball into the back of the net, while the defender merely needs to clear the ball away. And, no, I'm not just saying this because I used to be a centre-forward. The weaker combatant will usually be more inclined to defending. Sun Tzu's implication is that your first priority should always be to defend yourself because, as long as you are alive, you have a chance to win. If you prioritize defending, you increase your chance of staying alive, which is essential to any battle, and force your opponent to devote more energy and resources to overcoming your defences, which means his own defence is weakened. Because defending requires less effort and ability than attack, your opponent will grow weary and, eventually, make a mistake, which, if you are clever, you can exploit with a swift counter-attack.

In general terms, this is the philosophy behind Catenaccio, although a few important caveats explain why, thankfully, this tactical approach has not become the norm (and, indeed, is nowhere near as prevalent as it used to be in Italy). First, as Sun Tzu points out, you can secure yourself against defeat, but 'cannot make certain of defeating the enemy'. That's because the philosophy is predicated upon the opponent making a mistake and conceding an opportunity. But what if the opponent does not make a mistake? In a war, where there is no final whistle, one side will eventually make a mistake. But a football match lasts ninety minutes and it's possible that, in that time frame, your opponent will not make an error that affords you a chance, so the result is, at best, a draw, when the objective is victory. This is especially true when your opponent shares your safety-first outlook.

Also, defending may not be as physically tiring as attacking but it is often more mentally tiring. When your team has possession, and the ball is on the other side of the pitch, you can give yourself a mental breather, you're safe, you won't concede and you're not likely to be involved. You can relax, break your concentration, maybe even think of something creative or intelligent that may help you break down your opponent. However, if you are defending, your concentration needs to be 100 per cent, regardless of where the ball is. You do not have possession, which means that every moment that passes harbours potential danger. You may not do much running around, but you are constantly worrying, studying and watching your opponent, trying to figure out and anticipate their next move. It's tremendously draining psychologically, and late in the game it can lead to precisely the kind of mental errors you are trying to avoid. Ultimately, the point of the game is to win, not to avoid defeat. And this holds true in Italy as it does in England. To win, you need to score, which means – if you are a follower of Sun Tzu – you must devote some of your defensive resources to attacking. The instant you do this, you become vulnerable.

And, once you're vulnerable, it's a question of playing the odds. You cannot 'secure yourself against defeat', as Sun Tzu might say, because in football, unlike war, an individual mistake at your end or a piece of individual genius at the other can determine a goal. And that is well beyond your control.

The Tactical Dogma: Stuck on 4–4–2

Remember my boxer analogy? The Italian boxer worries about his opponent: first and foremost he is preoccupied with defending himself so he tries to gain any advantage he can. The English boxer gamely comes forward, unconcerned with what his opponent might do.

In Italy, tactics are a huge part of the game at every level: preparation, coaching, discourse, the fans. It's a country where you can wander into a bar and hear people talking about Lazio's flat back four and whether it wouldn't be better if one of the central defenders dropped off when facing teams with only one striker. Or, equally, you might hear a discussion of whether Serginho's overlapping runs are more effective than Marek Jankulovski's when Clarence Seedorf is in midfield, given the Dutchman's tendency to drift inside.

Italian football is full of numbers and schemes: 4–4–2, 3–5–2, 4–3–3, 4–3–2–1, 4–2–3–1, 4–3–1–2, 5–3–2, 5–4–1, 3–4–3. And those are just the formations. There are endless variations, from the 'diamond', to the man 'in the hole', to having two men 'in the hole'. And then the marking. It can be zonal, man-to-man or mixed, with or without a sweeper. Plus, the differences in style. You have teams who play slowly, almost at a South American pace, while others bomb forward at every opportunity. Some use the midfield to build play, others happily get the ball forward as quickly as they can, in perfect Charles Hughes style, bypassing the midfield.

There is a tactical variety in the Italian game that, perhaps, exists in no other league in the world. It is reflected in the formations and the philosophies, which range from arch-conservative Catenaccio to brazen, all-out attack.

To me this is entirely different from England, where the basic 4–4–2 ruled for so long. In the last decade, few teams have been consistently successful using any other formation. Martin O'Neill's Leicester used a 3–5–2, Sam Allardyce's Bolton employs the 4–5–1 and Manchester United likewise experimented with a 4–2–3–1 or 4–5–1 scheme. Then, of course, there is Chelsea, which employed a variety of formations under Ranieri and, with Mourinho, tends to prefer 4–3–3.

Everybody else traditionally has stuck to a rather rigid version of the 4–4–2, featuring almost exclusively a flat back four defending zonally and central midfielders, whose main job is destructive and ball-winning, rather than constructive. Of course, football is always evolving and, even as I write this, more and more clubs are trying a different formation, a version of the 4–5–1, which has been much criticized by both fans and the media.

I think most 4–5–1 schemes in England, with a few exceptions, consist of little more than taking off a striker and inserting a third central ball-winner in midfield. Tactically, they are rather simple and still in their infancy; few have yet had a chance to refine them and turn them into anything other than primarily defensive schemes, though the likes of Iain Dowie and David Moyes have done some interesting things with one-striker formations.

Still, when I came to England in 1996 it was one of the things that surprised me: the fact that most teams, by and large, played a similar brand of football using identical tactical schemes. Across Europe, teams were using all sorts of formations. At Juventus we had won the Champions' League with a 4–3–3 scheme, beating Ajax, which used a 3–3–1–3. Germany had won the European Championships with the 3–5–2 and, in fact, under Terry Venables, England had used the 'Christmas Tree' or 4–3–2–1 formation. Yet the Premiership was dominated by the basic, no frills 4–4–2.

I don't think it's surprising that Italy has far more tactical variety. As I have said, tactics, calculations and strategy are ingrained in the Italian approach to the game. Couple this tradition of finding solutions 'at the chalkboard' with the influence of the Coverciano coaching school – where tactics are analysed closely – and the result is a footballing culture based on tactical flexibility.

'Italian coaches are very evolved tactically. In fact, we're probably the most advanced in the world,' says Marcello Lippi. 'If you think about it, it's logical. A good manager has to have convictions, but those convictions must not be certainties. What's the difference? A certainty is immutable, it's a dogma. A conviction is a belief that, based on the circumstances, may or may not change. It's something on which you can build. As you grow as a manager, you learn and better yourself and re-evaluate your convictions. What may have been true before may no longer be true now. And so, because you have convictions and not certainties, you are ready to change your system. It may be because your opponents have started playing a certain way or because you have a different set of players or maybe the weather conditions. Whatever it is, being able to change your convictions is a sign of intelligence. I know it's a cliché, but, ultimately, the great coach is the one whose formation maximizes the strengths of his players. That is the ultimate objective.'

The idea is to find a formation that exalts the individual qualities of the players, in which the sum is greater than the parts. From a manager's perspective, again, there is a trade-off. You want your players to be comfortable in your system while leaving them free to express themselves and play to their strengths. Of course, at the same time, your team has to be balanced and organized. And, naturally, it has to be a tactical formation with which you, as manager, are thoroughly familiar.

As you can see, it's far from easy. But it's what we in Italy strive towards. We recognize the basic footballing dilemma: does a manager force his players to fit into his favoured formation or does he find a formation that enables him to field his best eleven? In England, until recently, there was no dilemma: the formation was 4–4–2, and the best eleven had to fit into it.

Elsewhere, though, it's one of football's basic debates: pragmatist v. idealist. And in Italy we have our fair share of the latter, such as Arrigo Sacchi and Zdenek Zeman, although most managers accept that their formation should be determined by the players at their disposal.

'I am convinced that you cannot always play the same way,' says Fabio Capello, who employed a variety of formations throughout his career. 'It all depends on the players you have.'

Mourinho agrees: 'Right now, for example, we play with

just one striker,' he says. 'But if the club goes and buys me one of the best strikers in the world, of course we might play with two strikers. You have to be ready to change it around based on the players you have.'

Coaches like Lippi, Capello and Giovanni Trapattoni, all phenomenally successful, embody, albeit in different ways, the pragmatic approach whereby tactics are determined by personnel. The Juventus side that I captained to the Champions' League crown in 1995–96 is a good example of this. Originally, Alex Del Piero and I were the strikers, but Fabrizio Ravanelli was in such exceptional form that Lippi found a system that would include a third striker.

'In the European Cup final against Ajax, Juventus had three up front and they kept playing the ball into space, exploiting the fact that the two Ajax full-backs were always looking to advance,' says Sir Alex Ferguson. 'Their tactics were spot-on. They should have killed the game by half-time.'

We took pride in our tactical ability in that Juve side. We understood the benefits of changing things round and trying different systems even though it often meant we had to work harder, both mentally and physically (when you're one of three forwards, you have to run that much more to help out the midfield). 'If you have smart players who understand tactics and are comfortable in multiple systems, then making frequent changes can be a big plus,' says Lippi. 'It's another weapon in your arsenal. Having said that, though, there are players who never learn how to play in a different system or in a different way. The more you try to teach them the more you confuse them and you run the risk of hurting their confidence. Equally, there are coaches who are very good at understanding the game but are completely inept at finding players to suit their formation. It's not that simple.'

Mourinho, himself a tactical chameleon – through his career he has alternated between the preferred 4–3–3 and a modified 4–4–2 – has a special appreciation for the kind of tactical versatility found in Italy: 'When I play against the Italians, I have no idea what I'm going to face. When I faced Lazio in the semi-finals of the UEFA Cup, they played a 4–5–1 in the first leg, then switched to three at the back for the return leg. They just adapt so easily to any formation. They think of football in relation to the opponent and change the way they play accordingly.'

That's anathema to British football. Changing systems is seen as a sign of weakness and insecurity. Then again traditionally there wasn't much reason to do it because almost every team played the same way, 4–4–2. The question then becomes: why is this the case?

'We English do not think about tactics,' David Platt explains. 'We always played 4–4–2 and, with a few exceptions, we're going to continue playing it. Besides, Charles Hughes's philosophy was based largely on 4–4–2. It's only in the past fifteen years that some of us have tried something different, like 4–3–3. The problem is that to play 4–3–3 you need wingers and we don't have any. There is another factor: the 4–4–2 is the easiest formation to play if you're poor technically and we've never been the best in terms of technique.'

Platt raises an interesting point: the idea that the English 4–4–2 is a result of the players the country produces. Indeed, to play 4–3–3 you need wingers; to play 4–3–1–2 you need a 'number ten', who plays between the lines; to play 3–5–2 you need wing-backs . . . If these players don't exist in England, you can't use the more exotic formations.

Is this a chicken-and-egg situation? In other words, does English football not play 4–3–3 because it doesn't produce wingers, or does it not produce wingers because it doesn't play 4–3–3? Youngsters generally adapt to the needs of the team. But what constitutes a winger? What if, say, Craig Bellamy had developed in an environment where everyone played 4–3–3? Would he be a centre-forward or a winger? Or what about Joe Cole? Under Glenn Roeder he was essentially a left-sided player in a midfield four, even though with his dribbling skills and vision he might have been better suited to playing in the hole or in a free role. This is not too dissimilar from what he does now at Chelsea with Mourinho. Yet in the English game players like that are square pegs in round holes. They simply don't fit. Glenn Hoddle, one of the most crystalline talents produced in England, was often harshly criticized and ended up going abroad. Matt Le Tissier avoided much of the criticism at club level because he stayed at Southampton, but he only won a few caps for England. Go back a few years and there are other examples, from Rodney Marsh to Stan Bowles.

I wonder if they would have been treated differently if there had been more tactical variety in England, if they had been allowed to interpret their positions in their own way, with their own quirks, with the team working on their behalf. I believe teams should maximize players' strengths and do what's best for the group. In some cases, it simply does not make sense for everyone to be treated and made to work in the same way. For example, if I have a Roberto Baggio on my team I may ask him not to run and chase players when we don't have possession. That's because, when we regain possession, I want him to be fresh and lucid, so he can weave his magic. As a coach, you want to see effort from everyone, but you don't want to see them run themselves into the ground.

'A number ten like that does not run, but you can have players who don't run,' says Mourinho. 'In our team at Chelsea we have three attacking players, but I don't want them chasing full-backs and making themselves tired. That's why I have a triangle in midfield, which slides laterally to do the defensive work. So, for example, Robben might not defend when their full-back comes forward with the ball. That's OK, because Lampard will then go across and challenge him and the other two midfielders will cover for him.'

Mourinho's belief, that it is not always desirable for all eleven players to 'work their socks off' (as I used to say when I was managing Chelsea), is rare in English football, where there is a kind of democratic ethos that everyone must work equally hard. It's an admirable idea, but in football it's impractical. Some players simply lack the work rate of others, and if you try to make them keep up, you may affect other aspects of their game. Just imagine if Romario had been born in Rotherham instead of Rio. Would he have made it as a footballer? Or would some drill sergeant of a manager have run him into the ground at an early age?

Andy Cale at the FA admits that perhaps English football is paying the price for a certain type of closed-mindedness. 'Only now are we beginning to produce managers who are a little bit different,' he says. 'I don't think it's down to the coaching courses we had before, though it's true that they were based more on technique than tactics. I think maybe we were a bit obtuse. We perhaps sat on our laurels after winning the World Cup in 1966.'

In many ways England is a conservative country and, without an established coaching course that illustrates a variety of methods, managers ended up preaching what they had known as players, which was, inevitably, the 4–4–2. It became a self-perpetuating cycle, passed down through the generations.

'Tradition is very important here. They play 4–4–2 and that's it,' says Eriksson. 'I don't know why exactly, I just know it's in their blood. They've done it all their lives and they see no reason to change. Among British managers, the only one I've seen who occasionally does things differently is Glenn Hoddle, but then again he played for many years abroad and maybe it's down to that.

'Change isn't easy,' he adds. 'You need to have a plan, you need to be able to explain it well and the players have to be able to accept it. That's why I did not change much. The only new thing I introduced was the diamond formation in midfield. For the players it was a completely new thing. We tried it in a few training sessions, they accepted it and it works. It's a sign that, at least on the England team, the players are open-minded.'

They may be open-minded, but events shortly after my chat with Eriksson, at Euro 2004, showed that they are not all comfortable with the diamond. The midfielders, led by captain David Beckham, approached Eriksson and said they were more comfortable in a flat midfield four. They asked to switch back to a normal 4–4–2 and, ever the pragmatist, Eriksson agreed. It shows that, even with a clever coach, intelligent players and a lot of goodwill, it's hard to give up the habit of a lifetime.

One man who happily goes against the grain and feels no special allegiance to the 4–4–2 is Sir Alex Ferguson. 'I don't know why English clubs are fixated on playing 4–4–2,' he says. 'I seldom play it. I learned to play with one striker up front when I was a player. I was a striker, but I lost my pace, so I decided to drop off the front. I found that nobody was picking me up, so I had time on the ball and found that I could make the passes I wanted to make.

'When I became manager of St Mirren, I implemented the system and I remember the players saying, "What kind of system is this?" I had a big argument with the directors. Later, at Aberdeen, I had Steve Archibald up front and Joe Harper dropping off behind. Then I got [Mark] McGhee and Archibald would drop behind. It was the same story at United. We had Mark Hughes and Brian McClair, then Mark Hughes and Eric Cantona, then Andy Cole and Eric Cantona, then Andy Cole or Dwight Yorke and Teddy Sheringham . . . What English teams always did was predictable. It's stupid to say, "You have to always have two up the park." If you do that, you only have one point of attack, whereas, if you have one guy dropping off, you have two points of attack.'

The issue with having multiple 'points of attack' is much debated in Italy. Indeed, it's the basis of what we call the *trequartista* (literally, three-quarter man), the guy 'in the hole' behind one or two strikers. The idea is that this player operates 'between the lines', behind the opposing midfield but not quite level with the defence. A player in this position is difficult to defend against, as Sir Alex points out. If a central defender picks him up, that defender is inevitably pulled out of position, leaving more room for the other striker. If one of the central midfielders drops back to mark him, the opposition then find themselves a man short in the middle of the park. And if, as often happens in England, the opposition hold their positions and make no adjustment, the player 'between the lines' has time on the ball. And his team has two points of attack: one through him and another through his colleague up the park.

Still, there is a certain irony in Sir Alex's words, which illustrates how tactics are talked about (or not talked about) in England. During the 2005–06 season, Manchester United tried out several formations, including the 4–2–3–1 and the 4–3–3, with decidedly mixed results. In fact, some fans started chanting 'Four–four–two!' to voice their disapproval. To them United was struggling because it had turned its back on tradition. Yet according to Sir Alex, United had only 'seldom' used 4–4–2.

Not everyone is so critical of the traditional 4–4–2. In fact, Arsène Wenger is a staunch believer. 'I think it's simply the most rational formation in most cases,' he says. 'In fact, it's the essence of reason. With a 4–4–2, sixty per cent of your players are occupying sixty per cent of the pitch. No other formation is as efficient in covering space. Of course, it also depends on the players you have. If I had Cafu and Roberto Carlos and both were in great form, then maybe I would also play 3–5–2, because I know they can both cover the whole flank on their own. But alas, I don't have Cafu and Roberto Carlos. And this means I have to use the 4–4–2, so that I can cover my flanks.'

I am not as wedded to any particular formation, believing that the tactical system should adjust to the players and not the other way round. In fact, I can sum up my ideal tactical scheme with three adjectives: rational, balanced and flexible.

A system must be rational because it has to suit the players at your disposal. That means not playing men out of position and, where possible, figuring out how to put your eleven best players on the pitch. Yet, at the same time – and I may appear to be contradicting myself – the system has to be balanced. You may have six Ronaldinhos in your squad, but you can't play them all at once (even though, rationally, it might make sense) because your team would be unbalanced. I know that 'balance' is often a by-word for being defensive and cautious, but that's not how I see it. Balance means finding an equilibrium that suits the coach's philosophy, whether it's offensive or defensive. It's no good having an aggressive 3–4–3 formation if your four guys in the middle of the park are all Claude Makelele types whose natural tendency is to sit deep and defend, primarily from central positions.

Finally, all systems need to be flexible. It is a huge advantage to have players who can comfortably change formation during the course of the season (or even a single game). It allows you to compensate for injuries or loss of form and can give you a tactical edge over your opponents. But flexibility is not just about changing formation: it's about changing the way players play within the same scheme. Thus, you can have a 4–4–2 where the full-backs push up aggressively, or another in which they sit. Same system, different interpretation.

While in Italy we undoubtedly overdo it on the tactical front, drilling tactical notions into the minds of footballers from an early age, it also ensures that our players are comfortable in a variety of systems. In England, tactical work is often seen as negative, or, at least, defensive. As we saw earlier, it is something 'the weak' do to gain an advantage they might not otherwise have. And, often, it is about stopping the opponent playing, rather than imposing your own game plan. At least, that's how it's viewed. In fact, many of the more sophisticated tacticians in the game, from Arrigo Sacchi to Louis Van Gaal, used tactical awareness as a weapon to break down the opponent. Still, that kind of approach requires hours of work at the blackboard, as well as endless repetition on the training pitch. While Italian footballers will put up with it (indeed, some are lost without it), in England most players bristle at this level of instruction.

'You need tactical discipline, you need tactical understanding and you need tactical work, but those are not usually a priority for English managers,' says Mourinho. 'I started as an assistant to Sir Bobby Robson. The training sessions began with some running and physical work, then some finishing and shooting on goal. And then we had a five-a-side. That was it.' The knock-on effect of this is clear. Players don't work on tactics so they don't think about tactics. They aren't used to worrying about positioning or adjustments beyond those they might do in a 4–4–2. As a result, they tend to be somewhat one-dimensional, comfortable in only one system and, often, one role.

'I can't believe that in England they don't teach young players to be multi-functional,' says Mourinho. 'To them it's just about knowing one position and playing that position. To them, a striker is a striker and that's it. For me, a striker is not just a striker. He is somebody who has to move, who has to cross, and who has to do this in a 4–4–2 or in a 4–3–3 or in a 3–5–2, each of which is different. I don't think you should take a youngster, say, aged between fourteen and eighteen and only teach him to play 4–4–2. You have to teach him different systems, make him comfortable in all of them. Because what happens if later he has a manager who likes to play 4–5–1 or 3–5–2? What happens to him then?'

The answer is that, in England, historically, it was highly unlikely that the player in question would ever work with a coach who used anything but the old traditional 4–4–2 so there was no need to learn other systems.

In Italy, many different managers employ so many different systems that it is essential for a player to be well grounded tactically. Changes of manager are frequent, which means that a player has to be ready to change systems. The current manager may use one system but, odds are, his replacement will use another. And some managers happily use multiple formations during a single game.

Learning to Be Flexible

Back to England. To some, tactical rigidity and obsession with 4–4–2 have resulted in long-standing under-achievement in European competition. 'Some managers in this country, not just English ones, don't do well in Europe because they never change,' says Sir Alex. 'They prepare their players in exactly the same way, home or away, regardless of who the opponent is. For example, they'll put two defensive midfielders as a shield in front of the back four and ask them to press the ball and win it back. But good European sides figure this out. They simply defend deeper or they keep the ball in other areas of the pitch.

'We at United do better in Europe than other sides because we change with every game,' he adds. 'Tactically, we always adjust to our opponents. We have to, because we know that every European opponent is changing to match us. And they're far better than English teams in terms of making life difficult, exploit the counter-attack, things like that.'

Sir Alex spoke at length throughout the 1990s about his quest for European success. Blessed with a successful team that dominated English football, he nevertheless seemed hexed when taking on certain sides, such as Marcello Lippi's Juventus. 'I remember playing Juve in the mid-1990s and thinking we were doing quite well,' he says. 'We get a throw-in near the corner flag. Gary Neville takes the throw and Alen Boksic goes up the other end and scores! He blows right through. Nicky Butt gets caught at the centre circle trying to defend, because both the centre-backs are in the Juve penalty area trying to score from the throw. That was it, one–nil and that was all they needed.

'We learned from that, we learned from those experiences,' he adds. 'Italians don't get caught on counter-attacks like that. We had to learn to do the same.'

Indeed, it is a credit to Sir Alex and to United that, by the end of the 1990s, they had learned to beat even Lippi's Juventus. The semi-final between the two teams, when United came back famously to win, advancing to that even more famous final in Barcelona against Bayern Munich, will be remembered as one of the club's greatest ever European nights.

United's success that season was as much about patience as anything else. Domestically they could overwhelm opponents, but on the European stage they had to learn to pick their spots, which does not come naturally in the English game where, traditionally, patience and slow build-ups have been frowned on as 'negative' football.

'To me attacking football happens when Makelele gets the ball and passes it to the central defender, who passes it to the right back, who comes forward and judges the situation,' says Mourinho. 'If he can do something he passes forward or runs with the ball, if not, he gives it back to Makelele who builds the attack again . . . That is attacking football. In England, attacking football is getting the ball to Makelele and having him hit it forward, no matter what, even if everybody is marked.

'Look, how many countries can you think of where a corner kick is treated with the same applause as a goal? One. It only happens in England. This is the only place where a corner kick is as good as a goal for the fans. And what is the best way to get a corner? Just kicking the ball into the box and pressing the second ball . . .'

Mourinho is a bit extreme, but his point is valid, and goes back to the old argument about possession not being integral to the English game. There are probably many reasons for this. It's part of Charles Hughes's legacy. English footballers have traditionally been less proficient technically so they tend to give the ball away. The colder weather causes players to run more, which means the game is played at a higher pace, which means more mistakes are made. And then there is the socio-cultural explanation: English crowds don't like to see the ball passed sideways and demand direct football.

There is an irony in all of this, which, I think, under-scores the changing attitudes among English fans towards what used to be called 'pretty' football. Arsène Wenger's Arsenal is one of the most admired sides in England, the side that most neutrals would want to watch. And yet it is not particularly 'English' in terms of personnel or foot-balling stereotypes. Their play is elaborate and intricate, the sideways pass as much a staple of their build-up as one of Thierry Henry's blistering runs.

To me this proves that football taste changes and evolves. However marked the national characteristics might be, there is a certain cross-pollination and homogenization. And, given that English football is as popular now as it has ever been, it may well be because fans prefer it as it is now.

The English game has been good at importing foreign ideas (as well as players and managers, of course), adapt-ing them to English traditions and growing. We've seen this happen with training techniques, facilities, diet, media coverage, club structure . . . the list goes on. The last area to fall to foreign influence is tactics: the English 4–4–2 still reigns supreme.

Does it matter? I think so. I don't think it's good for English football. First, it means English teams are limited in what they can do tactically, which is a problem, particularly against stronger opponents. It also means they can't tailor their tactics to the players at their disposal. So, for example, a team may have three of the best central defenders in the world, but, because it only knows how to play 4–4–2, one ends up either on the bench or out of position.

Indeed, that's exactly what many have said about the current England team. When you have three defenders of the calibre of John Terry, Rio Ferdinand and Sol Campbell – not to mention two outstanding alternatives like Ledley King and Jamie Carragher – a 3–5–2 scheme would seem a logical alternative.

Another negative effect of the 4–4–2 is that it does not allow for players with unique gifts or talents. Had Ronaldinho been born English, where would he have played in a 4–4–2? As one of two forwards on the shoulder of the last defender and making runs into the channel? As a central midfielder, asked to scamper around and win the 'second ball'? Or as a wide midfielder, making runs along the touchline and delivering crosses into the box? I wonder how many great English players have been penalized over the years because they did not fit into the traditional 4–4–2.

There is another reason why lack of variety is hurting the English game. Teams are so used to facing the 4–4–2, that when an opponent varies things they struggle to respond. An example of this is Arsenal, whose 4–4–2 was nominal, as Thierry Henry moved to the left and Dennis Bergkamp dropped off. It was the kind of formation that was very difficult for a traditional 4–4–2 side to counter, as Sir Alex Ferguson explains: 'Arsenal have done very well against the 4–4–2,' he says. 'Henry doesn't play through the middle, he goes into space and Bergkamp drops off. If the opposing right back goes forward, Henry goes into the space behind him and Pires cuts inside. That works very well, which is why I'm sure Arsenal would be very happy if everybody stayed with the 4–4–2. That's why some teams are starting to change a bit when they face Arsenal. For example, we always keep the right-back position filled when we play them . . . Henry needs space to play. If you give it to him he destroys you, but if you deny him space you've got a chance.'

Think about the three teams that have done best in the English game over the past five years or so. Manchester United, by Sir Alex Ferguson's own admission, 'seldom' plays a 4–4–2. Arsenal plays an unorthodox 4–4–2, with wonderful strikers like Henry and Bergkamp, who interpret the forward position in their own way. Chelsea uses a different system entirely: one striker, two wingers and a triangle in midfield. 'The English are always thinking in the same way,' says Mourinho. 'But the top teams are not playing a pure 4–4–2 and this is a problem for the others because their football is based on stopping pure 4–4–2. Look, if I have a triangle in midfield, [Claude] Makelele behind and two others just in front, I will always have an advantage against a pure 4–4–2 where the central midfielders are side by side. That's because I will always have an extra man. It starts with Makelele, who is between the lines. If nobody comes to him he can see the whole pitch and has time. If he gets closed down it means one of the two other central midfielders is open. If they are closed down and the other team's wingers come inside to help, it means there is space now for us on the flank, either for our own wingers or for our full-backs. There is nothing a pure 4–4–2 can do to stop things. That's why I think its popularity will come to an end in England. It has to. It does not work against teams like us.'

What this suggests to me is that the basic 4–4–2 is effective at shutting down a mirror image of itself, which occurs when the opposition also plays a 4–4–2. Yet against teams who do things a little differently, it can be a liability, which may partly explain the success of Chelsea, Arsenal and United (I say 'partly' because they also have exceptional players.)

Looking back, even Sir Alex, who had enjoyed years of success with a traditional four-man midfield, saw the need to change things shortly after winning the Treble. 'When we won the European Cup, we won it because we had a great front two of Andy Cole and Dwight Yorke who scored nineteen goals between them in Europe,' he says. 'Next season we lost games because we tried to play the same way as the year before and our opponents punished us. That's when I changed it around, by adding a third midfielder.'

That 'third midfielder' was Juan Sebastian Veron, the Premiership's then record signing. A big part of the media views the purchase of Veron as a mistake (though I'm told that opinion among United fans is divided) but it's interesting to note that United felt the need to change their formation and give themselves more options. It was as if Sir Alex realized that his traditional midfield four could only take United so far and that, in certain matches, it was best to have more tactical options.

Note that having more options does not necessarily mean chopping and changing the formation. It means being able to do so if required. And it means knowing how to adjust when the opposition plays in a certain way. 'My way is to have one major system plus a second system which also works and you can use sometimes against certain opponents because there are times when you need to make a change,' says Mourinho. 'Most of all, though, I want my players to be comfortable and to know everything about their role and the different ways to interpret it on the pitch. Generally speaking, while we analyse our opponent in great detail, in most cases, we do not change our formation according to the opponent. So if they have two strikers, we'll play with two central defenders. And if they have one striker, we'll still play with two central defenders. Of course, the difference is the way those two central defenders move and defend. That is what changes. Against one striker you play differently than against two strikers.'

The idea, of course, is that there are different ways of interpreting the same formation. And that's the key here. Because Mourinho's men can defend in three or four different ways within the same formation, he does not need to change things around as frequently. To do this you need players who are tactically aware, who are used to thinking in certain ways, who are versatile and comfortable in different types of situation.

'But the English footballer does not like to accept change,' says Ray Wilkins. 'The Italian player is accustomed to it, he enjoys it, he has no problem playing in a different position or with a different formation. I think it's because in Italy you spend much more time on tactics in training. You may even devote a whole afternoon session to it. Imagine that. Training in the afternoon. In England nobody trains in the afternoon. Why? Because the English manager is more than just a coach. He has thousands of other things to worry about. Or maybe because he is lazy and would rather be out on the golf course.'

Again, maybe my friend Wilkins is being a bit harsh. But I agree with his next point.

'Sooner or later we in English football are going to have to change,' he says. 'If you want to improve, you need to work more and improve your knowledge. This applies to players as well as managers.'

People see English football as conservative, yet in many ways it has been progressive and trailblazing and probably far more open in some respects than that of other nations. Yet one area which remains largely untouched by foreign influence is tactics. English clubs do very little tactical work, English players are not used to thinking in tactical terms and, as we've seen, there is a tremendous tactical uniformity to the game, one which, in the long run, is hurting English football.

The solution lies on several levels. Improving the coaching course, making it more academic and encouraging coaches to try new systems, would be a start. Equally, it's time to demand more of the players. We are talking about highly paid professionals; asking them to learn and apply more sophisticated tactical schemes is perfectly reasonable. This is particularly true if you can convince them (and then prove to them on the pitch) that tactical prowess makes them better players.

The main danger, and one that the English game would do well to avoid, is in replicating the tactical excesses of Italian football. There have been times and clubs, particularly in the past, where tactics became more important than technique and individual creativity, situations in which the game was reduced to chess, with both teams trying to stop the other playing. Tactical awareness does not necessarily equate with negative football. A clever tactician can use his knowledge to keep possession, to create chances, to take a variety of positive, attacking steps on the pitch.

That, to me, should be one of the goals of the English game: developing a way to make tactical awareness suit English football. Not the other way round.

Chapter Seven

Getting the Bullet

One of the most frequent complaints I hear from fellow managers is that there is little job security in coaching. Chairmen chop and change, hire and fire with abandon. And, typically, the manager shoulders all the blame for his team's mistakes. When we coaches are sacked we complain that we did not have enough time. And we are always given the impression that the pressure now is greater than it has ever been and a manager's life tougher. This applies to both Italy and England and it generally follows a familiar pattern. People call for a manager's head, then feel sorry for him afterwards.

I was curious to see, however, which country's clubs were quicker to hand out the proverbial bullet. And I wanted to know what became of former coaches and managers. How quickly did they get another job? How many 'second chances' were they allowed?

With this in mind, I looked at a four-year period, from August 2000 to June 2004, examining the managerial situations in the top two divisions in England and Italy. I counted the number of permanent managers each team had while in the top two divisions, discounting caretakers or interim bosses.

First, as you would expect, the figure of the long-term 'father-figure' boss, like Sir Alex Ferguson or Guy Roux of Auxerre, is extremely rare. In fact, of the thirty-six English clubs who spent all four years in either the Premiership or the First Division (as it was then known), only eleven kept the same manager throughout, or 30.6 per cent of the total. Is that high or low? Well, compare it with Italy. Of the twenty-nine clubs in Serie A or B during that period, just three kept the same manager: Roma (Fabio Capello), Chievo (Gigi Del Neri) and Perugia (Serse Cosmi). That's 10.3 per cent or only a third as many as in England.

The obvious conclusion is that Italian clubs are impatient and readily sack managers. The three Italian coaches who stayed the course for four years are an exception. As I write this, in January 2006, all three have changed clubs. Capello is at Juventus, Del Neri is unemployed, having taken charge of three different clubs (Porto, Roma and Palermo) in eighteen months, while Cosmi was sacked by Udinese, his second club after departing from Perugia (Genoa was the other). On the other hand, of the eleven 'English' managers, six are still in the same jobs they held in the autumn of 2000: Neil Warnock, Sir Alex Ferguson, Dario Gradi, Alan Curbishley, Sam Allardyce and Arsène Wenger.

What kind of a manager stays at the same club for four consecutive years? The implication is that he must be successful or the club would have sacked him. Yet if he is very successful he'll presumably want to move to a bigger club.

This helps to explain why there are so few long-standing managers in the Italian game. There is already a high turnover, which means that openings are constantly created near the top. Coaches who do well further down the line are soon given opportunities at bigger clubs. In England, managers stay in their jobs longer, which means there are fewer openings at bigger clubs so managers further down have fewer chances to move up. In that four-year period Italy's five most successful clubs – Roma, Lazio, Inter, Juventus and Milan – employed fifteen different managers. By contrast, England's big five – Arsenal, Chelsea, Manchester United, Liverpool and Newcastle – featured just six. And one, yours truly, was in charge for just a few months of those four seasons.

In Italy in those four years, the average Serie A or B side had 4.7 full-time managers, more than one per season. By contrast, the average English side had a seemingly more civilized 2.8. If you think about it, this is a massive disparity.

And the gap is even more impressive when you consider that the English managerial market is far more fluid than the Italian one. In England, a manager is allowed to take charge of more than one club in the same season. Thus Harry Redknapp moved from Portsmouth to Southampton mid-season in 2004–05 (and moved back the following year). In Italy, this would be illegal. If you manage one club you can't manage another until the following season, even if you're sacked. This means that it's far easier for the English to make managerial changes: they can effectively choose from unemployed and sacked managers and managers currently employed by other clubs. In Italy you have to limit your choice to unemployed managers who have been out of work since the previous season.

And yet, in spite of this, there are far more managerial

changes in Italy. Indeed, in some situations a manager is pretty much guaranteed the sack, such as when a team is relegated. Of the twelve clubs who were relegated from Serie A to Serie B in those four seasons, every one of them changed managers during the relegation season in an effort to avoid the drop. Yet of the twelve English clubs that went down in that period, six kept the same manager for the entire season.

Why are we Italians so quick with the pink slip? According to Franco Ferrari, of the Coverciano Academy, 'In Italy, we just look to the result, we don't care how we obtained it, it's all about the result,' he says. 'And if you lose, you're an idiot, period. It's not a question of playing well or building a base for the future, you have to win. That's the mentality. And I don't think it's a coincidence, but in other countries it's the opposite. There, it's not just about winning, winning alone is not enough. You also have to play good football.'

He's right. There's no other way to explain the absurdities of Italian football. There is such an impatience, such an obsession with the here and now, that club presidents will gladly go out and sack managers at whim. How else do you explain Cagliari having had four different managers by November in the 2005–06 season? Sometimes you get the sense that Italian chairmen would rather sack the whole team, but they can't do that so they vent their frustration on the manager.

In Italy, at the start of a season, the objectives for that year – as determined by the press, the fans and the chairman – are outlined. And, typically, they are very specific. For three or four teams it's winning the *scudetto*; for another two or three it's qualifying for the Champions'

League. A further few must win a place in the UEFA Cup, while another three or four are striving for a comfortable mid-table finish. All of the others are struggling not to go down. With this in mind, it's not hard to see that the winners will be few and far between. The manager who takes the *scudetto* is a winner, of course, as will be one or two others who have qualified for Europe and, perhaps, one or two who have kept their relegation-earmarked teams up or over-achieved their way to a mid-table spot at the end of the season. But that's it. Everybody else is a loser. Everybody else has either failed and is fired, or is grudgingly given a second chance.

It goes without saying that this situation is neither healthy nor logical. It's not good for the game because there is no stability and no job security. How should a player feel about a manager if he knows that, statistically, he won't last the season? And how can a manager get the best out of his players in those conditions? Indeed, how is a manager supposed to build for the future – blooding youngsters, instilling a work ethic, teaching a tactical system – when he knows he will be judged only on the present?

English managers are comparatively as secure as civil servants. But that, too, is changing, particularly in the lower leagues: 'Warwick University did a study which found that, in the last nine seasons, year on year, sixty per cent of Football League clubs changed their managers,' says John Barnwell, of the League Managers' Association. 'That's a massive number. Things are a bit better in the Premier League, where only one in four changes managers year on year. In our opinion, there are two main reasons for this. The first is that the clubs make the wrong choices and appoint the wrong people. And the second is that too many of our managers are simply not prepared.'

Coming from the head of the League Managers' Association, that's quite an indictment. Then again, Barnwell is a straight-shooter, unafraid to speak his mind.

'We're in a society where it's all about having everything and having it straight away,' he says. 'There is no more patience, everything has to be instantaneous, starting with success and gratification. We have instant coffee, fast food, the Internet . . . Nobody is willing to wait, nobody wants to grow slowly. Quality is a distant memory. I'm honest when I say that many young managers are sent out there without the necessary skills and I feel bad for them. Football is vulnerable because the pressure is enormous. Everybody is ready to criticize but, too often, the critics understand and know very little.'

Sacked Managers: Recycle or Incinerate?

My research shows that while English clubs are far more reluctant to sack managers and generally afford them more time at the helm, it is much more difficult for an English boss to get another job after he has been fired. In Italy, the turnover rate is far higher, and managers rarely find themselves out of work for long.

In the four years I analysed, ninety-seven managers worked full-time in the top two divisions of English football. Of those, twenty-four managed two or more clubs and two (Steve Bruce and Glenn Hoddle) managed as many as three clubs. That means 24.7 per cent were given a second chance and two per cent were afforded a third chance.

In Italy there were 104 managers of whom fifty-two took charge of more than one club: that's exactly 50 per cent! Twenty-two managers coached three or more teams, 21.2 per cent against England's two per cent. In fact, no fewer than ten (9.6 per cent) had four different stints in charge during the four seasons we looked at. These numbers underscore a fundamental difference between England and Italy. In Italy, we are far quicker to decide that a manager's *stint* is a failure, but we are far more reluctant to determine that the manager *himself* is a failure. Italian football lets managers back in time and again, believing that they always have something to contribute.

In English football a manager is given every chance to fail before he is let go. Managerial tenures are far longer – it's common for a boss to talk about a three- or four-year plan and his chairman will give him the time to work. The problem occurs after the manager in question is sacked: then he is viewed as 'damaged goods'. He may get another opportunity further down in the same division or possibly a division below. If he fails again, however, unless he has a big reputation, it will be difficult for him to find another job.

'In 1999, we at the League Managers' Association had about three hundred managers on our books,' says Barnwell. 'Of them, do you know how many were still managing in 2004? Twenty-eight. Another seventy-one recycled themselves and are somehow still in the game. They're assistants or scouts, or they work with kids. But the other two hundred – they're gone! They no longer exist in football. Just imagine how much talent and knowledge was lost as a result.

'It all goes back to the same problem. A lack of

preparation. Finding your first job is not very difficult. The youngster comes in, without being prepared, he thinks he knows everything but then, sooner or later, he gets the sack. And because he is not prepared nobody offers him another job so he leaves football. We at the LMA are convinced that if every manager had the benefit of a proper coaching course they would at least have a chance. They would have the foundation to learn from their mistakes and setbacks. Sure, managers would still get the sack but they would have a better chance of staying in the game.'

I wonder how many great managers have been lost to the English game because of this. It seems to be a peculiarly English thing: few other footballing nations have this attitude.

There are many different reasons why a manager and a club might part ways, and while the coach is always responsible for his side, it is not always his fault when things go wrong. Furthermore, he might have made a mistake but he is not necessarily a bad manager. And there is plenty of truth in the old maxim that 'You learn more in defeat than in victory.'

Since 2001 Rafa Benitez has won two Liga titles, a UEFA Cup and, of course, the Champions' League, making him one of the most successful managers around right now. Had he been English, rather than Spanish, he would probably never have had the chance to take charge of clubs like Valencia or Liverpool. Having worked in Real Madrid's youth system, he was given his first management job in 1995–96, at Valladolid. He was sacked after six months, with the side last in the table. His successor kept them up, which is never a good reference for the previous manager. Nor is the fact that, the following year, they qualified for the UEFA Cup.

Still, Benitez bounced back immediately, getting the nod at Osasuna, in the Spanish second division. The club had big plans, but he was shown the door after just nine matches as Osasuna were third from bottom. His next appointment was at tiny Extremadura, a rural club based in a small town, also in the second division. This time he pulled off a minor miracle in his first season, winning promotion to the top flight. But the euphoria didn't last: the following year, 1998–99, Extremadura were relegated and Benitez was gone.

So Benitez was let go three times in his first four years as a manager. Twice he lasted six months or less, and each time he left a club they were stuck in the relegation zone. Most people looking at this record would probably have taken him aside, put an arm round him and said, 'Rafa, mate, why don't you go and do something else? You're clearly not cut out to be a manager.' And they would have been dead wrong. He was given another shot at Tenerife, in the Spanish second division, which led to the Valencia job and, eventually, Liverpool and European glory. How did it happen? Was Benitez simply unlucky at his earlier jobs? Did circumstances conspire against him? Or was he responsible for his own failure, making poor decisions?

The answer is probably a bit of everything. He might not have been entirely responsible for his sackings, but there are probably things that, with hindsight, he would have done differently. But that's OK. Because – and this is the fundamental point – good managers learn from their mistakes. Benitez gained valuable experience and learned a tremendous amount even though things did not work out on the pitch.

In Italy, being sacked is not a capital offence. Neither does it scar you for life. If you look at some of the most successful managers around, you'll see that an unusually high proportion have, at some point or another, been unceremoniously sacked. Marcello Lippi, the Italy boss, was fired four times, and Carlo Ancelotti twice, first by Parma and then by Juventus (the latter after two consecutive second-place finishes). Even Giovanni Trapattoni, the most successful manager in the history of the Italian game, was sacked in mid-season by Cagliari in 1995–96 and by Stuttgart in 2005–06. Each man came back to a prestigious job at a big club.

But the epitome of the 'recycled' Italian manager is veteran boss Gigi Simoni. He has managed no fewer than sixteen different clubs in thirty-one years of coaching. In the seven seasons between 1998 and 2005 he coached seven different clubs, including Inter, Napoli and CSKA Sofia. In his long career, he has won eight promotions, been relegated four times and sacked during the season on four occasions. He is a clever, pragmatic coach, who is valued and respected throughout Italy for his experience. I don't think a character such as Simoni could exist in England. He would simply never get another job.

In England this is largely unthinkable. Once you have been sacked by a big club you usually take a step down. After leaving the England job, Glenn Hoddle went to Southampton, where he did well, earning himself a move to Tottenham. There, he struggled, and his next job was at Wolves, outside the Premiership. In Italy, this tends not to happen. Alberto Zaccheroni was sacked by Milan, then had spells at Lazio and Inter immediately afterwards. Ancelotti was let go by Juventus but landed at Milan. And after Lippi was sacked by Inter following the first match of the season, he returned to Juventus.

Italian clubs are much more willing to recycle managers. This is a positive, and, I think, intelligent approach. In football, a good manager learns from his mistakes, just like a good leader anywhere, in any profession. 'I think the English are wrong with their attitude,' says Fabio Capello. 'You screw up once and that's it, you're gone. What about the experience you gain? Isn't that worth something? In Italy we have a lot of flaws, but at least I think we judge managers on their merit not simply on their most recent record.'

In England, few remember that a certain Sir Alex Ferguson was let go by St Mirren at the age of thirty-seven in 1978. What if Aberdeen had viewed him as damaged goods and not given him a second chance? It's safe to say that the history of British football would have taken a very different turn.

There is a certain inconsistency here in both Italian and English football. Italian clubs will sack a manager based on most recent results. Sometimes even a month's run of losses is enough for him to get the bullet. In that sense their vision is incredibly short-sighted. They like to use certain buzzwords: they will claim that their manager is part of a long-term 'project' and that they want to open a 'cycle' of success, but in reality, they are focused on the here and now, the immediate results. In Italy everybody knows the story of Sir Alex Ferguson and how he won nothing in his first four years at Old Trafford, then conquered the footballing world. The story is told almost as a kind of parable, a way of educating clubs, fans and the media in the virtues of patience. Typically, it is met with smiles and the shaking of heads, as if such patience were, indeed, wonderful but could only exist in a faraway mysterious land, such as England. Consider the case of Hector Cuper at Inter. In his first year in charge, he finished third, losing the *scudetto* on the last day of the season after leading for much of the campaign. The following year he finished second and reached the semi-final of the Champions' League. And the year after that, as a reward, he was sacked after six matches. This is Italian football. Nobody can go empty-handed at a big club for more than two seasons without getting the sack.

Managers know this all too well, which is why they often pay little attention to medium-term planning because they know that that is not what they will be judged on. And yet, funnily enough, when it comes to hiring a manager, Italian clubs look at the big picture. If he was recently fired, they'll consider the circumstances of the sacking, they'll study the way his teams play, they'll do research on his personality. And, most of all, they will try to work out whether he has grown as a manager in his most recent experience. That is the exact reverse of English clubs: when a manager is in employment, a club will often give him plenty of time. If the fans are unhappy with the results, the club will defend the manager and point to medium-term and long-term objectives. They will preach patience at every turn and, in most cases, practise what they preach. Yet when they are looking to fill a vacancy, they will be just as irrational as the Italians are in sacking managers. They will hardly ever consider out-of-work managers, except in special circumstances, the thinking being that if you're out of work you can't be very good. Remember the managerial changes during the 2004–05 Premiership season? At Southampton, Paul Sturrock was replaced by Steve Wigley, who was already at the club as a coach. Wigley, in turn, was replaced by Harry Redknapp, who was at Portsmouth. When Redknapp left Portsmouth, director of football Velimir Zajec took his place, later to be replaced by Alain Perrin, who was unemployed.

In fact, Perrin and Bryan Robson (who replaced Gary Megson) at West Brom were the only unemployed managers called to fill Premiership vacancies. Martin Jol (who replaced Jacques Santini) at Tottenham and Stuart Pearce (who stepped in for Kevin Keegan) at Manchester City were already at the clubs in a coaching role. At Newcastle, when Sir Bobby Robson was let go, they turned to Graeme Souness of Blackburn. And Souness's place at Ewood Park was taken by Mark Hughes, who was coaching the Welsh national team. Thus, out of nine managerial changes in 2004–05 only two went to un-employed managers, and one of those, Bryan Robson, was a local hero and club legend. The implication is that clubs look primarily to very recent success as evidence of a manager's ability.

I am baffled as to why English clubs, who are so good at seeing the bigger picture and not being swayed by results in sacking managers, become so results-driven when hiring an ex-novo. Here, Italian football can learn from English foot-ball – and vice versa.

What Makes a Good Manager?

If we accept that managers should be judged on more than results what should clubs look for? What *are* the qualities and characteristics of a good manager?

I've wondered about this for a long time, both when I was a player, later as a manager and now that I have a bit more time on my hands.

'In my opinion, a manager's job has three components,' says Arsène Wenger. 'He needs to work in these three different areas and be judged separately in each of them. The first, obviously, is results and the quality of the football shown on the pitch. However, you must always remember that these are short-term results. A new manager is not going to make a big difference in the first six months. He simply won't have had time to work with the players. Of course, in reality, if things go well, he'll get all the praise. If they go badly, he'll be criticized. But the truth is that, after so little time, the team is not really his.'

I'm pretty much in agreement with that. You can't escape results: the fans demand it, the players demand it and, frankly, it's the right thing to do. You can't say, 'Well, we're not going to play well or get decent results for the next two years but, don't worry, after that, we'll be great.' If you did, it would not be football.

Also it *does* take time for a manager to mould his team into the kind of side he wants. I saw this when I took over from Ruud Gullit at Chelsea: it was mid-season and I knew there wasn't much I could do until the summer.

'The second parameter is the ability of the manager to help players progress on an individual level,' Wenger continues. 'I am convinced that only ten to fifteen per cent of players perform at their best anywhere, at any club, with any manager. The development and performance of the other eighty-five to ninety per cent is determined by the environment of the team, the work of the coaches, the relationship with teammates. And you must know how to judge this. If your club buys players who potentially perform at a hundred per cent but only reach sixty under your stewardship, you may still win the league if everybody else's players only have a performance potential of, say, fifty per cent. You have better players so you win. But that does not mean you're doing a good job. Doing a good job means taking your players as close as possible to their performance potential, making them the best players they can possibly be. That should be your absolute priority, along with results.'

I believe this point is too often overlooked, possibly because there is no objective way of assessing players. But everyone recognizes that certain clubs have better players and probably do not require great managerial skills. At the same time, there are clubs with weaker squads who overachieve, which is often down to the work of the manager or coaching staff. Indeed, we can all think of players who are outstanding under one manager and mediocre under another. They fall into the 85 to 90 per cent category that Wenger spoke about. A clever manager can turn mediocre players into good ones and good players into great ones.

Having said that, it is often difficult for clubs to judge this quality in a manager. That's because they tend instinctively not to belittle the abilities of their own players. Thus, if a previously mediocre player starts doing very well under a new manager, the club will probably say that the player was good all along: he simply did not work hard enough previously or had the wrong kind of manager (and it took a clever club chairman to appoint the right manager). A club simply won't say to their manager, 'Yes, that central defender is actually a big donkey but thanks to the work you're doing, he plays like Beckenbauer,' although there are probably times when they should . . .

'Finally, the third parameter is the impact the manager is having long-term at club level,' concludes Wenger. 'And here we go into the philosophy of play, the club's infrastructure, the image of the club. These are not things that you measure week on week, month on month or even year on year. You have to take a step back. How is the club seen? Where are they now compared to five years ago? Ten years ago? Twenty years ago? These things happen on a macro level, and they are often subjective. Yet they are no less important.'

In Italy, few managers reach the point where they can be judged on Wenger's third parameter. They are usually sacked, or move on, well before that. While it is true that in Italy it is also harder for a manager to have an impact on that level because of the *direttore sportivo*, the sporting director, who handles transfers and contractual issues, it is equally true that, given time, an outstanding coach can rework the whole image of a club. Arrigo Sacchi at Milan is an example of this: he left a legacy of organization and entertainment that endured even after his departure. And, in a different way, Gigi Del Neri at Chievo became synonymous with a certain brand of direct football and a plucky-underdog image.

In England, there are more examples of this third parameter of progress. Exhibits one and two are, of course, Wenger and Sir Alex Ferguson. Their way of doing things and their personality have become synonymous with Arsenal and Manchester United. The same could be said for Alan Curbishley at Charlton, Sam Allardyce at Bolton and David Moyes at Everton. North of the border, Martin O'Neill's Celtic was much the same, before his departure in the summer of 2005. Each of these clubs was revamped and reshaped by its manager, reaching new heights that went beyond results on the pitch.

Wenger's analysis of a manager's goals is cogent, but the question remains: what qualities does a manager need to attain them? My old teammate Fabrizio Ravanelli used to say, 'Coaches are like parents . . . They raise their children,' and there's a certain wisdom in this – not because footballers are childish or impressionable, but because a coach controls most of a player's environment in much the same way that a parent controls their child's. Naturally, you can't isolate your child: he or she will go to school or to a crèche and interact with other children, maybe watch television, but you as a parent are their main guiding force. It is much the same with coaches: they are the main professional influence and they are the ones who set the tone for the squad. They can create the good team atmosphere, the solid work habits and the mutual respect that are often crucial to success. Indeed, often a top club's success lies in the little things the manager does, in the seemingly irrelevant details.

For example, I am always struck that when a foreigner arrives at Milan, it is usually about three months before he starts doing media interviews in Italian. By then, he is usually conversationally fluent, even if he did not speak a word of Italian before his arrival. I was curious about this since it doesn't happen at most other clubs. Some guys have been in Italy for years and can't speak decent Italian, just as some foreigners in the Premiership can hardly string together a sentence in English after several seasons.

When I asked Adriano Galliani, vice-president of Milan, why his players all seemed so gifted in the language department he told me, 'We make it a priority. As soon as they arrive we provide them with Italian teachers and we make sure they learn the language. We make it clear it is something we expect. And they all learn very quickly.'

Of course, anyone can hire a language tutor for their foreign players. But the difference is that, at Milan, they learn quickly. And, believe me, when you are a twenty-something millionaire living in a new country, worrying about earning a place in your new team, language lessons are not likely to be your priority. And that's why the really good, well-run clubs foster the kind of environment in which players want to put in the time with a tutor.

It's just an example. In fact, some of the best and highest paid managers in the world concede that a coach can only do so much. When I asked around about which attribute or character trait was most important for a manager, more than one said, 'To have good players in your squad.' And they were only half joking. 'You can have the best coach in the world, but if he does not have good players he's never going to win anything,' says Eriksson. 'So Empoli will never win the *scudetto*, it does not matter who is coaching them. But the opposite is also true. If you manage Real Madrid it is hard not to win something.'

Obviously there is only so much a manager can do without talent. Giovanni Trapattoni used to say, 'A good manager can make a team five per cent better, but a bad manager can make a team thirty per cent worse' – it's easier to ruin a team than it is to improve it. Some teams win in spite of their managers, not because of them. And there are teams who make their managers look very good. On this point, Wenger is in agreement: 'Everybody knows the secret to winning. It's the players,' he says. 'At most, a manager might make five per cent of difference, improving the performance or making it worse. But that is it. The history of football is made by players, not managers. Real Madrid had Di Stefano and Puskas so they won. Milan had Van Basten and Gullit, so they won. I don't think it was the managers who made them win. It was the players.

'However, the managers still played a very important part,' he continues. 'They are the ones who put the team together in the summer and put them in the right physical and mental condition to perform. I think that's where most of the manager's job is done, putting the team together and preparing them for the season. After that, you just let them go and there isn't much you can do. Almost everything must be done before the season starts.' With clubs typically playing at weekends and midweek, and with travel days, there isn't much time to work.

Fabio Capello disputes this. 'I could say I'm like Wenger in that sense, but I'd be lying,' he says. 'I think you continue to work all year. Players need the eye of the boss looking over them. That's how they work and improve. He can say what he likes, but unless you have a group with three or four leaders – and I mean strong leaders who can motivate the whole team and drag it along – you as a coach have to stay on top of the players and you have to make them work. Because they can improve during the season, just as they can get worse. And that's why they need the eye of the boss looking over them.'

I'm not sure that Capello and Wenger's positions are quite that far apart, though the former clearly believes in tweaking and making continual adjustments, as well as keeping a very close eye on his players. Wenger seems to give his men more freedom, but perhaps this is because he has been in charge for nearly ten years and therefore his system is ingrained in the club and its players. He does not need to be so vigilant because Arsenal's system is proven and there are veterans such as Thierry Henry, Robert Pires and Ashley Cole who know it inside out and can inspire and motivate the others.

The point about selecting the right players is crucial, though. And, on this issue, most of the managers I spoke to were in agreement.

'There are, broadly speaking, two factors to consider,' says José Mourinho. 'You look at the player's profile and then you look at what needs you have. So, for example, if somebody wanted to sell me Gigi Buffon right now, I would say no, thank you. Sure, he's the best goalkeeper in the world, but we don't need him. Of course, if I say that, it might be a mistake. But that is football. You make mistakes and you learn from them. We made a mistake with Mateja Kezman, who hardly ever scored for us. So you may laugh at me over that, but that's reality, mistakes are made. This is also why it is so important to have a good team of scouts and assistants. Because you as a manager might be able to travel once or twice to see a player, but you can't do it ten times. And sometimes that's what is required.'

Capello agrees, though he suggests that a good manager will make fewer mistakes than most. 'When I am putting together a team and I ask the club to buy me somebody, I don't do it just for the sake of doing it,' he says. 'I only buy players who will make the team tangibly and demonstrably better. Otherwise, I don't want them. I don't want a guy who is not going to clearly make my team better. Why should I?

'You know, people say that Capello is a good coach because his clubs buy him good players,' he adds. 'That's not true. Capello is a good manager because he chooses good players to play for him. Just look at the facts. There are clubs who buy ten guys every year and get nowhere. Now that I'm here and they're buying the right guys it's a different story.'

Getting the right players in is only the first part of the job. Once they are there, you have to get the best out of them. This aspect of man-management is seen by many as the single most difficult part of the job. 'I think the training side and the tactical side are very important, but they are things which a person can learn,' says Eriksson. 'What is even more important is taking your players and turning them into a unit, a team, and then managing that team in the right way. The bigger their players are, the tougher it is, because they tend to have stronger and stronger personalities. A manager has to be prepared for this.'

According to Mourinho, the problem is that you can't prepare yourself for it. It's not a skill you can learn. You are either predisposed to manage people or you are not. 'You can study, you can improve, you can learn with experience and from your mistakes, but in the end, knowing how to lead and how to control a group is something which must come to you naturally,' he says. 'I did things in the past that I would never do now so I learn from that and I evolve. But I had to have the capacity to lead at the beginning. Then, later, through study and experience I refined it.'

Years ago, shortly after winning the *scudetto* with Milan in 1987–88, Arrigo Sacchi said that managing and motivating footballers was no different from handling any group of people, whether it was a team of accountants, a battalion of soldiers or a crew of construction workers. The leadership and management skills were transferable, the technical skills were not.

'To lead effectively is the most difficult thing you can do in football,' says Mourinho. 'You are leading a group of men of different mentalities, different cultures, and different ages towards a common goal. Even when the group is united, there are natural differences. For example, at Chelsea we have a fantastic group, we can feel it, but if you look in our dressing room, you will see four black players over there, seven English over here, the three Portuguese in that corner . . . How do you lead a group which is so different?' Mourinho has highlighted a challenge that we rarely talk about but which makes the game totally different from that of ten or twenty years ago. It's not uncommon to have men from ten or fifteen different countries in a playing squad, often with a foreign manager.

In my first full season in charge at Chelsea, twenty-nine players made appearances in the first team. They came from twelve different countries: Holland, Italy, England, Uruguay, Romania, France, Denmark, Russia, Finland, Norway, Spain and Nigeria. Contrast that with, say, the Celtic side that won the European Cup in 1967: every member of that team was born within a twenty-five-mile radius of Celtic Park. Actually, I don't need to go that far back. When I made my professional début at Cremonese in 1980–81, not only was our entire team Italian, most of the players, like me, hailed from the north of the country. Ten years later, I was in the Sampdoria side that won the Serie A title. We were probably considered an exotic team because we had three foreign players: a Slovenian, Srecko Katanec, a Brazilian, Toninho Cerezo, and a Soviet, Aleksei Mikhailichenko. Our coach, Vujadin Boskov, was a Serb. It was a tiny number of foreigners. And, with the overwhelming majority being Italian, the side was run according to Italian customs. The foreign players adapted to our way of doing things. They had no choice.

When I was managing Chelsea, it was a different story. We had eleven English players but only four – Graeme Le Saux, Jody Morris, Michael Duberry and our captain Dennis Wise – were regulars. There was no 'critical mass' from a single nation: we were conscious of being an English club, but we knew there could not be a 'one-size-fits-all' culture. I am not surprised to hear that Mourinho is facing some of those same challenges today: 'Your first objective is to build a group and try to make them understand that they are all the same, there are rules for everyone, but at the same time everyone is different,' he says. 'What I mean by this is that when I relate to them within a group they are all the same, but when I deal with them individually they are different. I must deal with an individual man to man, tailoring what I say, based on his personality and his priorities.

'For example, if I have to shout at John Terry after a poor game and call him an effing disgrace, I can do that, because I know that in the next match he will be super-motivated to prove me wrong and will be the best player on the pitch,' he adds. 'But if I say the same thing to William Gallas, the next game he won't want to play for me. To me this is the single most difficult thing to do . . . knowing how to treat people differently and still be fair or, at least, appear fair. It's not something you can study.'

This is something that is always difficult for managers. All managers accept that you get the best out of some players by yelling and screaming, but with others a hug and a cuddle is the best way to go. I think this difference is cultural – in some cultures shouting is never done – and individual: some people simply do not react well to confrontation. What can be difficult, though, is handling the star player, the guy who is special and can determine the difference between the team's success and failure. If he is late for training do you punish him by leaving him on the bench, as you would with other players? If he looks lazy while running drills, do you rebuke him in front of the others?

This is where theoretical football often clashes with harsh reality. In theoretical football, a manager is fair and just and leads by example. He may treat his players individually – as Mourinho outlined above – but he shows no favouritism. That's the theory. The reality is that a manager has to answer to his employers, the club. And the club is neither a democracy nor a Sunday school teaching values and ethics. It is a business concerned primarily with winning. Therefore, if the £10 million striker on £60,000 a week turns up late for training the club may not want to treat him in the same way as the eighteen-year-old training with the first team. Especially if that striker scores a goal in every other game.

It's a fine line that a manager needs to walk. I loathe

favouritism and believe that the biggest star should be held to the same standards of behaviour as the third-choice goalkeeper. However, I also believe that you have to be mindful of the club's priorities and also of what the squad is willing to accept. It's fairly well known, for example, that when he was at Napoli Diego Maradona was occasionally late for training, and at the end of each summer he was regularly late back from his holiday in Argentina. The club could have fined and disciplined him. But would it have been in their best interest to do so? Probably not. Maradona's occasional tardiness affected neither his performance nor his effort. And, indeed, none of his teammates begrudged him the special treatment. In those circumstances, preferential treatment can be acceptable, provided the club and the players support it.

When Brazilian midfielder Paulo Roberto Falcao joined Roma in 1982, he told the club that he did not train on the day before a match: it unsettled him physically and he would not do it. The manager, Nils Liedholm, accepted it, as did the rest of the squad. Falcao still spent time with the team during the training sessions and, of course, on the pitch performed at a high level. This was enough for the players. Shortly after coming to England, Sir Alex faced a slightly different disciplinary issue. His advice underscores the importance of picking your battles: 'When I first arrived at Manchester United, there was a problem with drinking among some players at the club,' says Sir Alex. 'I told them, "I'm not going to change, so that means you'll have to change." I always tell young coaches, don't seek confrontation, it will come to you, just be prepared. And, if you do get into a fight, make sure you can win it.'

His advice is reminiscent of our old friend Machiavelli, who suggested avoiding all battles except for those where victory is assured. In Sir Alex's case it was especially difficult because he was a young manager who had just arrived in England and he was taking on some of the biggest names at United, as well as a culture that was deeply ingrained in the English game. Yet he obviously got his calculations right. And he made sure he could win before he went into battle.

Mourinho emulates another great military thinker, Colin Powell. 'When I need to get people's opinions, I always ask them to give me theirs before I give my own,' he says. 'As a leader, you have to do that, because if you speak first, your words will influence what they say and you don't want that. You want them to be candid. I have always done that, without even thinking about it. Yet recently I read Colin Powell's book and I found out that he does the same thing. He said it is a sign of good leadership.'

Mourinho, like Capello, excels in another important aspect of management: dealing with fringe players and those who rarely get to play. Increasingly, top clubs have very large squads, and the reality is that a manager counts on no more than sixteen or seventeen players. What do you do with the others? Do you speak to them? If so, how?

In my first managerial job, I tried everything. I tried calling players into my office individually, explaining why they were not going to be picked. I tried treating everyone the same and not saying anything unless asked, figuring that the team sheet would do the talking. And I tried a hybrid method, dealing with some players in one way, others in another. There is no foolproof way to do it: you have to handle each player individually. Some guys might not want an explanation for why they are left out: they might feel patronized, particularly if they can see that the player starting in their place is clearly better than they are. Others might feel lost and discouraged if you do not put an arm round them.

I think there are two rules to follow here. First, you must never justify yourself. As a manager, you are responsible for making decisions and it is your rear end on the line if things don't work out. Once you start explaining you undermine your position. Second, players must know – whether because they figure it out for themselves or you tell them directly – why they are on the bench or in the stands. Of course, if you have Andriy Shevchenko and Thierry Henry starting ahead of you, it's not difficult to understand. The tricky part is when the situation is not quite so clear-cut, when a player can win a spot in the starting eleven if he can improve in certain areas. As a manager, it's crucial that the left-out player knows what he needs to do to play his way into the side.

In a perfect world, players would be happy just training, getting paid and being ready when called upon, even if it's only once every six months. The reality is that footballers are human, they know they have a short career and they want to play. Keeping them happy and motivated is difficult and a special skill. I think Mourinho's gift for dialogue is at the heart of his success in this department.

This 'dialogue' between a boss and his employees – or, in our case, coach and players – is essential and valuable to a manager. The problem is that the players have to be accustomed to and comfortable with speaking their minds to their boss. In Italy the players embrace the opportunity for dialogue with the manager far more than is usual in England. 'For me discussion is something I always seek out,' says Eriksson. 'It's just the way I am. And in that sense there is much more dialogue, many more questions. They want to know what we're doing, why we're doing it and so on. In England sometimes I find that the players are not very curious. And so I have to flush them out. I split them into groups of four or five and meet with them individually to try and understand what they are thinking. At first here in England they were shocked and surprised. They did not know what to say. But then they became very receptive to this method.'

Eriksson's experience shows that, although not inherently 'English', dialogue can be easily and profitably introduced. 'With football being the way it is today, having an open dialogue with your players is crucial,' says Marcello Lippi. 'I speak to them often and I have to say it really does enrich me in so many ways: culturally, tactically, technically, socially . . . these are the things which improve a manager, not things you read in books.' (Except this one, of course.)

Real-world management MBAs will probably recognize what Lippi and Eriksson are talking about. It's a basic business-school principle: lower-level employees will often have suggestions and solutions that escape CEOs because they are on the ground dealing with the company's business directly every day.

Some believe that the extensive common ground between coaching a football club and an MBA handbook indicates that a successful manager, like Mourinho or Capello, could easily run, say, a pharmaceutical company. And that the CEO of a major corporation could head

Juventus or Manchester United. I wouldn't go that far. The man-management qualities are important, but there are many other technical skills that a football manager must have, skills that you only gain from growing up in football or at least studying it seriously. Here again, though, we find a difference in expectation between Italy and England. In Italy, public opinion routinely analyses a manager's work with a fine-tooth comb. How is the tactical system working? What are the fitness levels like? What kind of physical preparation is being done? Which players are improving under his guidance?

What you rarely hear there is what you almost always hear in England: talk of passion, inspiration and enthusiasm, and whether or not the manager is transmitting them to his players. In England, more so than in Italy, everything is personalized: a manager's character is on the line every time his team takes to the pitch. He is judged on how much (or how little) he has inspired his players. I don't think it's a coincidence either that when Eriksson is criticized it is usually for his laid-back, calm demeanour, which is seen as 'lack of passion'. The notion that a coach could be more muted, relaxed, maybe even less passionate, and still be a good leader of men seems unfathomable in England. 'I suppose it's normal that in England they don't judge a coach or even a match based on tactics because they all play the same way,' says Lippi. 'There is no innovation. And so the only way to differentiate English managers is in their character, their passion, their approach and how well they relate to their players. It's never a question of tactics because they are all the same.'

Beware the Foreigner

Because they are two great 'schools' of football, both Italy and England view the outsider with a degree of suspicion. Interestingly, though, I think this has changed a little over the years. Some time ago, Italian football went through a phase of employing foreign managers – it has gone through several, actually. In the early years, when the Italian game was in its infancy, many managers were British, because the clubs were founded by Britons living in Italy. Another flurry of foreign coaches arrived in the 1960s. Helenio Herrera, from Argentina, led Inter to two European Cups. Paraguayan Heriberto Herrera won a title at Juventus, as did the Croatian Ljubisa Brocic and the Czech Cestmir Vycpalek. The next generation, broadly speaking, came in the 1980s, led by Nils Liedholm, Sven-Goran Eriksson and Vujadin Boskov. By then, however, while we admired and appreciated foreign coaches in Italy, we were always sceptical about whether or not they could do well. Four of the most successful coaches in South American football – Sebastiao Lazaroni (Fiorentina), Oscar Washington Tabarez (Milan), Carlos Bianchi (Roma) and Cesar Luis Menotti (Sampdoria) – came and went without leaving much of a trace in the Italian game. Perhaps we felt that our game was so layered and complex, so draining on the man in charge, that only Italians or foreigners who had spent long periods in Italy – like Zeman, Eriksson and Liedholm – could grasp it successfully.

In England, I think there is a different attitude. Unless you have proved yourself in a big league very recently, you are viewed with a scepticism that is far more overt than it is in Italy. When Wenger took over at Arsenal in 1996, one newspaper famously splashed across its back page 'Arsène Who?' Granted, he had spent the previous two seasons in Japan, but he had won a French league title, the French Cup at Monaco, and had reached the final of the Cupwinners' Cup. To treat him as a nobody, some Forrest Gump who had stumbled into Highbury, was bizarre. I can't imagine a similar reaction in Italy.

Wenger was taken aback and bemused: 'Right away they told me I would never win anything, not just because I was unknown but because I was a foreigner. The papers were full of articles illustrating exactly why a foreigner was never going to win the English title. Faced with this situation, I tried to open a dialogue with everybody. I tried to be open and inquisitive. I really wanted to learn their way of thinking and why they felt the way they did. I don't know if I succeeded, but I do know that, at least within Arsenal, it fostered a dynamism, a sense of reciprocal discovery which helped me a lot.'

Mourinho arrived in England under different auspices. He was the reigning European champion and his Porto side had knocked out Manchester United. The year before, he had won the UEFA Cup, defeating another British side, Celtic, in the final. And yet he, too, was greeted with profound scepticism. 'I became European champion on 26 May, on 28 May I arrived in London and I was greeted like a nobody, with a bunch of question marks,' he says. 'What do I have to add? Can I adapt to the English game? Why do I think I can win the Premiership in my first season when nobody has ever done it? Do I have enough experience? Have I ever worked with top players? Do I know how hard English football is? English football this, English football that. I don't want to say that

I wasn't respected, but to them, they are *here* and people who come from abroad are *here* . . .' As he does this, he moves his hand from above his head to his waist. There is little doubt about what he means: those who come from abroad are at first considered below those who have established themselves in England. 'Even if you are a European champion like I am, you still have to prove that you belong on their level in the Premiership,' he says. 'I can only imagine how difficult it must have been for Wenger. He wasn't European champion, he came from Japan!

'It's simple,' he continues. 'I could not have come to England if I had not been European champion. I could not. The English feel that this is a special country, with special football and, even if you are good, it's not easy for you to adapt. They believe their football is more difficult, that it is unlikely that you will be able to add something. I don't think they are anti-foreigner, I don't believe that at all. I do think, however, that they are sceptical of foreigners and whether they can adapt to their football, because they genuinely believe their football is different and special.'

It is interesting to note that Wenger, Eriksson, Mourinho and Rafa Benitez all had to prove themselves from nothing when they came to England. I suspect there are deep-seated socio-cultural reasons for this. England is a 'confident' nation, at least outwardly. Italy is, too, at least when it comes to football. By contrast, Portugal has long suffered from a certain insecurity and lack of self-belief. 'So in Portugal, when a guy like [Giovanni] Trapattoni arrives everybody is excited,' says Mourinho. 'He takes over at Benfica and everybody is talking about how this gives Portugal prestige, how Italian eyes are going to be watching Portuguese football, how he is the old master and we have so much to learn. Of course, if he does not succeed, he will get criticized, that's normal. But at the beginning all foreigners are welcomed with open arms. It was the same thing with [Graeme] Souness and [Sir Bobby] Robson. They had a fantastic welcome. Sometimes you have to leave by the back door, but, when you first arrive, in Portugal you are always welcomed.'

I was made to feel very welcome when I arrived in England, unlike Mourinho and Wenger perhaps, although that was probably because I came under different circumstances: I was still playing, I had just won the European Cup, I was among the first wave of foreign players so there was a lot of curiosity about us.

What was unusual was the reaction when I became player-manager of Chelsea. My appointment was questioned far more in Italy – how could a thirty-three-year-old with no experience run a top-flight football club and play at the same time? – than it was in England. True, I was not coming from abroad, but I had only spent eighteen months or so at Chelsea as a player when I was appointed. I was still 'foreign' in so many ways. I believe my achievement as a player somehow justified my appointment in the eyes of some. Because I had a successful playing career – unlike Wenger and Mourinho – I was entitled to respect as a manager, even though I was foreign and still new to the English game.

My Managerial Obsession

Looking back, I did not know what to expect when I took on the Chelsea job. I soon realized how such a job can consume you, occupying all your energy, mental and physical, all the time. There were moments when I might be watching television or relaxing with my family, trying to get away from the game, and images would pop into my mind. I'd see Dennis Wise's positioning in midfield or Marcel Desailly's marking on set-pieces or perhaps Gianfranco Zola coming back to help out the midfield. And I would inevitably find myself thinking about football once again. Perhaps it is like a drug addiction: it's all you think about, you can't escape it and the pressure wears you down. I had always been focused on football as a player, but this level of obsession was almost scary.

Years later when I spoke about it with Sir Alex Ferguson, he reassured me that what I had been through was normal. Something similar had happened to him, which is partly why he got involved in horse-racing and with Rock of Gibraltar. When he finished with horses, he had decided, aged sixty-four, to take up golf. (I was shocked that he – as a football manager and a Scot – had not been playing golf all his life . . .) 'You can think about the game too much as a manager,' he said. 'That's what happened to me a few years ago. I was too focused. I had trouble thinking about anything that was not football. It's as if I was in a fog all the time, unable to relate to anything. The only time I would snap out of it and find clarity was in football. That's when I got into other interests,' he adds. 'I had to. You need to be able to disconnect. Otherwise, management consumes you until there is nothing left.'

Sir Alex's words may seem extreme, but I know where he's coming from. If you are a passionate and competitive manager and you are in charge of a team, this is how you live. There is no down-time, there is no time off. Your mind shuts out everything else until all that matters is the football and specifically your team. Anything else is a distraction. The ability to balance management and private life is a skill that must be learned, particularly if, like me, Sir Alex and many others, you're a bit of a workaholic.

I suppose that part of what drives you to work so hard is the knowledge that your fate rests with eleven young men. It can be a chilling thought. 'Even today the most difficult thing for me is to say, "OK, guys, I believe in you, my career is in your hands," and mean it,' says Wenger. 'And you have to mean it. You have to have total faith in your players because, if you don't have confidence in them, they will realize it and their performance will drop. Having faith means being an optimist, being convinced that they will reach all their objectives. But it's hard, because in the end your career, your livelihood, everything you have worked so hard to build is in their hands.

'I have seen some exceptional managers fail for that very reason,' he adds. 'They were unable to put their total faith in the players. And the players noticed.'

Learning to trust your players implicitly is not easy, particularly if you have played at a high level and know what constitutes a good footballer. Yet you must learn to do it. It is the greatest leap of faith of all.

The Other

Chapter Eight

Chasing the Big Bucks: A Way to Keep Score?

We've looked at the various forces shaping the development of a player, from early coaching to socio-cultural factors and even the weather. But there is another set of influences which has a profound effect on how a footballer is made. It comes from outside the footballing world. I'm talking about the way footballers are perceived in the media and by the man on the street. Throughout Europe footballers have gone from being admired sportsmen to celebrities, with everything that that entails, particularly the financial rewards. Today, the top players are like individual corporations, with an annual turnover in tens of millions of pounds. But even the next few levels of players, those who are regulars in the top flight without being superstars, find themselves earning disproportionately large amounts of money compared to what they would have been paid when I started playing.

Many players of my generation joke that if they had been born just five years later, they would have retired as wealthy men, without having to work a single day for the rest of their lives. Of course, players have always complained about this, insisting that the next generation had it easier. But the change has been staggering, particularly in England.

In 1990 John Barnes made headlines when he signed a £6,000-a-week deal with Liverpool. At the time, it seemed like an outrageous amount and all sorts of people came out of the woodwork to moralize about the future of football and whether it could be sustained. Today, the highest-paid players in the Premiership earn £100,000 a week. What I find amazing is how much Barnes's £6,000 a week would be worth today. Once you adjust for inflation it would work out to £8771.86. Which means that the highest-paid players in the Premiership today earn more than eleven times what the highest-paid player earned just fifteen years ago.

It's an astonishing statistic, and one that is worth reflecting on. Barnes, the superstar of his era, made no more than many squad players at mid-table clubs today. In Italy, the boom in wages came perhaps a decade before, but it was no less significant. All of a sudden players found that, with one contract, they were set for life. As with all radical changes, it has taken a while for football to digest. 'For managers, it's not easy to keep it all in check,' says Sir Alex Ferguson. 'One minute a player is a nobody, the next minute they're all over the press and they've got a million-pound contract. Back in the day when everyone was the same, we all made twenty pounds a week.'

In some ways, particularly for young players, money should not be an issue. On a youth contract, you earn a few hundred pounds a month, and whether you sign for £1,000 or £10,000 a week it does not make much difference: either way it's more money than you can imagine at eighteen.

Except it does make a difference: footballers are human and, to many, wages are a way of 'keeping score', a means of knowing where you stand vis-à-vis your colleagues. That's what most of the 'greed' stories are about. Last season there was much talk in the media about the contract extensions of Roma's Antonio Cassano and Liverpool's Steven Gerrard. Both had initially turned down what seemed like enormous offers, somewhere in the region of £60,000 a week. That's £3 million a year! Now, it's difficult to explain to a 'normal' person in a 'normal' job why £3 million a year is not enough. Most people could live well for the rest of their lives on a £3 million lump sum. Also, it's hard to believe that either player's life would change substantially if he made another million pounds in a season. After all, there is only so much you can buy. And, in the cases of Cassano and Gerrard, neither strikes me as the extravagant type. Conventional wisdom would blame the agents, no doubt, for 'corrupting' their clients. And it's obvious that the more a player earns, the more his agent makes since they are normally paid a percentage commission. Yet it is not quite so simple. A good agent worries about a player's profile. If the player is squeaky clean and generally well liked, he can make a lot of money in endorsements. If, on the other hand, he is seen as greedy and selfish, few companies will want to link their products with him. And once you develop a reputation as a 'bad egg', it's difficult to shake off. Look at Nicolas Anelka. Whether it is his fault or not, he suffers from a negative image, owing to his contract disputes and personal run-ins. Early in his career he was starring for Arsenal and Real Madrid, but now he is in Turkey, at Fenerbache. A player of his ability, two years younger than Thierry Henry, should be at a bigger club in a bigger league.

Of course, some agents drive a hard bargain, but I don't think they're always the ones planting ideas in players' heads so much as responding to their clients' requests. To me it comes back to 'keeping score'. If you make X amount more than another player in the same position, you are somehow better or smarter because you got a better deal. Some players define their worth by the size of their pay cheque. Nobody likes to be taken advantage of, and when a player sees that a colleague of equal or lesser ability who plays the same position earns £1–£2 million more per season, he will feel exploited, or that his agent is not doing his job properly. 'I tell my young players, "You don't need to chase money, money will come to you,"' says Sir Alex. 'But today you're dealing with a different individual.'

I can see both sides of the argument. As a coach, you don't want players worrying about how much they earn and whether their colleagues make more or less than they do. You just want them to be happy and focused. What it takes to make a player happy, however, has changed, partly because there is far more money in the game and partly because we talk about wages more than ever. It is simply more of an issue than it used to be and, in some ways, I don't fault young players for wanting the best deal they can get. Footballers are fragile, a career can end at any time and if you, as a twenty-year-old, can sign a contract that will secure your future and that of your family, who is to say it's wrong?

That said, I agree with Sir Alex that, once you've reached a certain level of financial security, chasing money can be counter-productive. It can turn into an unnecessary distraction, whether you're doing advertisements, endorsements or simply banging on the door of the club each year in search of a better deal. A man can spend only so much money, but for some, it appears sometimes as if they define themselves by their bank balance rather than by caps, goals or trophies.

The Bosman Balance of Power

The issue was further exacerbated by the Bosman rule, which granted players free agency. This means that when a player's contract expires he can move to another club without his old club receiving a penny in return. Today it sounds perfectly reasonable that an unattached player should be allowed to sell his services to the team of his choice, but for a long time things were rather different.

As we know, for most of the twentieth century, when a player's contract expired he remained the property of the club who had only to pay him a nominal wage to retain his registration. If another club wanted to sign him, they had to agree a fee with the club. In the early 1980s, UEFA realized how unfair the system was to the players and helped to change the regulations so that when a contract ended a player could move, with a fee determined according to the 'UEFA parameter', a formula that took into account the player's age and wages. If you wanted to sign an out-of-contract player, you had to pay the parameter. There was no getting round it. And, if you had the misfortune to be an out-of-contract player, you had two options: you either found a club to pay your UEFA parameter (or, if you had the money, paid it yourself) or you were forced to sit out. Under UEFA regulations, after one year the parameter was halved, and after two years you were officially a free agent. Of course, that meant not playing competitive football and not drawing a salary for a long time, which is something most players were loath to do. Jean-Marc Bosman, the Belgian footballer, found himself in that position. His contract had expired and, while he had found a new club, he could not join them because they could not afford to pay his UEFA parameter. He took UEFA to the European Court and eventually changed the history of the game.

I was one of the first beneficiaries of the Bosman ruling in the summer of 1996. My contract with Juventus expired and I was able to join Chelsea on a 'Bosman' transfer. This meant that Chelsea did not have to pay for my registration. The impact of cases like this is hard to overstate. The balance of power swung from the clubs to the players virtually overnight and added another layer of complexity to the player-club relationship.

'Clubs lost control once freedom of contract began,' says Sir Alex. 'Don't get me wrong, I don't think the previous system was fair, but I think it was better for players in terms of their relationship with the manager. It was a direct relationship: you, the manager and nobody else. Today, it's all changed.' Indeed, Bosman made an agent nearly indispensable to a player. I hired one for the first time in my life just after the Bosman ruling. As a well-established veteran, I was able to maintain the personal relationships I had built, but I can see that it would be different for many players, particularly young ones. Once Bosman kicked in, the relationship with clubs became necessarily adversarial, at least at certain times.

To clubs, having a star player (or, at least, a player whom they considered an asset) enter the final year of his contract without a new deal was a terrifying prospect. It meant that he could walk out and join another club at the end of the season without any kind of compensation paid to his present club. In an age where the bean-counters think of players primarily as assets on the club's balance sheet this is of paramount importance. Virtually overnight, an asset worth £10–£20 million can disappear. This is especially serious in Italy where, at some clubs, a certain amount of 'creative' (albeit legal) accounting has led to some players being given vastly inflated valuations in the club's books. Therefore clubs have a vested interest in making sure that those players they wish to hold on to sign their contract extensions nice and early. Otherwise, a game of 'chicken' ensues, a kind of psychological warfare as the 'tipping point' approaches. In this case, the tipping point is the moment at which it is no longer in the player's interest to accept or even consider the club's offer. If you wanted to represent it graphically it would look something like this:

YEARS TO GO: 2   ADVANTAGE: CLUB
YEARS TO GO: 1.5   ADVANTAGE: EVEN ('Tipping
                      point')
YEARS TO GO: 1   ADVANTAGE: PLAYER
YEARS TO GO: 0.5   PLAYER HAS NO SPECIAL
                      INCENTIVE TO SIGN

This is a generalization, of course, based on a number of assumptions, such as the player's performance and the club's financial situation remaining constant. Yet, by and large, it tends to hold true. The irony is that the side with the advantage is least likely to want to extend the contract.

Thus, when a player has two years left, he will begin to worry about his future – all players, particularly in the latter half of their careers, are aware that the clock is ticking and they are one bad injury away from retirement. He will want to extend his contract by another two or three seasons, thereby giving his family some security and ridding himself of worry. In some cases, perhaps more than the cynics imagine, the player may simply want to tie himself to the club for as long as possible because he's genuinely happy there and has grown attached to the team.

From the club's perspective, this is a big commitment, which is why they are in no hurry to negotiate. The player is under contract, he isn't going anywhere, and the club has the advantage. Only the club can offer what the player craves – security – as they are the only ones with whom the player and his agents can talk at this point in his contract. It's not uncommon at this stage for a player to sign for a little less than expected in exchange for a long-term deal. Effectively, the club holds all the cards. For example, Rio Ferdinand, at Manchester United, extended his deal in the summer of 2005, reportedly without receiving that much sought-after pay rise.

With eighteen months to go, we reach the tipping point, with both sides negotiating on a level playing-field. Eighteen months is too long for a player to 'hardball' the club and simply hold out for a better contract. By the same token, the clubs are all too aware that with each day that passes they lose leverage. From a neutral's perspective, all things being equal, this is the best and most logical time for a contract extension: it's the point at which the player earns the most realistic wage. By the time a player has a year left, he has the upper hand. He can take his time, turning down offers until he gets what he wants. And, of course, in the last six months of his contract, when he is allowed to negotiate with other clubs, not just his own, he becomes effectively an under-contract free agent. At this point, he holds all the cards. Strictly speaking his club is no different from any other and he can simply sell his services to the highest bidder.

Of course, plenty of other factors affect this sequence of events – it is just a general guide. Many players – believe it or not – are not motivated only by money. They do not simply gravitate towards the highest bidder. An economist might say that they are 'irrational', as the stock market is at times. There are obvious examples of this. Some are extreme: in 2004 Paolo Di Canio rescinded the one-year contract extension he had signed with Charlton Athletic to return to Lazio, the club where he had started his career. Reportedly, in leaving Charlton by mutual consent, Paolo took a 75 per cent pay cut, which cost him some £750,000 a year. In his case, other factors came into play: Lazio was the club he had supported all his life, he was financially secure and he was thirty-six, which meant he knew it was now or never in terms of returning home.

Other examples are, perhaps, less extreme but no less relevant. In the last few years of his career Dennis Bergkamp went from one-year deal to one-year deal at Arsenal, because it is club policy to give one-year extensions to players after a certain age. From a purely economic standpoint, Bergkamp had to be mad to accept this situation. Other clubs could probably have offered him more money and certainly have given him a two- or maybe even three-year commitment. Accepting Arsenal's offer did not make sense: the situation was totally weighted in the club's favour. Yet clearly Bergkamp did not mind because he placed other values ahead of his finances. He was happy at Arsenal, his family was settled in north London, he was probably quietly confident that he would play well enough to get a new deal year after year.

Another type of situation exists that does not follow the above pattern. It is the case of a player who signs a long-term contract, then far surpasses expectations straight away. It could be that a young player breaks into the first team, then becomes an international soon after, or perhaps someone like Wayne Rooney or Zlatan Ibrahimovic who joins a club, then quickly establishes himself as one of the team's key players, proving he probably deserves more money. In these cases, you generally see a convergence of intention: both sides want to get the deal done and neither has the upper hand. The player, of course, wants to earn his just rewards: he wants the kind of contract comparable to a superstar's. In theory, the club could wait a little while before adjusting his wages but, most likely, they want him to have a fair market-value contract. That's because – and we're talking about very few men here – the player in question is the kind of star you build a team round and it is imperative that he is kept happy. It is not worth saving a few million at this stage in his career if it means jeopardizing his future at the club. In these situations, both parties try to reach a quick, amicable solution.

Contract negotiations are as much about bluffing, faking and deceiving the other party as anything else. The club wants to pay as little as possible for the player's services; the player, via his agent, wants to get as much as he can. That means sounding out other clubs to make it seem as if the player has plenty of offers. It's the oldest trick in the book. An agent has a client who would like a new and improved contract so he puts out the word that there is lots of interest in him from other clubs. He leaks this to the press, to other agents and to clubs. He may get his client to do a few press interviews, just to keep his name in the public eye. In short, he does what he needs to do to get an improved figure.

Across the barricade, clubs use the same methods. They'll stall on talks, they'll spread the word that a player is 'greedy', sometimes inflating his contract demands. In some cases they may use their friends in the media to turn the fans against him, questioning his loyalty to the club. These things go on regularly in Italy and in England. It's all part of the negotiating game and, within reason, it has to be accepted. What is far more questionable is the treatment players in Italy receive from clubs when their contracts are up for renewal.

It came to the fore in the 2005–06 season and really bothered me, particularly because the situation was so different in Italy from that in England, Germany and other countries. Udinese striker Vincenzo Iaquinta and Roma starlet Antonio Cassano both began the season in the final year of their contracts. Both, of course, are outstanding players, Italian internationals approaching their prime. At the time, Cassano was twenty-three, Iaquinta twenty-five, and many felt their contract extensions were long overdue, regardless of whether either player was going to stay on at the club.

Udinese are generally a selling club so it appeared unlikely that Iaquinta would stay much longer, but it seemed a given that he would re-sign so that the club could earn a transfer fee from his sale. Cassano's situation was slightly different in that it was by no means certain he would be sold since Roma are a big club and the president, Franco Sensi, indicated repeatedly that he was an important part of their future. However, given Roma's financial difficulties, many accepted that he would most likely be on his way, particularly if he could fetch a sizeable transfer fee. To do this, though, he had to extend his contract, like Iaquinta.

The season began, the players were nine months away from being free to leave on Bosman transfers and neither had extended his contract. Both were offered sizeable pay rises and both felt they were worth more. And while I suppose they knew their contract extensions were likely to be a formality as they were likely to be sold on, they felt they deserved a better deal, not least because there was no guarantee that they would be sold: by holding out until their contracts expired they were pretty much guaranteed hefty pay rises by moving on free transfers.

The clubs, however, would not stand for this and ended up taking drastic action. Iaquinta was dropped from the team and sent to train separately, even though he was Udinese's leading scorer and was establishing himself as a prolific international with Italy. Cassano's 'disappearance' was more subtle. The club suspended him: he was said to be 'out of form', treated as a foreign object and kept well away from the first team. Iaquinta's 'exile' lasted several weeks until he signed his new contract. By Christmas 2005, Cassano's situation was still uncertain: he had made several fleeting appearances but was largely kept far away from first-team Serie A football. In January 2006 he moved to Real Madrid for a cut-rate £3 million.

It does not take a genius to figure out that Cassano and Iaquinta were victims of undue pressure from their clubs. The clubs used whatever leverage they had. Effectively it was a 'lockout', the exact reverse of a strike. The clubs knew that, without first-team football, Cassano and Iaquinta would have almost no chance of making it into Italy's squad for the 2006 World Cup. Indeed, Marcello Lippi, the Italy boss, said as much, indicating that he would only call upon those players who were getting playing time.

True, to some it may appear to have been cutting off your nose to spite your face, but the clubs knew what they were doing. They took a calculated risk. They figured that the best-case scenario to be had in hardballing Cassano and Iaquinta would be worth tens of millions of euros. The players would not be able to deal with lack of first-team football and they would have to come to terms. The worst-case scenario, of course, was that without their star players Roma and Udinese would be relegated. Yet that was a far-fetched scenario: both clubs were clearly strong enough to stay up. Thus, all of a sudden, it began to make sense, at least as a business decision. The pros outweighed the cons. And business prevailed over football.

I understand the concept that a player is contracted not to play, but rather to be fit and ready to play. The decision of playing or not rests with the coach. Fine. Yet the decision should be a purely footballing and, perhaps, disciplinary decision. It should not be based on something as petty as failing to sign a new contract. In this case, it sent out completely the wrong message. What it said was, 'Cassano[Iaquinta] is a very good player. And by dropping him we are a worse team. But it is more important to us that we be able to sell him and make some money back, than it is for us to have him in the line-up and thus be a better side.' Essentially, that was the message the fans received. And it was very damaging. Negotiations are tough – that's their nature – but to go so far was wrong, although it may have been within the clubs' legal rights. I realize there are times when players – sometimes egged on by agents, sometimes acting on their own – turn the tables on their employers, negotiating with other clubs while still under contract and occasionally even signing post-dated contracts. Yet just as a player is wrong if he goes on strike to demand higher wages or a new contract, a lockout – provided the player is performing on the training pitch – is nothing more than the club's equivalent of throwing toys out of the pram.

I wonder why we in Italy feel the need to go so far. Because, make no mistake, this is a peculiarly Italian phenomenon. A few years ago Roy Keane, then captain of Manchester United, let his contract run all the way down yet he was not dropped, left out or bullied into signing (I suppose bullying someone like Keane would be a tall order indeed). In the 2005–06 season, Robert Pires at Arsenal and Michael Ballack at Bayern Munich played for much of the year while in the last season of their contracts. And while negotiations went on long and hard for both players, dropping them was never an option. Neither was there any talk of them being affected by uncertainty over their future. They each had a contract and they simply got on with it. As for the clubs, they were grateful to have those players. Their philosophy seemed to be: 'It would be great if they extended their deal and stayed with us and it's true that we might lose them but, in the meantime, let's get the best out of them.'

To me that's the healthy way of dealing with things. It recognizes that, after all, we're still talking about football clubs – or, at least, multi-national corporations whose main business is football, not buying, growing and selling players as if they were plants from a nursery. Indeed, at the beginning of the 2005–06 season, Bayern Munich had no fewer than ten players in the last year of their contracts. They did not make a big deal of it. Nobody was threatened. They simply accepted the situation, in particular the player's right not to extend his contract.

How Much Should You Pay?

The section above is just one example of the profound ways in which the Bosman ruling affected football. The knock-on effect manifests itself in many ways and, often, is not quite as clear-cut as it seems. For example, Bosman signings seem like a great little piece of business, largely because they're free, yet this is not always the case. Allow me to give you an example.

Let's say Chelsea need to sign a striker and have a budget of £10 million to spend on a transfer fee and a four-year contract. The Chelsea manager identifies two possible targets, Carlos Kickaball and Bruno Bidone (OK, the names are silly, work with me here . . .). Kickaball is looking for wages of £1 million a year and costs £6 million in transfer fees. Bidone, on the other hand, is out of contract and demands £2 million a year in wages. Last season, Bidone and Kickaball both made the same amount of money, around £1 million. However, Bidone reckons he can ask for more money since anybody wishing to sign him does not have to pay a transfer fee.

Here's the quiz question for you. If Bidone and Kickaball are of the same age and ability, which one do you sign?

You probably said Bidone. He's the cheaper option, after all. If you give him a four-year deal, it will cost the club £8 million (four years at £2 million a season). Kickaball, on the other hand, would cost just £4 million in wages (four years at £1 million a season), but you would also have to pay £6 million in transfer fees, bringing the total to £10 million.

Many club managers think in that way. And, in many ways, it makes sense, because you are getting the player you want and saving yourself two million pounds. But what if some of his teammates are annoyed because Bidone earns £2 million a season? After all, he's no better than Kickaball, who makes half as much. That's when the problems start: other players come forward and begin to ask questions. Your star players may be on less money than Bidone and feel entitled to demand more since, after all, they are better players. Let's say you have a young striker who came through the ranks and, in his first season as a professional, scores more goals than Bidone. Can you justify paying him less? Do you give him a £2 million-a-season contract straight away? How do you explain his wages to others? How do you tell them that they need to earn less money simply because they came through the ranks or because a transfer fee was paid? Is it their fault that they weren't free transfers?

Many clubs have dealt with this by adjusting the other players' wages, with Bidone's salary as the benchmark. At the highest level, this side-effect of the Bosman ruling is what has driven the boom in wages, with the fact that, of course, footballers are human and will compare themselves to their colleagues.

To some degree, perhaps, these comparisons have always been around in football. Maybe Sandro Mazzola worried that Gianni Rivera made more than he did, and maybe Jimmy Greaves felt he should be paid more than Bobby Charlton. Yet whatever differences there might have been back then, they were minimal. Today we are talking about millions of pounds or euros. It is one of the factors that is widening the gulf between footballers and the average fan.

The issue isn't so much about massive wages. Ultimately, these are determined by the market. Clubs don't pay a Thierry Henry or a Francesco Totti millions per season because they happen to like them or because they are generous guys. They pay them enormous amounts because they believe Henry and Totti can help to generate that much more revenue for the club. All too often the media and the clubs do a less than good job when it comes to explaining the link between a player's wages and the amount he generates for the club. Too often people will come out and say, 'Well, they pay Kickaball a million a year and he helped get them to the FA Cup final and into the top six in the Premiership.' That may be true, but it's simplistic.

The real question in determining Kickaball's wages is

far more complex and it's directly tied to economics. For Kickaball contributes far more than his playing skills to a club. In fact, all professional footballers – albeit to varying degrees – contribute much more than mere ability to a team. In a perfect world, you could even determine Kickaball's ideal wage if you ask the following questions.

1. How does he affect the club's position in the league?
This is difficult to calculate, but it's an estimate of how Kickaball helps (or hurts) the club's position. If he improves the side, they'll finish higher in the league and consequently get a bigger slice of the television pie. Or vice versa.

Incidentally, there is a huge difference here between England, where the Premiership rights are sold collectively, and Italy, where each club sells them individually. In England the correlation is much stronger than it is in Italy: gaining one or two places in your Premiership standing can mean several million more in television money. There is still a considerable link in Italy: most television contracts are annual. If a team does well, it can negotiate for the following season from a slightly stronger position.

Then there is the Champions' League. If a team finishes in the top two in the league, they qualify automatically for the competition, which may provide further revenue; if they finish third or fourth, they enter the competition's qualifying rounds.

2. How does he affect the club's performance in Cup competitions?
Much like before, the question is whether Kickaball has

helped the team and to what degree. The further a team goes in a cup competition, whether domestic or European, the more it can earn from television rights and box-office receipts, since the team will be playing additional matches. This is much more of a factor in England than it is in Italy. For a number of reasons, there is little popular interest in the Coppa Italia and even in the UEFA Cup. Reaching the final of either adds little to a club's coffers. In England, on the other hand, despite falling attendances in both the FA Cup and the League Cup competitions, a good cup run can be a huge money-spinner for a club.

3. Does Kickaball increase attendance?

Gate receipts used to represent the bulk of a club's revenues, but now they often bring in less than a third. Still, signing a big-name player who will 'put bums on seats' still makes a difference. If Kickaball is an exciting or popular player, he will boost attendance without question. The trick is determining how much, if anything, he contributes to the gate. When Gianfranco Zola returned to his native Sardinia to join Cagliari, attendance there increased by 64.7 per cent! As I write this, six months after his departure, Cagliari's average gates have fallen 28.8 per cent. Such cases are rare and often increased attendance goes hand in hand with a winning team – because fans want to see good players, not bad ones, and good players make teams better. And, of course, fans would rather see teams win than lose so it's hard to judge whether higher attendance is a result of the player's popularity or what he contributes on the pitch.

4. How does Kickaball affect merchandising sales?

This is generally simpler to calculate: it is related to the player's popularity. Clubs keep close tabs on this: they want to know exactly whose shirts the fans are buying. For them, it's practically pure profit. We've all heard the stories of Real Madrid selling millions of David Beckham shirts around the world. The thing to determine, of course, is why people bought them. How many did so because they were primarily Beckham fans who, if he had played for Scunthorpe United, would have bought a Scunthorpe United jersey? And how many were Real Madrid fans who, if Beckham weren't there, would have bought another player's shirt?

5. How much, if at all, does Kickaball contribute to the club's sponsorship and other ancillary revenues?

In the mid-1990s, Nike invested heavily in Ronaldo as their pitchman. When he moved to Inter Milan, they invested in the club. The link between the two was obvious. Indeed, it was reported that Nike's sponsorship contract with Inter included a clause that stipulated the club would receive less money if Ronaldo left.

Whenever a player of such magnitude moves, the issue of sponsors and kit suppliers becomes paramount. And it can work both ways. If at the time of Ronaldo's move Inter's kit had been supplied by, say, Adidas, Nike might have thought twice about it. Or they might have done their best to get in there, using Ronaldo as a 'Trojan horse' to oust Adidas. Either way, you can be sure that expressions like 'synergy' and 'maximizing sponsor value' would have been thrown about, both by the club and the sponsors. There are other examples. When the midfielder

Li Tie joined Everton, the club were sponsored in his first season by a Chinese company. When Hidetoshi Nakata, easily the most famous Asian footballer, moved to Perugia in 1998 he helped to draw all sorts of revenue to the club and effectively became the game's first self-financing player. The revenue streams he generated – tours of the club, merchandising, sponsorship, television rights of Perugia games in Japan – were staggering and more than enough to justify his wages.

Agents: The Men Who Make It All Possible

The top players earn so much money because they generate even more. Even Sir Alex Ferguson, who instituted a wage structure at Old Trafford, concedes that, compared to other sports, at the highest level footballers may even be underpaid. 'It's not a bad thing [that foot-ballers earn more than ever these days],' he says. 'When you compare them to golfers or American football and basketball players, footballers are well down the line.'

Indeed, the highest paid footballer in the world earns around £6.7 million (10 million euros) in wages per season. By contrast, Shaquille O'Neal, of the Miami Heat, makes around £11.2 million (16.5 million euros). In fact, as I write this, there were no fewer than twenty-nine National Basketball Association stars who earned more than ten million euros, more than the world's best-paid footballer.

But football does relatively well compared to golf and American football. On the PGA Tour, it is rare for more than three or four players to be earning in excess of US $4 million a year. And, of course, the PGA Tour is the ultimate example of performance-related pay. The above earnings are prize money and, of course, it's an individual sport. In the National Football League (NFL), only a few players would earn as much as the top footballers, with the added drawback that their contracts are largely unguaranteed. Given the high risk of injury in a sport like American football and the massive amount of television revenue it generates, you almost wonder if some of the stars aren't underpaid.

In football, it is often hard to establish just how much a player ought to be paid. In theory, because we live in a free market economy, this should be decided by market forces, Adam Smith's 'invisible hand'. Smith was an eighteenth-century economist who wrote *The Wealth of Nations* in which he argued, among other things, that through the laws of supply and demand markets sorted themselves out, establishing fair prices, rewarding better products and ensuring everyone was satisfied.

Players are 'suppliers', who sell their services, and clubs are 'buyers', who hire them. The 'invisible hand' ensures that players are paid what the market can bear. Or so the theory goes, because this only happens in a 'perfect market'. A 'perfect market' is a free market that has no entry or mobility barriers and, most of all, flawless information. In other words, people are free to do business with whomever they choose, they are fully aware of what is available on the market ('perfect information') and they have total and free access to it. Well, football isn't like that. Even the most knowledgeable scouts and executives have a limited view of what is on offer. And players often know little about other potential employers, particularly those abroad.

All this makes for an inefficient market, in which players are easily exploited and clubs are continually making costly errors. So football generated that most controversial of figures: the agent. The catch-all word 'agent' includes those who represent players, helping them negotiate contracts with clubs and sponsors, and 'middlemen', who act on behalf of clubs to find suitable players. An agent protects a player from being taken advantage of and ensures that he gets the best possible deal from a club, or he brings together buyers and sellers (clubs and players) who might not otherwise come in contact with each other. This makes the market more efficient, because it gives everyone more and better choice. At least, that is how an agent would justify their role in the game.

In my personal experience, I managed to go a long time without hiring one. When I signed my first professional contract, with Cremonese, my father came with me. When I extended my deal with them, I was represented by the Associazione Italiana Calciatori, Italy's version of the Professional Footballers' Association. Incidentally, the PFA in England offer a similar service and one which, in my opinion, players would do well to use. They only take a small percentage and, obviously, they don't have any hidden interests. It's not right for everyone but if, like me, you enjoy a degree of independence and do not want to be tied to an agent, it may be the right solution.

For most of my career, it never occurred to me that I would need an agent to look after me. Perhaps football was different back then. Without question there are few chairmen left like the late Paolo Mantovani, who was president of Sampdoria when I joined in the summer of 1984. He was the classic father-figure chairman, a throwback to another era. He loved the club and saw players, coaches, fans, the media as members of an extended family.

I remember meeting with him to discuss the terms of my contract: 'If you like, we can decide right now how much money you are going to make for the next five years,' he said, 'but if you were my own son I would advise you differently. Because you are young and talented, I think you're only going to get better. And so, rather than locking you into a long-term contract, where we give you a pre-set wage that rises each year, I think it is better if we decide how much to pay you this season and leave the amount for next year blank. At the end of this season we'll get together and determine how much you should make next year. And so on. That way, it will work out in your favour. You'll earn more every year.' Sure enough, that was what happened.

Today, if a player signed a blank contract, the men in white coats would most likely cart him away. It would be insane. Suppose Mantovani had decided to screw me? What if I had been injured? It was risky from Mantovani's perspective too. He could not simply tell me to honour my contract: he had to sit down and negotiate with me every twelve months, which made it more difficult for him to budget. I could have demanded a higher wage and there would have been nothing he could do about it, other than sell me. It's difficult to imagine a chairman offering that level of trust today to a youngster he hardly knows. Although Mantovani and I developed a close relationship over the years, he did not know me at all when I first walked into his office: I was just a promising striker for whom his club had paid a considerable sum.

Would my interests have been better served if I had had an agent? Probably not, but only because I was happy with the wages I was earning and I had no desire to move. But Mantovani kept me satisfied. If I had had an agent, my relationship with Mantovani would have been very different. One of my teammates, Luca Pellegrini, became the first Sampdoria player at the time to be represented by an agent, a local lawyer. When Mantovani saw that Pellegrini had shown up with another man, he said, 'Pardon me, but who is this gentleman?'

'He's my lawyer. He is advising me on the contract,' Pellegrini replied.

'I see,' said Mantovani, getting up to leave. 'In that case, I am going to have to ask you to return in a few days so that I can have my lawyer present. In my experience, lawyers should talk to other lawyers.'

And that was it. Once the 'foreign object' of agents or lawyers was thrown into the mix, Mantovani's spell was broken. The old way of doing business – on trust and a handshake – was gone for ever.

Nowadays I yearn for Mantovani's paternalistic way of doing business – you really felt as if he was looking out for you and never felt the need to question him – but I know how few of his kind there are in football, and how many young footballers have been misled and exploited. In that sense, agents are necessary.

When I think back to my time at Samp, I see how different my relationship with Mantovani and the club would have been if I had had an agent. My agent would have advised me to sign a deal whereby I knew exactly how much money I would be getting year on year. From a security standpoint, it would have been the smart thing to do. I was twenty. I might have shattered my knee at any time. Career over. A long-term contract would also have proved that the club was committed to me. It meant that, if I played poorly, they could not simply offload me. Also the agent would have known better than I how much young players of similar ability were earning at other clubs – he would have had a better sense of my 'market value'.

In my first year, we won the Coppa Italia and finished fourth in Serie A. The following season I won my first caps for Italy and was called up to the 1986 World Cup squad. Again, from my agent's perspective, that would have been the perfect time to discuss a new contract. But to do this he had to know what my options were elsewhere. He would probably have had to make discreet enquiries with other clubs. Would they put in a bid for me? How much could they pay me? He would have had to plant some stories in the papers. And he would probably have had to spread the word that either I was 'unhappy' at Sampdoria or that I 'wanted a club to match my ambition'. That is how business is done. One of two things would have happened. Another club would have come in for me – maybe Milan, Juventus, Barcelona – and my career would have taken a totally different course. Or Mantovani would have bowed to my agent's demands. And the same ritual would have repeated itself every two years.

I probably would not have stayed at Sampdoria for eight seasons, as I did; I would never have experienced the incredible feeling of leading that small provincial club to the *scudetto* one year and the European Cup final the next. Indeed, even if I had stayed, my relationship with

Mantovani, who had a profound influence on my life, as a footballer and as a man, would not have been the same. I think most of all that I would not have made decisions with my heart, only with my head. And I am so grateful to have had the privilege of following my heart on many occasions.

My case is not typical but it was worth relating it to illustrate the impact an agent can have. My story had a happy ending. Countless others don't because players are ill advised – or even unadvised.

In 1992, when I left Sampdoria to join Juventus, I knew I would never have the same relationship with a president. I trusted Mantovani, and that was why, when it came time to discuss my contract with Juve, I did not hire an agent but asked Mantovani to negotiate on my behalf. I told him that I was moving to Italy's richest club and felt that I deserved to be among the best-paid players in Serie A.

Again, when you take a step back, you realize just how unusual my decision was. Talk about conflict of interest. He was selling me to Juventus and, at the same time, negotiating my wages there. He would have had every incentive to negotiate a relatively low salary for me: clearly, the less Juventus had to pay me in wages, the more they would have left over to pay to him as my transfer fee. Yet Mantovani had given me his word. There was no question he would not get me the best possible deal.

If It Sounds Too Good To Be True . . .

During the 1995–96 season, my final year at Juventus, I understood that it was best to move on. I had been offered an extension but it was clear to me that I did not fit into the club's plans. In January, I decided I would leave that summer. I was not yet thirty-two and ready for a new challenge. I felt as if I could go anywhere and, since the Bosman ruling had just come into effect, my options were nearly limitless. For bureaucratic reasons, the UEFA parameter had not yet been removed within Italy, which meant that if I joined another Italian club a fee would be payable. But if I moved to a foreign club, my new team would not have to pay a transfer fee.

The problem for me was to establish who was interested in my services. How could I possibly know? I might have had a sense in Italy, but abroad? And, if someone did rate me, how would they know how to get in touch with me? How would we communicate? How would we even begin to talk about contracts? It became clear to me then I needed an agent.

Agents fulfil an important function: they make the market more efficient, they bring people together and they look out for players' interests. But they cannot go unchecked. There should be a clear distinction between agents working for players and agents working for clubs. The former should be paid by players, the latter by the clubs. This is the best way to ensure a separation of interests. Some agents object that they are at the mercy of the players' whims: they say it's just not feasible for them to invoice their clients, because footballers don't pay up. And while they could, theoretically, take them to court over unpaid bills, in practice no agent likes to do that – they don't want to develop a reputation as a litigious guy who sues his clients. These days, it's easy for a player to cancel his agreement with an agent.

Thus, the agents claim, they have no choice but to go after the clubs for payment. Part of me feels the agents are exaggerating. I find it difficult to accept that, particularly at the highest level, my colleagues could be so brazen and selfish that they would simply turn their backs on their agents and not pay them. Then again, particularly with young players, I can see that some might. They would find it difficult to justify giving away five per cent of their salary because somebody had helped them sign a contract. Naturally, there is an irony in this: they are happy to sign a contract that stipulates the club must pay them X amount of money over Y number of years but they won't honour a contract they signed with an agent.

There is a simple solution. All you have to do is make the clubs responsible for deducting the commission fees from the players' wages and paying them to the agents. It would safeguard agents, while eliminating possible conflicts of interest. National associations, like the FA or the FIGC, could make it mandatory for all transactions without much difficulty.

Rotten to the Core: the 'Bung' System

At the highest level, a professional footballer needs an army of specialists to help him. 'You're not just signing a player, you're signing his profile and the people who present it,' recalls Sir Alex. 'When we signed [Juan Sebastian] Veron there must have been half a dozen people there representing him . . . I didn't even know who was who.'

As Chelsea manager, my job was to focus on the playing squad and recommend players I wanted the club to sign.

As such, I was working more in the continental style, identifying players but leaving the business side to others. Yet I've been in football long enough – and I've spoken to enough people – to understand that there are very serious problems related to the way players change clubs.

You may or may not be familiar with the word 'bung'. It's an important part of many transfers today, in England and in Italy. A bung is an illegal payment, but to illustrate how it might typically work, let's enlist the help of our old friend Carlos Kickaball.

Kickaball plays for Castelpiccolo, in Serie A. His agent is a guy named Pino Procuratore. Castelpiccolo's chairman, Paolo Presidente, and the club's sporting director, Dino Diesse, call Procuratore and discuss Kickaball's future. They agree that perhaps it's time for the club to cash in on Kickaball, who could be worth as much as £2 million. Procuratore stipulates that the transfer can go ahead provided his client can move to a big club in England or Italy.

Diesse calls up his trusted friend, another agent, Andrea Agente, and asks if he can find a club for Kickaball in England. Agente knows a few people who do business in the Premiership but rather than approaching clubs directly, he rings up his colleague Michael Middleman, an agent who acts as a sort of broker, bringing together foreign players and English clubs. Middleman makes a few calls and eventually learns that George Gaffer, the manager at Smallsbury Village FC, is keen to sign Kickaball. Gaffer tells his club's chief executive, Brian Bossman, who is delighted at the prospect of bringing in a top player like Kickaball and happily releases the funds. A brief negotiation follows and, a few days later, the tabloid newspapers scream: 'Smallsbury Sign £3m Star Kickaball!'

Wait! £3 million? Wasn't the asking price £2 million? Yes. But there are commissions on top of that. First, there is Kickaball's agent, Procuratore. He'll want to be paid. And since it has become customary for clubs to pay player agents, the odds are that his fee will have to be paid by Smallsbury. Then there is the man hired by Castelpiccolo to sell Kickaball, Andrea Agente, and his English counterpart, Michael Middleman. They need to be paid too, and their cut will come from the commission paid on the transfer. So you've got these three guys – Procuratore, Agente and Middleman – who share a commission amounting to £1 million. Sometimes they might invoice individually; sometimes it goes to one person who parcels it out to the other two. For our purposes, let's pretend that Procuratore, Kickaball's agent, earns £300,000 in fees, while the two intermediaries, Agente and Middleman, pocket £350,000 each. Either way, Smallsbury are paying out £1 million in commissions on a transfer whose cumulative total is £3 million! Sounds crazy, right? Sounds like Procuratore, Agente and Middleman have the best jobs in the world, right?

Maybe, maybe not. Or, rather, the job is good, just not as good as it seems. Because the sad truth is that, all too often, the money doesn't stay with the agents. It gets 'bunged' back to people at the clubs. In our example, Agente might pay £100,000 each to Diesse and his boss, Presidente, Castelpiccolo's chairman, leaving a £150,000 'finder's fee' for himself. Why should Diesse and Presidente demand money? Well, because they chose to sell Kickaball and, had it not been for that decision, there would have been no transfer and nobody would have profited. Also, they picked Agente to help find a buyer. They did not have to choose *him* – after all, Kickaball is a famous player. The £100,000 kicked back to Presidente and Diesse is Agente's way of saying thank you to them for allowing him to do business.

Meanwhile, something similar is happening at the English end. Michael Middleman needs to make sure that George Gaffer, the manager, and Brian Bossman, the chief executive, are also 'taken care of'. After all, it was Gaffer who decided to sign Kickaball, and it was Bossman who authorized the release of funds to buy him. Without them, there would have been no deal. Middleman, out of his £350,000 pay-off, might divert, say, £100,000 each to Gaffer and Bossman, keeping the rest for himself.

And Procuratore? Kickaball's agent? Does he get to hang on to his £300,000 commission or does he need to split it with someone? In our example, let's pretend that it's all his. Let's say he made a 'very good deal' with Kickaball. 'Don't worry about me, Carlos,' Procuratore might have said. 'I'll get Smallsbury Village to pay me my commission. You won't have to pay me a single penny!'

Gaffer and Bossman are more than pleased to pay Procuratore a £300,000 commission. Why? Well, maybe because Procuratore bungs them back £50,000 each. Or maybe because Procuratore persuades Kickaball to accept a three-year contract worth £1 million a year, instead of the £1.5 million per season he might have received if Procuratore had negotiated hard on behalf of his client. Instead of paying Kickaball £4.5 million over three years, Smallsbury have to pay him just £3 million, which is far more attractive. Indeed, all of a sudden the £300,000 commission paid to Procuratore looks like a real bargain, particularly when a third of it is making its way back into the pockets of Gaffer and Bossman.

Here's a quick recap. Smallsbury Village pay out a total of £3 million. Two million of that goes into Castelpiccolo's coffers. Of the remaining million, £200,000 goes to Pino Procuratore, Kickaball's player agent; £150,000 is paid to Andrea Agente, the intermediary hired by Castelpiccolo; and another £150,000 makes its way to Michael Middleman, the English intermediary Agente contacted. Dino Diesse, Castelpiccolo's sporting director, and Paolo Presidente, Castelpiccolo's president, make around £100,000 each on the deal, while George Gaffer, Smallsbury's manager, and Brian Bossman, the club's chief executive, 'earn' around £150,000 a head.

Depressing, isn't it? That's a million pounds disappearing *en route* from Smallsbury to Castelpiccolo. And, what's more, these days, with the proliferation of off-shore companies and fiscal lawyers specializing in 'tax avoidance', most or all of that money is tax-free. 'Tax avoidance' differs from tax evasion in that it is a legal way of not paying taxes through a variety of schemes, such as trusts and off-shore companies. Of course, it requires clever and expensive tax lawyers to put it in place because the legislation is always changing, which is why it's generally something only the rich can take advantage of. And, as you can imagine, people who 'earn' such commissions on a single transfer are rich.

I don't want to be a demagogue here – I don't want simply to blame agents for taking big commissions. What those who see agents as the source of all evil seem to forget is that, as I mentioned before, they serve a useful purpose. But there are plenty of 'bad' ones, the worst of whom effectively steal money from the clubs. There is no other word for it. Having said that, many among the media, the fans and the governing bodies ignore an obvious point: it takes two to steal. When I say some agents 'steal' money from clubs I don't mean that they break into the club safe at night and make off with a sackful of cash. No. Somebody opens the door, invites them in and takes a share of the spoils. Whenever people rail against 'bungs' and 'illegal payments' in football, they ought to rail against collusion too. Because none of this would be possible without the consent of those at the clubs who allow this to continue and profit from it. Some people make light of it, others take it as the natural state of affairs. Some say it happens in other industries too. I don't know about that, but I do know that other industries are not necessarily built on passion and love as football is. I also know there is nothing funny about it: this money comes from the supporters. It's the supporters who pay the wages of chief executives and managers, presidents and sporting directors. They put their trust in those people, they hope they will run the club in a way that is fair, honourable and in the best interests of their team.

It makes my blood boil to think that, all too often, those men steal shamelessly from the people whose hard-earned cash gives them the opportunity to make a living from football in the first place. Some say it has always been this way, but it hasn't. Agents only became wide-spread in football during the early 1990s. And the size of contracts and transfer fees only began to expand to current levels in the mid-1990s. Before that, there probably wasn't much thieving in the shape of bungs because there wasn't so much to steal.

What can be done? The difficulty is in ascertaining how widespread this practice is and how close the guilty parties are to the power structure, in England and in Italy. It's difficult for the leagues – the Premier League in England, the Lega Calcio in Italy – to police because, ultimately, those bodies answer directly to the clubs and some clubs have no interest in changing the status quo. There is also a sense among the people who run football that it would take too much effort to deal with it. Those who are honest have little incentive to do something about it as it does not directly affect them and because they have other, more pressing concerns. The FAs in either country have a little more independence in that they represent the game as a whole, not just the top flight. But they, too, are under the influence of the clubs. This is especially true in Italy, but also in England. It's unthinkable for either country to elect an FA chief executive who does not have the approval of that nation's big clubs.

So you have to go higher. But to whom? The government? The sad truth is that government ministers are overburdened and underfunded when it comes to something like this. And it might prove politically unpopular if they tried to make a case against a high-profile team or popular club official who pleaded innocence.

Those best placed to police this situation and perhaps even end it are the folk at the Inland Revenue and their counterparts in Italy. The kickbacks to club officials are not declared, which is tax evasion. It's sad that football can't enforce the few rules it makes for itself. Then again, that was how Al Capone was finally busted: the tax police got him.

Not long ago it was common practice for footballers to be paid a little extra 'under the table'. It happened at many clubs, and when I was young, I benefited from it. But that was the way things operated. As a young player you didn't have any choice. And, from what I hear, it was common in England, particularly in the ticketless days of turnstiles, when fans turned up, paid cash and walked in. I've heard stories of 'chairmen's turnstiles' where all the money from a particular turnstile found its way into the chairman's back pocket. Naturally the fans who entered via that turnstile would not feature in the official attendance figures, which was why sometimes you would see a suspiciously low attendance rating in the newspapers the next day when the game had appeared to be a sell-out.

There is a difference between events that happened twenty years ago (when football clubs were not run as proper businesses and there was a lot less money in the game), which, for better or worse, were the norm at the time, and the brazen theft that is taking bungs. Taking bungs, paying bungs, sharing bungs – these are crimes in so many ways and tax evasion is just one of them.

We are left with a situation in which some are crooked, some are clueless and know nothing, and some are honest and know who the crooked are but, for a variety of reasons, cannot or will not speak out. Perhaps they have more suspicions than facts. Perhaps they do not want to upset the status quo. Perhaps the rot is so widespread they figure it won't make any difference. Perhaps they feel they will be frozen out by their colleagues if they blow the whistle. Or perhaps they don't feel it's their job to play crusader.

I hope that things change, but it will take time. I don't think the public at large knows or understands enough of what goes on in certain cases. When they do – and it will be up to the healthy parts of football to shine a light on the rotten bits – I think they will be sufficiently outraged to demand change. And, if the public is outraged, the sponsors will take notice and they, too, will join the battle. At that point, football will have to clean itself up.

Speaking of sponsors, they may yet serve as a civilizing force in football. I know many purists complain about the commercialization of the game and lament that, to a sponsor, football is simply a way of flogging a product. That may be true. But it does not mean that the interests of sponsors and fans are not the same, at least in certain cases. Fans want a healthy, honest, competitive sport. Sponsors want something that is at least perceived to be the same. They don't want to associate their product with something corrupt or boring. If the game deteriorates, if people start losing faith in the transparency of the competition and its protagonists (a process that – as we'll see – has already begun in Italy and may develop in England), the sponsors may be the ones with the clout to make a difference. Because, ultimately, their money fuels the game. And if change is going to happen in football, you cannot leave the sponsors out of the equation.

Who We Are and How We Appear . . .

Even now, the notion of 'image rights' for a footballer seems bizarre to me. Every time I hear about an average footballer with a multi-million-pound image-rights contract I wonder whether there isn't an ulterior motive. I suspect that in many cases of disproportionately large image-rights deals, they may exist to pay certain people discreetly.

Of course, for some there are legitimate issues of image and branding – David Beckham is the obvious one, but there are others, players whose image is instantly worth X amount to advertisers and sponsors. It's only right that they look after it and reach some sort of understanding with the club. The difficulty lies in establishing how much of the image is down to the individual and how much to the club.

After all, if footballers all looked the same and wore shirts with no names and numbers on them, we would be rooting for clubs, not individuals. Indeed, there would be no individuals, just the team. No player could argue that he's a bigger star than a teammate because nobody would be able to tell them apart. That's why many footballers feel the need to establish their own image, to differentiate themselves so that they can exploit it.

'This is an era where you need to be seen, you need an image,' says Sir Alex, 'so players present themselves differently, with earrings, tattoos, agents . . . Notice how the goal celebrations have changed as well. Today, when a player scores a goal, he turns away from his teammates for his own self-acclaim. You rarely see a player celebrating with his teammates, staying in the goal area and having them all come to him.'

The idea is that a player can create his own parallel brand, partly based on his football, partly on his demeanour off the pitch. A player with the right 'brand image' will probably gain all sorts of advantages, and not just in commercial terms. But the key is in being seen. This may explain why, in branding terms, golfers are among the most loved by advertisers. They have long careers (which means that, after you have built a brand, you can reap the rewards for decades), they are highly visible and they have plenty of opportunity to express their personalities.

By contrast, despite the huge popularity of the sport, American football players are relatively unloved in marketing terms. There are several reasons for this – short careers, it's a team sport – but the single biggest is that these guys wear helmets, which means you don't see what they look like. A big part of the logic behind branding is to have a product associated with a player (like Nike and Michael Jordan). Every time you see Player X you think of Product Y, or so the sponsors hope. The problem is that, if Player X happens to be an American football player and he endorses a product while he's in 'civilian' clothes, most people won't recognize him because they're used to seeing him in his helmet. Footballers rank somewhere between golfers and American footballers so they need to make themselves stand out. Of course, the best way is to do things on the pitch that others can't. If you score a hat-trick every week, you'll have no trouble in standing out. But because this is not an easy thing to achieve, some find other ways to brand themselves. The ultimate example of this comes from tennis, in which Anna Kournikova was easily the most famous woman player without having won a single tournament. This was no accident: she and her advisers nurtured her image. True, she was born beautiful, but her beauty was used in a very clever commercial way that another tennis player, who was pre-occupied exclusively with the athletic side of things, might not have pursued.

Some maintain that Beckham's celebrity status is not just a result of his footballing ability but of a variety of other factors: his wife, the way he dresses, the way he looks, etc. It's difficult to argue with them. If Beckham was ugly, married to an unknown and dressed like the average punter, he would not be the most famous foot-baller in the world. He has chosen a certain image and lifestyle that, with his football ability, have made him the game's biggest celebrity.

Beckham is far from the only one. Anyone who has seen Rino Gattuso play will know what I'm talking about. With his goatee, gestures to the crowd and pinballing around the pitch, the Milan midfielder also has an image. And it continues off the pitch in the things he says, which are often heartfelt and aimed at the fans.

Rio Ferdinand has a different image: his is more refined, hip and cool. His hairstyle and the way he dresses speak to a different audience. The 'Rio brand' is nothing like the 'Gattuso brand' or, indeed, the 'Beckham brand'.

I don't think it's wrong for a player to cultivate his image. It would be hypocritical if I did. After all, in my youth I changed my look several times in several different ways. I've had my share of tattoos and, in terms of hair-style, I went for the skinhead look *and* bleached-blond mop. Of course, branding was the furthest thing from my mind: I did it to express myself, have fun. It was who I was. From what I know, Beckham and the others are only doing the same. They are being who they want to be. But, deep down, there is a traditionalist streak in the game, a conservatism, a sense that fame is something you gain on footballing merit. And that is where the resentment from certain quarters comes into play. Beckham is more famous than others who, perhaps, are better players. This is very upsetting to some: they feel that celebrity status has to relate only to footballing ability.

'Rio is a good example,' says Dave Boyle, deputy chief executive of Supporters Direct, the government task force that looks after fans' interests. 'His advisers talk of music, fashion, books . . . they want to build upon the Rio brand. But fans say to us that it's about the football and what does that have to do with brands? To them, Rio is a footballer, not a celebrity. They are comfortable, I think, with rising wages as long as the focus is on football.

'But, in their eyes, Ferdinand does not have the good grace to be humble,' he adds. 'It's the same with Beckham. His image says, "Look at the money I make, look at the fancy clothes I wear at these charity galas." Roy Keane also makes a lot of money, but he lets the football do the talking. It's very British, but there's a sense that it's OK to make a lot of money as long as you're not ostentatious about it.'

I see inconsistency there. Both Ferdinand and Beckham have done lots of charity work, exploiting their fame and image to help raise money for good causes. It seems a paradox that Beckham, for example, should be criticized for being photographed at a charity ball wearing flash clothes. It's almost as if he would be better off sitting at home counting his money. At least that way he would not be 'flash'. And 'flash' is not something you want to be. Not if you're an English footballer anyway. 'Beckham is flash, which is why I think some of the fans at Manchester

United never really took to him,' says Boyle. 'He didn't fit the Mancunian work ethic. You see, Manchester United is a global brand, but it's very much rooted in Manchester and Manchester values. Now, here was a guy who was as comfortable on the fashion pages as on the sports pages . . .

'George Best was a celebrity too, of course, but with him it was different,' he adds. 'His celebrity did not manifest itself on the catwalk. It was about getting drunk and going to bed with lots of women. That's something Mancunians could relate to. It's what they would do if they could. Faced with the choice of being Beckham and leading his life, or Best, they would all choose Best.'

This will probably change. We will come to accept that the relationship between celebrity and football is not what it once was. Previously, celebrity was a by-product of football: it grew in proportion to a player's achievements on the pitch. Now football is still the basis of celebrity (let's not forget that if Beckham were an ordinary or even a 'very good' player, he would not have the fame he enjoys today), but the two are no longer proportionally related. Image acts as a co-efficient and has a multiplier effect. You can represent it in a formula:

f = football achievement, i = image, c = celebrity status

It used to be that $f = c$. Now, it's $f \times i = c$

There is an addendum to that, of course: $c = £$. The greater the celebrity, the more revenue generated. It raises the stakes tremendously. Not only are players judged in sporting terms (by the fans, the press, the football fraternity), they are also judged in business terms (by the clubs, the sponsors, the agents).

Chapter Nine

Referees: Here to Serve the Game?

I like to think that the referee is something you need to play football and that he's no different from the ball or, indeed, the goalposts. Sometimes, like the ball, he might take a bad bounce or swerve unexpectedly or be less than true in his movements. But he is part of the game, a neutral element, neither good nor bad. He's essentially a tool.

That's what I like to think, but referees are not inanimate objects. They are humans. Like inanimate objects, they can be improved. Companies spend millions on research and development to make a 'better' football, and over the years we've improved the training techniques and attitudes of our referees. Now they are probably better than they've ever been. But they are far from perfect. Just as we don't have the perfect football, we don't have a perfect referee. But perhaps the difference is that the football's 'errors' are random, while those of the referee can be caused by countless factors: poor positioning, poor eyesight, being conned by a player, nerves, or intimidation by clubs, institutions or fans . . .

While we may reasonably expect one day to produce the 'perfect' football, we cannot expect our referees to be flawless. Refereeing is not merely about making decisions – if it were, theoretically, a robot could do a better job – it's about psychology and control. And once you venture into those grey areas, mistakes are bound to happen.

Still, that doesn't mean we cannot improve our referees *and* our attitude towards them. To understand this a little better, I talked to two of the best in the business, Pierluigi Collina (now retired) and Graham Poll, officials widely regarded as number one in Italy and in England respectively. Both men love football and both have been in the game as long as most professionals if not longer. But for a quirk of nature that saw them blessed with refereeing rather than football skills, they never made it as players.

'I always played football at my works team, but then I changed jobs and my new job didn't have a team,' says Poll. 'I thought I'd try refereeing because I wanted to stay involved.'

Collina's story is not much different: 'I can't remember my life without football. I started as a very small child,' he recalls. 'I started playing as soon as I could kick the ball. I played right through into my teens. Then, at seventeen, my best friend had the brilliant idea of enrolling in a refereeing course and harassed me until I joined him. I agreed, not because I was convinced but partly because I was curious and partly because I felt like doing something a little different . . .'

Amazing as it sounds, two of the best officials of our time became referees almost accidentally. But maybe it's not so remarkable – after all, it's not as if children grow up dreaming of becoming referees . . . 'Very few people want to be a referee,' says Poll. 'It's something you just fall into. Maybe you got an injury, or maybe, like me, you no longer had a team and instead of finding a new one you decided to be a referee. Seldom is there actually a desire to be a referee because, well, when you don't know about it, it's not such an attractive job.'

Poll and Collina started refereeing some twenty-five years ago. It's safe to say that the game changed more in that last quarter-century than it did in the previous fifty years. 'When I compare what football was like in 1977, when I made my début, to what it is like in 2005, it's like comparing the present to the Jurassic era,' Collina says. 'Honestly. The football played back then was a different sport.' Indeed, some might suggest that it was a sport, while today's game is part spectacle, part entertainment and part business.

'We're in a different industry now,' says Poll. 'Football is an entertainment industry, it's no longer a sport. The same goes for us, the referees. We're professionals now. And our attitude towards football is different. It's more about being efficient and minimizing mistakes. Before you just did what you did.'

The introduction of professionalism was the most obvious change for referees, and it became easier to hold them to account for their decisions. From their perspective, it obviously made it easier to train and prepare properly for matches. 'As with most things there are good and bad aspects to having professional referees,' Poll says. 'I used to have to work virtually a full day and then drive to the match. I'd be tired before I'd even start the game. And, if you're tired, you're going to make mistakes, your decision-making isn't going to be crisp, your positioning isn't going to be as good.

'Certainly from that point of view it's better . . .

However, it used to be that, by Monday, you could forget about the game. Now I have to sit there with a DVD showing every incident from multiple angles and at multiple speeds, and I then have to analyse it. I have to ask myself, is this making me a better referee or am I overanalysing things? Am I becoming too technical? Am I complicating things? It's a very simple game and there are only seventeen laws. In some ways I think maybe we should just let things flow naturally . . .'

It's the price you pay for professionalism, some might say. Now that referees are paid to officiate, we expect them to be as good as they can be. And that means preparing between matches. How can a referee prepare? By training, so that they are physically fit, and by analysing their past performance. At least, that would seem to be the obvious answer. To Collina, however, there is another area in which a referee can prepare: 'Some referees don't want to know anything about the teams before they go on to the pitch. I am the opposite,' he says. 'The night before the 2002 World Cup final between Germany and Brazil, I stayed up until dawn watching every single game the two teams had played in that competition. I wanted to know the players as best I could.'

Collina had a specific reason for 'scouting' the players in such detail. It is probably at the heart of why he was such a successful referee: he used his knowledge of each club to predict what they would do on the pitch. 'Obviously as a referee you're always going to be one step behind, because you're reacting to the players,' he says. 'But if you can guess what is going to happen, you can minimize that initial reaction gap.

'For example, some teams, particularly English ones,

like to send the ball wide and then look for the cross. Well, if you know this ahead of time, it's a tremendous help because it means you will position yourself accordingly on the pitch. Another team might prefer to cut inside from a wide position and run at central defenders. Again, if you are familiar with this you'll put yourself in the right position to best judge what is about to happen.'

Now that Collina has retired, he is more than happy to reveal his 'secrets'. I knew referees prepared for matches, but I had not expected such intense research. And indeed Collina goes further: 'Certain teams have certain characteristics, but certain players have certain characteristics as well and you have to take those into account too,' he says. 'For example, if I'm refereeing an Inter match in which [Sinisa] Mihailovic is playing, I know there is a good chance that he will move to the left of the defence and launch a fifty-yard pass for Obafemi Martins to chase. Now, obviously, I am not as fast as the ball. In fact, I am not as fast as Martins either. So I have to anticipate what will happen. And the second I see Mihailovic move to the left of the defence, I check Martins's position. If it appears he's looking to make a run, I'll position myself accordingly, perhaps beginning my movement up the pitch so I can be ready for Mihailovic's long ball.

'Or, for example, take [Alex] Del Piero,' he adds. 'Having refereed him so many times I know his tendencies. If he has the ball wide on the left, he almost always comes inside and rarely goes down the line. The point is that if you know how play might develop, it is far simpler to referee.'

It occurs to me that Collina probably knows more

about players in the game than most scouts or coaches. He has to: he must watch them constantly because they hold one of the keys to his performance. As a player, you don't think of yourself as predictable, though I suppose many of us are, at least to Collina.

'It doesn't work with everyone,' Collina explains. 'If you're dealing with a Totti or a Ronaldinho, it's nearly impossible to know what's going to happen, both for you and for the opposing manager. As a team, Arsenal are like that. It was very hard for me to know where the ball was going to go and what movements they were going to make. It's fun to watch, but from a refereeing perspective it's certainly a challenge.'

Collina speaks about what we might term the 'technical' side of refereeing. There is no psychology here, it's simply about giving yourself the best possible view of each incident. That means having the fitness to keep up, the experience to know how to position yourself and, if you use Collina's method, an individual knowledge of players and teams that allows you to anticipate what will happen, thereby gaining valuable seconds.

But then there is the other huge part of refereeing, the intangible part, the discretionary part. It is probably here that officials draw the most criticism. It's not so much about what they see or don't see, but about how they handle what they do see. It is here that, often, there appears to be a contrast between the laws of the game and the referees' discretion. On the one hand, you want consistency but on the other you need 'common sense'.

'Twice a year UEFA's top fifty referees get together and the analogy we use is that of the game as a thoroughbred horse,' says Poll. 'If you have a thoroughbred horse, you want to see it expressing itself so you don't tie it to a post. But you don't let it run free either, because it will run away from you. You have to build a corral around it and let it express itself within that corral.

'The corral is the way you apply the laws of the game,' he goes on. 'You don't tie yourself slavishly to the laws. That's why sometimes you see some perceived inconsistencies.'

These 'inconsistencies', as Poll calls them, are at the heart of one of the trickier issues of the game. We've all seen referees sanction differently what appear to be identical fouls in different games. In fact, we've seen referees sanction fouls differently at different times in the same match. I can understand why this happens: sometimes referees use their discretion based on the flow of the game. They force themselves to look at the bigger picture and act accordingly.

'I am there to serve the game,' says Poll. 'I am not there for Graham Poll. I am there for football. Within the framework of the laws I have to do what is credible on that day. So, if Tottenham and Arsenal are playing they may need someone who can understand the passion and allow the game to flow because this is indicative of English football. And if it's the Milan derby, it's more about free kicks, control, dead-ball situations. You need to keep the temperature down. The temperament of the players is more volatile.

'In a different match, in a different temperature, I may speak more or less,' adds Poll. 'If it's a certain intense game I may speak for longer, because I want to take the temperature out of the match . . . This pot which is boiling up, I want it to simmer down. In a situation like that I may speak to a player for a long time, to calm him down and calm the other players down, and re-establish myself as in control of the game. It all depends on the situation.'

Mourinho also points to the discretion exercised by certain referees, particularly English ones: 'It's fantastic,' he says. 'The objective of the referees in England is to finish eleven versus eleven. In other countries, their objective is to keep control. They don't care about the quality of the game or the spectacle on the pitch. What they want is to protect themselves and, to do this, they impose discipline by pulling out cards. It doesn't matter to them if it's ten versus ten, nine versus nine or even eight versus eight. In England, the referee has much more discretion – he can even go against the rules sometimes, if it is going to help the game.'

The English referees' use of discretion is reflected in the fact that they are constantly eager to engage the players in dialogue. English officials are always keen to have a word, share a joke, or lecture a player when necessary. They believe in adopting an informal, schoolmasterly manner. Many Italian referees seem actively to avoid dialogue or human contact with the players. It's as if they don't want to fraternize with them, as if they want to maintain a certain distance. It's also why they sometimes give the impression of enjoying it a little too much when they pull out a card.

I realize why the distinction exists. Referees represent authority: they should be faceless and treat everyone the same. In the same way judges wear robes and wigs: they lose their individuality and instead represent a larger ideal, the law. As a defendant, you don't want the prosecutor and the judge to be too chummy, cracking jokes and slapping each other on the back. But a football pitch is not a court, and an amicable relationship between referee and players, perhaps peppered with humour, can defuse tension.

This 'common sense' approach, tailoring the officiating to the situation, makes sense, although it leaves referees open to criticism because people see inconsistencies between one game and the next. They point out, quite rightly, that each game is not just an individual episode, it's part of a larger whole. Imagine you have two players – our old friends Bidone and Kickaball – who commit the same foul in different matches. Bidone's foul comes towards the end of a good-natured 2–0 victory and it's the first bad foul of the day. Kickaball commits his foul in a tight derby, with tackles flying in. Shortly before his foul, the referee has just warned the two captains about the behaviour of the players.

Which of the two gets booked? That's right, Kickaball. His booking sends a message to both sets of players: it signals that the referee is ready to come down hard on foul play. He wants to show the players he won't be intimidated and make sure that he maintains his authority over the match. There is nothing wrong with this in the context of the game. In fact, it's excellent refereeing. Where it can become a problem is in the larger context of a season. Kickaball gets booked, Bidone does not. It could mean that Kickaball is suspended and Bidone isn't. And that affects not just the game they are playing in, the one in which they committed the foul, but the next match. Their opponents in that game can face Kickaball's team without Kickaball, which is quite an advantage. The team against which Kickaball committed the foul meanwhile got no advantage out of it: he stayed on the pitch for ninety minutes.

I'm not sure how you solve this problem. Philosophically, I'm all for common-sense discretionary refereeing. Yet I am all too aware of the dangers and how it can become unfair over the course of a season. This is particularly true in a country like Italy, where the press, clubs and fans are bound to pick up on things and hammer the referees. In England referees enjoy a relatively smooth ride.

The Dark Conspiracy Against Us . . .

'If I were a referee I am a hundred per cent sure that I would much rather work in England than in Italy,' says Sven-Goran Eriksson. 'This country is fantastic for referees. Nobody questions their decisions and, most of all, nobody ever questions their honesty.'

He may be exaggerating a little. In the last few years England has severely criticized referees (especially foreign ones, as Urs Meier, the Swiss official who disallowed Sol Campbell's goal at Euro 2004, discovered), but we are light years away from Italy. In fact, even in the Meier case, the papers leading the witch-hunt were tabloids, which take a rather playful attitude towards the sport, while the heavyweight broadsheets were more muted. In Italy, there is no distinction. The 'serious' papers go after referees with as much gusto as the daily sports papers.

'I prefer the English approach as a manager too,' says Eriksson. 'The more time I spent in Italy, the more I became like an Italian. My first year in Italy, I still had the Swedish mentality. I wasn't interested in things like the draw to determine who our referee would be in the next match. Then, year after year, I noticed I was changing. My last season in Italy, I waited for the referees' assignments to come out with great anticipation. And I began asking myself whether the referee was honest . . . Think about it. This is what we spend time worrying about in Italy. What the hell are we supposed to do if he's not honest? Change tactics because a referee might not be honest? If you think about it, it's madness.'

Indeed it is. But the referees' assignments, which come out every Wednesday ahead of the weekend's matches, are huge news in Italy. It's as if a parallel sport is based around match officials. But, unlike most sports, the sport of referee-watching has no winners, only a group of frustrated individuals.

Most Italian conspiracy theorists will tell you that the only time referees were assigned by a random draw, rather than to specific matches by a referees' association, Verona won the title. Yes, little Verona, who captured the *scudetto* in 1984–85. The implication is clear. In 1984–85, referees' names were drawn out of a hat for the last time. This meant that the luck of the draw determined which official attended a match so 'big' teams could not assign themselves 'friendly' referees – or make sure that Verona got a referee who would 'sort them out' by making them drop points. Conspiracy theorists maintain that the system changed after that season to ensure that a small provincial team could never again win the title. And, indeed, since then, in typical Italian fashion, the system has changed almost annually. We've had the Referees' Association assigning specific officials to specific games (as is the case in England), the logic being that some matches are tougher than others and therefore should be given to higher-rated referees. We've had a hybrid system, whereby fixtures were divided into tiers according to difficulty, referees placed in each tier (supposedly according to ability), then a draw made within each tier. And we've tried both having one man in charge and, until 2004–05, two men, one allegedly looking out for northern teams, the other closer to the Roman teams, because the clubs could not agree on one person and vetoed each other's choice.

At this level, I don't believe in conspiracy. Even the Verona argument is rather weak. For starters, they weren't a no-hope provincial side: the year before they were sixth, in 1982–83 they finished fourth, and the team included Italian internationals, such as Pietro Fanna, Antonio di Gennaro, Beppe Galderisi and Roberto Tricella, the magnificent German strongman Hans-Peter Briegel, and the Danish striker Preben Elkjaer Larsen, then one of the best in the world. That year, the two pre-season favourites, Roma and Juventus, struggled for a number of reasons. Roma, coached by Eriksson in his first Italian season, was hit by a rash of injuries, while Juve's ageing team found that it could only focus on one target and chose the European Cup (which they eventually won on the night of the Heysel stadium tragedy). Milan were by no means a powerhouse (it was only their second year back in Serie A), Inter were in transition, and Diego Maradona had only just arrived at Napoli. It was a season in which everyone faltered and Verona was simply more consistent.

I might also add that Verona was not the only small provincial side to win the *scudetto* in the last twenty years. My Sampdoria team took it in 1990–91. We, too, had a very good team, but you would hardly call us or our chairman part of Italian football's aristocracy. Which suggests to me that if a big conspiracy was afoot it must have taken a year off in 1990–91.

It's hard to see similar conspiracy theories taking hold in England, largely because referees are rarely discussed, either by fans or the media, 'only when something really, really big happens, like in Manchester United–Tottenham,' Mourinho says, referring to referee Mark Clattenburg who did not see the ball cross Roy Carroll's goal line. 'I'll give you an example. We had the same referee twice last season and in two games, with two controversial decisions, he cost us five points. If I were in Portugal I would come out and say, "The referee has something against us," so that the next time he referees us, he is already under pressure. He will want to be careful not to appear anti our team. Here in England, I can't do that, because nobody remembers who he is. Nobody wants to talk about him. In Portugal I can create big problems for a referee. Here I can't do a thing. There is much more respect for the institutions and, because of that, everybody behaves differently.'

It's refreshing to hear Mourinho candidly admit that he would 'create problems' for a referee who had made two mistakes against him. It's one of the oldest tricks, which preys upon basic psychology. If you give an interview before a match and say, 'I don't think that referee likes us, he's always trying to hurt us. I hope he can have a good game, I really do, because his natural instinct is to be against my team,' you can have a profound effect on the game. The referee will be aware of what you said and may go out of his way to prove he is not biased. In doing so, he may give you the benefit of the doubt on more than one occasion. The public will be scrutinizing the match, mindful of what you said, which will only increase the pressure on the referee: he will know that if he rules against your team, you'll be joined in protest by the media. In Italy, every manager – indeed, every player – knows this. Not everybody engages in it, but everyone is aware of the mind game played by referees and coaches.

'I thought it was bizarre when the referee's name would be announced and my teammates would all immediately begin talking about him and discussing his merits,' says Ray Wilkins. 'I really did not care, but to them it was vitally important.'

Marcel Desailly agrees: 'In Italy, I knew all the referees,' he says. 'All of them. It was impossible not to know them, it was the only topic of discussion, both in the papers and in the dressing room. Here in England, on the other hand, they are never talked about. Honestly, I could not tell you the name of a single English referee. They all look the same, at least to me.'

Earlier in this book I talked about how in Italy we are prone to thinking cynically, to expecting the worst. We assume that nothing is as it seems, that there is always something behind it. We even have a word for it: *dietrologia*, literally 'backology' – the study of what is 'at the back', or 'behind'.

'There is always a conspiracy, always a vendetta . . .' says Graham Poll. 'I officiated at a World Cup game involving Italy, and after the match the centre-forward came up to me and said, "The assistant killed you." His thinking was that the linesman had made some mistakes to ruin my reputation as a referee in this tournament.' So, the linesman couldn't just have had a bad day: there must have been something behind his poor performance.

'People in Italy are more insulting, in England they are more abusive,' says Poll. In Italy angry fans accuse referees of being corrupt while in England they call them incompetent. 'Neither is particularly pleasant. But I would rather be called useless than corrupt. I'm happy that in England, we're never accused of intentionally favouring one team over another. We have to have that credibility in decision-making.'

The problem is that facile suspicions undermine credibility. They plant the seed of doubt: 'What if there is a conspiracy?' Part of the problem is that, when people believe that others are conspiring against them, they themselves begin to conspire. Sometimes I am shocked at the degree to which we are ready to believe the worst of others. One of the reasons Collina retired from the game in the summer of 2005 was that the Referees' Association had criticized him for not asking permission in writing before he signed a sponsorship contract with Opel. The fear was that, since Opel sponsor Milan, it would be inappropriate for them also to sponsor a referee.

I laugh when I think about it. Who were Chelsea's shirt sponsors during the 2004–05 season? Emirates. Who is sponsoring Arsenal's new stadium at Ashburton Grove? Emirates. And who also sponsored the Premiership referees, all of them, with their logo proudly displayed on the referees' jerseys? That's right . . . Emirates!

An Italian cynic would draw his own conclusions: 'Chelsea and Arsenal finished first and second in the Premiership. Well, of course they would. Their sponsors also sponsor the referees!'

Sticking to the Rulebook

Fortunately, this attitude is almost unknown in England. I believe that English referees are not under constant suspicion because of the way in which they officiate. 'Italian and English referees reflect the football that is played in their respective countries,' says Desailly. 'In Italy, where people are more clever and tricky and there are more tactical fouls, it's obvious that referees blow their whistles more often. In England, they let play go on, partly because there is less of the above, and partly because this is what the fans want.'

His impressions are backed up by the facts. In Serie A, there are 60 per cent more red cards (0.31 compared to 0.18) per match and 20 per cent more yellow cards (3.80 compared to 3.09) than there are in the Premiership. But the real difference is in fouls. On average, a Serie A match features fourteen more than a Premiership game. This is particularly surprising when you consider that English football is played at a higher pace so there are more collisions and more contact between players. 'And that's another reason why I prefer English referees,' says Arsène Wenger. 'I don't like constant interruptions. In fact, the more a referee uses his whistle, the more he is encouraging diving and cheating. It's best to let the game flow.'

Everybody wants the game 'to flow'. I have yet to meet someone who says, 'I like it when a football match doesn't flow. I love hearing the whistle and knowing that things are going to stop and there's going to be a lot of standing around, waving of arms and arguing. Those are my favourite bits.' However, when it's our striker who is man-handled in the penalty area or it's our goalkeeper who is shoved when he's coming out to collect a corner, we feel differently. It's only human, of course. The problem becomes serious, though, when, as in Italy, the media replay individual incidents over and over again. More often than not, they crucify referees for not calling fouls rather than for the ones they sanction. 'In Italy unfortunately the referees are victims of the *moviolisti* [the analysts who endlessly replay incidents on television],' says Fabio Capello. 'They are obsessed with whether there is contact, whether the leg or arm is here or there. It's crazy. If you watch a basketball game you see players pushing and shoving each other all over the place and it's OK. In football, as soon as they touch you it's a foul. They simply call too many fouls.'

'The excuse they give is that they're protecting the stars, the gifted players,' he adds, 'but in fact they're protecting nothing. They're protecting weaklings and pansies. We don't need that. I much prefer the English way, where technique and skill goes hand in hand with physical prowess. It's a shame, though, because in fact Italian referees are very good. It's just that, because of the way they are treated by the media, they have this Sword of Damocles over their heads.'

Of course, English football and Italian football do not exist in a vacuum. They can't just make up their own rules: they have to answer to FIFA, the game's governing body. And FIFA, judging from the rankings of Italian referees compared to English ones, seems to believe that the Italian way of officiating is better. As Ray Wilkins points out, this creates a problem for English clubs: 'It's one of the bigger hurdles we face,' he says. 'In England you'll see a two-footed tackle go unpunished and, as usual, we English come out and say, "Well, that's never been a foul, why should it be given?" The problem comes when our players go into the Champions' League or the national team and, all of a sudden, that tackle becomes a bookable offence. They then collect yellow and red cards because the rest of the world views it differently. You need consistency.'

How to achieve consistency? Does England become like the rest of the footballing world or does the rest of the world adopt English ways? To me, the answer is that while it would be great to bring the rest of the world closer to England – we want to see the game flow – England will have to take the first step. Because the rest of the world is happy to go on without England. In fact, that is what has been happening and English football has suffered the consequences.

'English referees are a big problem for us when we play in Europe,' says Mourinho. 'There is just a difference in psychology. For example, in the Champions' League, the referees are always calling attacking fouls, when a striker fouls a defender. In England, a forward can jump on a defender's head and it's not a foul. In Europe, the whistle goes immediately. I don't want to say which philosophy is better, but I do think we should get some consistency.'

I've asked myself many times what lies at the heart of the inconsistency. It's understandable that Italian referees call more fouls because they are under greater scrutiny. After all, Italy is the country where every week there are shows like *Il Processo* (literally *The Trial*), which consist of replaying incidents in super-slow motion, and second-guessing each referee's decision. There are similar shows on every national network and also on many local stations.

It's not surprising that an Italian referee 'covers his bases' by ensuring he doesn't miss any sanctionable fouls.

The English referee has a different priority. He wants the game to flow in the fairest and most pleasant way. Sometimes that means not respecting the letter of the law. He has greater powers of discretion than his Italian colleague and he is not afraid to use them. 'Statistically the Italian referee intervenes more, that's true, but a good referee adapts himself to the type of match it is, not the other way round,' says Collina. 'He has to tailor his style to what the game needs and what the players expect.

'If I am officiating a Scotland v. England international and I start whistling every contact, the players are going to question that. I'm obviously talking here about grey areas. Black and white areas will always be sanctioned, of course. It's those dubious ones, the ones which could go either way, that's where you as a referee have to be sensitive.'

So, referees adapt to the expectations of the two teams. But what happens when you have two teams with different expectations? Things get tricky.

'The most difficult game to referee is when you have one mentality, say an Italian or Spanish or Greek mentality, against a north-European mentality,' says Poll. 'That's where the referee has to find common ground because he can't simply say, "I do things this way." There are twenty-two other people out there and you have to find that common ground and maintain your credibility. It's not easy.'

It's in the nature of football that things are done differently in different countries. And just as certain tackles are tolerated in England but sanctioned in Italy, the reverse happens with shirt-pulling. In Italy, particularly in set-pieces, players often grab each other in an attempt to gain leverage or hold back the opponent. I think it is counterproductive to tolerate this, as is allowing those flying English tackles in midfield. We saw an example of it at Euro 2004, when Marco Materazzi gave away a penalty against Bulgaria for doing things in a way that he does them week in, week out in Serie A: using his arms to defend the opponent's header. As a striker, one of the fouls I find most annoying is the defender holding you back in the box. To me, this kind of foul is frustrating as your opponent makes no attempt to get the ball or to do anything positive. It's just about stopping you. I'd like to see every one of those fouls punished with a penalty, if it takes place in the area.

I know people will say that often the shoving or grabbing is mutual. Well, if that's the case, book both players. That will stop them. Others might say that if you give penalties for shirt-grabbing, you'll end up with six or seven penalties in a game. So be it. You can be sure that shirt-grabbing won't last long.

But if it is to be stamped out, it has to be a concerted effort. Giving the occasional penalty won't help. In fact, it will have the opposite effect. When a penalty for shirt-pulling is given, you often see more shirt-pulling throughout the rest of the game. The reason for this is simple: players figure that no referee will dare to give more than one penalty for such an offence in a single game.

To make matters worse, an unwritten rule, particularly in Italy, states that a simple foul in the box is rarely sufficient to get a penalty. You need more. That's why fouls sanctioned in the middle of the park often go unpunished in the penalty area. Sometimes it feels as if there are two sets of rules, one for the penalty area and one outside it.

Another area of inconsistency is that, all things being equal, defenders get away with far more than strikers. You see this clearly in set-pieces where players are jockeying for position, or when two players go up to head the ball. When the shoving, grabbing or elbowing is mutual, referees tend to punish the forward. I've seen a defender practically get inside a striker's shirt, but the moment the striker gives him a little nudge to free himself, the referee blows the whistle. Year after year, we see the same players leading the league in fouls. In England it's usually Alan Shearer, in Italy it's Luca Toni or Bernardo Corradi, someone like that. They aren't dirty players: they commit many fouls because their actions are judged differently from those of the men who mark them.

There is a plausible explanation for the 'double standard'. Punishing the striker simply yields a free kick in the box to the defending team. It's hardly controversial, not the kind of thing anybody will talk about after the final whistle. Punishing the defender is far more difficult. It invariably means granting a penalty, with all the controversy and acrimony that's sure to follow. I am not suggesting that referees bottle it, but I do feel that the consequence of a decision sometimes weighs on their minds more than it should.

Mourinho also has his pet hate among infractions: the 'tactical' foul, aimed only at stopping the opponent's rhythm. 'It is a foul they don't punish enough here in England,' he says. 'It's the foul whose only objective is to kill the attacking situation. It's purely tactical. I remember facing Everton, who had [Tomas] Gravesen and [Lee] Carsley. It was tactical fouling, over and over, for ninety minutes. In other countries players like that would be sent off for persistent fouling. Here in England they not only get away with it, they are allowed to influence the game.'

The tactical foul is an example of something imported into the English game. Following the Bosman ruling in 1996, Europe's top leagues welcomed a flood of foreign players. The impact was enormous: it precipitated a convergence of styles, tactics and attitudes. Some suggest that the foreign influence has brought gamesmanship and, particularly, diving into a previously innocent English game. Poll begs to differ: 'I really don't see diving as something we've been importing to this country from abroad,' he says. 'It's true, there are more foreign players diving than English players. But that's because there are more foreign players than English players!'

I suspect he is being charitable here. To me there is little question that, while there are more English players today who are ready to let themselves fall to 'win a penalty', it remains something that occurs far more frequently abroad and in that sense remains foreign to the English game. The fact that the media and the supporters are so opposed to it is a sign of how alien it is. In fact, as Mourinho points out, the hatred felt for gamesmanship is so strong that many foreign players who used to dive change after arriving in England: 'You are pushed to behave differently here, you don't really have a choice,' says Mourinho. 'If you cheat you have no chance of being admired. Even your own supporters will dislike you. So what do you do? Well, the way is not to be stupid, but not to cheat either. If there is a foul, you have to fall. But if there is no contact, stay on your feet. I call it "helping the referee to make a decision". That's not cheating. It's helping him by showing that you have been fouled.'

I understand Mourinho's position. As a striker you know there are times when you are clearly fouled but stay on your feet. In fact, I would go further: you can be fouled without being touched. The rules even specify this. Let me explain. If I'm running with the ball, and a defender comes in to slide-tackle me, I have two options. I can either let him run into me, thereby winning a free kick but also risking injury. Or I can try to jump out of the way, which may mean I end up on the ground without having been touched. If I choose the latter option, odds are I won't win a free kick. And, to me, this is unfair. If the defender's slide-tackle is clearly going to be a foul, I don't see why I have to run into him to prove the point. Why do I have to help the referee make a decision, particularly if I risk getting myself injured? And yet in our football culture 'winning a penalty' is a sign of skill and intelligence, and encourages cheating. At the heart of it is the fact that cheats view the referee as an opponent to be tricked. And that's all wrong, says Collina. 'You're never actually cheating the referee, even though you may think you are,' he says. 'You may cause the referee to make a mistake, but that's it. The one who you are really cheating is your opponent, your colleague, the one who, next year, may be your teammate. You're committing fraud against him, not against the referee.

'Think about it,' he adds. 'It's not a victimless crime. Your cheating may cause a team to be relegated, a manager to be sacked or a player to be sold. Some people compare it to bluffing in poker, but it's nothing like that.

Bluffing is the equivalent of making a dummy run or feinting one way, then going the other. This is the equivalent of stealing the chips from the dealer. It's just wrong and has nothing to do with football.'

You would have to have your head in the sand not to realize that this kind of behaviour is far more frequent in Italy than in England.

'Look, I wish I could always say good things about what happens in my own country but sometimes you just have to admit that things are better elsewhere,' says Collina. 'I'm talking in terms of footballing culture, not society as a whole. If you're talking about society as a whole, well, I don't think Italy has anything to learn from England . . .'

If Machiavelli Were Managing, He Would Be a Whinger . . .

I'll avoid getting into that sociological discussion. But I do agree that the notion of English 'fair play' and 'sportsmanship' is more than a cliché. In terms of ethical footballing culture, Italy has more to learn from England than vice versa. You don't change sporting culture overnight, of course. It takes decades, if not longer. But, in the meantime, steps can be taken to deal with very real problems.

In Italy there is a culture of whingeing. And it's not whingeing for the sake of whingeing, it's 'calculated whingeing'. If a controversial decision goes against you, it is always a good idea to cry, scream, shout and complain about it. At least, this is the case if you see things from a Machiavellian perspective. I'm pretty sure that if Machiavelli were advising a Serie A coach, he would say:

'The main negative of whingeing is that some people don't like it and will think less of you. If you are a good leader your own supporters will continue to like you even if you whinge, so you needn't worry about *them*. Equally, you don't need to worry if your enemies think less of you because you whinge. After all, they are your enemies and they dislike you regardless. In fact, the only people who should concern you are the neutrals. Those among them who don't like whingers will be put off by your behaviour. But that's the only negative.

'Now consider the positives. Many of your friends will instantly believe that you have been robbed and victimized. They will think that the powers-that-be are against you and that they, not you, are responsible for the loss. This is useful because it buys you time. It is also useful because it fosters a siege mentality, an us versus them attitude within your own team. If you can blame defeat on the referees, rather than on your players' poor performance, it won't affect their confidence. And the players will continue to back you in the media and with the supporters, which is always helpful.

'But there is another reason to whinge and perhaps it's the single most important. The more and the louder you whinge, the more attention you get, particularly if the media are on your side. If people start believing everyone is against you, they'll be extra careful the next time you step on to the pitch. The press, the public, the FA . . . they'll all watch the officiating closely next time around to see if, in fact, there is a plot against you. When that happens, the referee will be under pressure to appear fair. And this could well see you get an edge on some of the more controversial decisions . . .'

I think this sums up the Machiavellian view quite well. And the last point touches on one of the more delicate issues referees have to deal with: psychological pressure. This can range from mind-games to pre-match comments about the referee, which are intended not to curry outright favour but to ensure that, when in doubt, the referee errs in the 'right' direction.

The most basic form of this pressure is what in Italy we call 'psychological subjection'. It is used to explain why fifty–fifty decisions are generally made in big clubs' favour. When a referee is sure, there's no problem: referees aren't blatantly biased. The problem arises when he is not 100 per cent sure. In these situations, he will tend unconsciously to favour the bigger club. The reason for this is clear: it's far worse to make a mistake that damages, say, Manchester United or Juventus than a small club like Southampton or Brescia. A mistake against a big club will receive lots of media attention and be talked about for the whole week (or even longer in Italy). You will be known as the referee who made a big blunder and upset millions of fans. Your image will suffer. A mistake that hurts a smaller club is not ideal either, but it will receive little attention, at least on national level.

In Italy, we worked out our theory of 'psychological subjection' years ago, but it has become an issue in England too, as Poll explains: 'We worked with a sports psychologist who talks about the conscious mind and the subconscious mind. The conscious mind is what we can control. You're not going to say "I'm going to give this penalty because it's Manchester United and not give it because it's Southampton." That would compromise your independence. But what happens in your subconscious mind is something you can't always control. In fact, it's something you seldom control. So we try to deal with it by acknowledging that this is a real danger and because it's a danger we put it in the front of our mind. We *have* to acknowledge it. There is a very real possibility it can happen. Because of the way the media report things, it's far more newsworthy if Manchester United are denied a penalty.'

That's one of the things I like about Poll: he's not afraid to face problems head on. Psychological subjection won't go away and, beyond making people aware of it, there is no good way to fight it. The best antidote is to have referees who are 100 per cent sure 100 per cent of the time. Which, of course, isn't easy. But at least it's a goal towards which to strive.

A Few Modest Proposals . . .

The independence of referees is crucial. In an ideal world, they would have no link to the national FA or the leagues. I'd like to see them as a self-perpetuating group, working independently and answering directly to FIFA and UEFA. Their relationship with the leagues should be simply to provide officials for matches.

In addition, particularly now that referees are professional, I would treat them as a 'club'. They would all live in some kind of convenient central location – maybe Coverciano, near Florence, in Italy, and somewhere in the Midlands in England – working as a football club does. They would have their own executives, their own coaches, their own fitness trainers, and they would train together most days. I realize this would mean that those who are married would have to move their families, but surely this is not too much to ask, given that they are now full-time professionals.

Each referee would have a three-year deal with the Referees' Association making him entirely independent of the FA. The idea is to create a sense of unity among them, and make them feel strong, protected and independent. With all the travel and stress, a referee's life is tough enough. At least this way he would have a support network.

It would also be beneficial if referees were encouraged to appear in the post-match press conference and speak to the media, clarifying some of their decisions, perhaps after watching a quick highlight summary of the contentious incidents. Some may feel this would put them under greater pressure, but Poll welcomes the idea: 'In terms of talking to the press, I'm more than happy explaining and clarifying, though I should never find myself justifying my decisions. The issue I personally have is that when I speak out I'm accused of wanting to be a media star. So it's something which either all of us referees do or which none of us do. I think it would be constructive if we were present at the post-match press conference,' he adds. 'It would be interesting to see the managers' reactions. You are more careful choosing your words when someone is present than when someone is not . . .'

If done properly, this kind of exercise could defuse controversy immediately. If there has been an obvious mistake, the referee could admit his error. If something needs to be clarified, he can explain it. Of course, some people will always be unhappy. But many contentious incidents that would otherwise undermine a referee's credibility and make his job more difficult could be explained quickly and easily immediately after the game. I also think it would limit the inflammatory and often insulting comments that, sometimes, we managers are prone to make about referees, and would add to the transparency surrounding them.

Granted, it's much more of an issue in Italy, but these changes would benefit the English game. It's important that people understand referees are professional athletes, like footballers, and they, too, are competing. Like all competitors they make mistakes, but their integrity and goodwill are separate issues. With this in mind, I would like to see a league table of referees compiled and made public. In fact, it already effectively exists. At each match an assessor in the stands evaluates the referee's performance. Based on his report, the official is given a score. This is used to determine the hierarchy of referees – who gets the big games and who is demoted to the Championship or Serie B. Why not make it public?

'Well, there are plus points to doing so,' says Poll. 'It would certainly deflate a few egos. But it would also raise some problems. How would a team feel if they got the fifteenth best referee? And if a team is in first place, would they always get the number-one-ranked referee? What you would then get is disputes about who gets appointed where.'

The details of how to work the system are open to discussion. The Referees' Association could determine which matches were toughest and assign an official accordingly, just as they do now. I think teams would accept this – it doesn't take a genius to figure out that Roma v. Lazio or Manchester United v. Arsenal are tougher to officiate at than, say, Treviso v. Roma or Tottenham v. Birmingham. And, obviously, you would have the usual rules restricting referees from officiating over the same teams more than a certain number of times each season, and barring them from working with sides from their home town.

Such a system would help tremendously, particularly in Italy. It would eliminate, or limit, speculation on why certain clubs are assigned certain referees. And it would bring some much-overdue respect at least to those referees who are near the top of the table. If an official is number two in the country, you as a fan may not like him, but you have to respect the fact that he is the second-best official.

With regard to the laws of the game, I'm a bit of a traditionalist. But there are a few innovations I'd like to see. In Brazil referees are given a little can of what looks like spray paint that they use to mark the distance on free kicks. When they assign a free kick, they count off ten yards and spray a straight line on the pitch, marking the exact distance that the wall has to observe. It's a simple, effective way to combat encroachment, which has always been a problem in Italy and is increasingly an issue in the Premiership.

That one was easy. My next suggestion is somewhat more controversial. I would like the clock to stop whenever the ball is not in play, as it does in basketball or ice hockey. This would have two immediate effects: first, it would help eliminate time-wasting – there would be no point in rolling around feigning an injury or taking for ever before a goal kick because the clock would only start once the ball is in play. It is amazing how little football is actually played over the ninety minutes. At the 1990

World Cup, the ball was in play on average for fifty-two minutes, and in some games it was as low as forty-five. Today the average is around fifty-five minutes. FIFA have urged referees to grant more injury time, but if the ball is in play for only fifty-five minutes, you can't expect an official to grant an additional thirty-five of injury time, can you?

I think the answer is to have two thirty-minute halves and stop the clock every time play is interrupted by the referee's whistle. FIFA have said that the game should strive to keep the ball in play for sixty minutes and I agree. Overall, matches would not be any longer, and might even be shorter because there would be less time-wasting and gamesmanship. And there would be more action. The idea has lurked in the background for several years, but now it's time to take it seriously. It would change neither the nature nor the fabric of the game.

I would also change the off-side rule so that it only applies in the final third of the pitch. This would have an even greater effect on the game, because it would stretch teams, forcing them to defend deeper and creating more space in the middle of the park. If the off-side rule applies only in the final third, strikers can play further up the pitch, the space between defence and midfield increases, as does the space between midfield and attack. All of a sudden congested and cluttered areas free up and the game becomes far more open.

I can think of three obvious reasons why this is desirable. First, it would favour the more skilful players, because they would have more room to operate. Second, it would lead to more goals (or, at least, more attempts). Third, it would cut down on off-sides and, particularly, controversial off-side decisions. The vast majority of mistakes on off-side decisions are made when the distance is great between the player and the ball at the time of the pass. When you think about it, the reason for this is plain: the linesman would have to be looking in two different directions at once. But if off-sides only applied in the final third, there would be fewer such situations because the space in which it could happen would be smaller so it would be far easier to call.

Then there is the issue of technology and video replays. Surely we can all agree on the use of goal-line technology. 'All referees are in favour of technology if it's matter-of-fact technology, such as whether or not the ball is in play along the goal line or whether or not it crossed the line for a goal,' says Poll. 'We saw it when Spain played Korea in the World Cup. But on matters of opinion or conjecture, I don't see how it would help. It would make the referee dither, it would make him consult with video too often.'

Indeed, if video evidence were to be introduced, there would have to be strict rules surrounding it. The last thing the game needs is endless interruptions. But there is scope at least to analyse the possibility. And if it is introduced, it should not become a burden or an interference for the referee. That is why we might do well to apply some principles from American football's use of replays and combine them with some of the characteristics of our own football.

First, any decision overturned on video replay must be indisputable. In other words, there can be no grey areas. It must clearly prove the referee wrong. For this reason, it would only come into play on technical issues, where discretion is not a factor. Did the ball cross the line? Was the player off-side? Those are the questions that would be resolved.

Second, the referee himself would review the video. This way, you maintain consistency, since the same person has the final say throughout the match, and you do not undermine his authority. You simply give the referee another chance to view an incident. You could easily have a monitor at pitch-side, connected to an editing suite.

Third, to ensure the game is not constantly interrupted, I would limit the number of video replays allowed per game to two per half. The referee would have a maximum of ninety seconds – calculated from the time he reaches the monitor – to make his decision. In that time he should be able to see at least six or seven replays of the incident. Let's say it takes him thirty seconds to reach the sideline and another thirty seconds to return to the pitch, the whole thing should not last more than three minutes. If all four replays occur during a game, there would be a maximum of twelve minutes added on. It may seem a lot, but it's a small price to pay if it helps the game.

Finally, and this is perhaps the crucial point, I would leave it up to the teams to decide when replay is used. Each team would get one 'challenge' per half. If, from the bench, they think the referee got something wrong, they would signal the fourth official, who would arrange the video replay. Obviously this would involve each team having someone – a coach, a scout – watching the game on a monitor at pitch-side, which would not be difficult to arrange.

Of course, you're probably wondering how it would be applied to off-sides. I would envisage having the referee's assistant signal as normal, but the referee could overrule him by not blowing his whistle if he felt the decision was close and that one of the teams might challenge it. The players would play to the whistle, which would be blown once the attacking team either lost possession or scored a goal. At that point, if there was no challenge, the off-side would stand. If there was a challenge and it was successful, play would continue as normal, and if it was unsuccessful (if the original off-side call was correct) you'd go back to the off-side. It sounds far more complicated than it is, believe me.

I am not entirely convinced by video replays, just outlining how they could be used if they are introduced. However, the power and authority of the match officials must be preserved: video replays must be an aid, not an alternative, to the referee. By placing the onus of 'challenging' his decisions on the teams – and limiting the number and duration – we will speed up the game and, hopefully, make coaches think twice before they complain about the officiating.

Chapter Ten

A Virtuous Cycle? How Football and the Media Use Each Other

So far we've limited our analysis mainly to the football pitch, looking at players and coaches, where they come from and where they're going. But that's just the core of football, the basic building blocks. The game does not exist in a vacuum: other forces act on it, from supporters to the media to business. Some are local phenomena, reflecting national cultures and mores, others are by-products of globalization, striking England and Italy in equal measure.

Please forgive the business slang but, increasingly, I'm realizing how many aspects of the game are directly tied to economics. One is the relationship between the game and the media, a rapport which is (or should be) all about synergy – which my dictionary defines as 'a mutually beneficial conjunction of distinct elements'.

The idea is that football and the media need each other, that they succeed and grow together, both benefiting from a virtuous cycle. Football gives the media something to talk about, write about and cover on television. It generates ratings and sells newspapers, because people are interested in it and want to watch, hear or read about it.

At the same time, the media provide football with free advertising. They turn clubs and footballers into stars, attracting new fans to the game. Everyone benefits when football is popular.

Given this situation, you would think that football and the media have a happy, harmonious working relationship. Alas, not so. Quite the opposite, in fact. It's one of the few things Italy and England have in common: an often testy relationship between football and the media.

At the heart of the difficulty is that their objectives only partially overlap. Football is happy to have the media serve it as a gigantic advertising apparatus, as long as it is just that: a form of advertising that attracts new customers and consolidates existing ones. That's what supporters are to many clubs in this age of business-driven football: customers.

To the media, football is a convenient source from which to fill airtime or column inches. Unlike most other news, football is refreshingly predictable. A business editor does not know when the stock market is going to crash. A crime editor has no idea when a serial killer is going to strike. But a sports editor knows exactly when Manchester United is going to take on Arsenal, or Juventus host Milan because it's written in the fixture list. And covering football is relatively cheap. Journalists are allowed into matches for free and you don't often have to send them to exotic locations or kit them out with bulletproof vests.

The problem for the media is that, while they are happy to cover football, they don't want simply to provide free advertising. They see themselves as having a duty to report on football as they report on politics, war and crime. They value their independence and want their journalism to be unbiased and comprehensive. And this is a problem for football: while football is happy to help the media in a promotional capacity, it would prefer them not to report on the less savoury aspects. Having their 'customers' read that there is turmoil at the club, seeing their new centre-half described as a donkey or their football as 'boring' is unpleasant and bad for business. It fuels a negative image of the club and potentially leads to disaffection.

Of course, the media are not blameless. They don't want to be promotional tools so they avoid the press-release stories that clubs try to champion. But they need to fill their airtime or papers. So, all too often they effectively 'create' news. They'll use a player's remark out of context, they'll ask leading questions in an interview, they'll run stories based on sources who have an axe to grind . . . In short, they love controversy as much as football clubs hate it. This is partly why all clubs have websites and some of the bigger ones run television stations and magazines. To them, these are purely promotional tools. It is not journalism, it is not 'all the news that's fit to print'. It is basically one giant commercial advert.

And that's at the heart of the tension between football and the media. Football wants free advertising. The media want what they consider 'journalism' but which, at times, can be little more than muckraking.

The Inquisitor and the Storyteller

In Italy, the football media are very developed and very

powerful. No detail goes unexamined. There is an Italian term, 'calcio parlato', literally 'spoken football', which neatly sums up the cottage industry that football has spawned: incessant chatter about transfers, hypothetical or otherwise, and lots of controversy.

In Italy, it feels sometimes as if there is too much coverage. There are three daily sports papers, plus half a dozen national papers with several pages of football coverage every day, and the local press, with even more extensive coverage of local clubs. In terms of television, the state broadcaster RAI and its commercial rivals, Mediaset and La7, run daily half-hour sports bulletins, while local television stations (at least three or four in most Italian cities) include daily reports from training. Then, of course, there is SportItalia, a twenty-four-hour free-to-air channel with rolling sports news and, via satellite, Sky Italia, with three daily half-hour sports bulletins. And we haven't even mentioned radio. In addition to the national broadcasters, in Rome alone, there are half a dozen local sports-talk stations, some of which cover training sessions and press conferences as if they were the World Cup final.

'There is an attention to detail and an obsession with tiny little things that would be unheard of in other countries,' says Marcello Lippi. 'Everything is dissected, the manager is taken apart, cut into tiny little pieces and then they do a public biopsy to find out exactly what happened. Why was the defence so high up the pitch? Why did that player make that run? Why was this player taken off? They're basically trying to put you under pressure, they want to catch you out.'

The Italian press has real power, if not over the clubs

then in relating the game to the fans. So the powers-that-be try to control it. 'They've become like political parties,' Lippi adds. '*Corriere dello Sport* champions Roma and Lazio. *Gazzetta* defends Milan and Inter. *Tuttosport* is all about Juventus. One week you get one paper defending referees at all costs while another attacks them mercilessly. And then they switch around.

'Because sport has some power, politicians naturally want to be involved,' he says. 'Some of those sports shows look like political shows, with politicians there pontificating on the game. What does an MP have to do with football? Nothing at all, but it doesn't matter.'

Indeed, the link between politics and football in Italy is well established and not just because the prime minister owns a football club. Many politicians speak out regularly about football in their capacity as fans. Indeed, the allegiance of any MP interested in the game is well known.

English media coverage is far more contained. The nine national newspapers and the local press offer a fair amount of daily reporting but, in terms of column inches, it is far less than is available in Italy. In broadcasting the difference is stark. Apart from Sky Sports' rolling news service, the only daily sports bulletin on television is on BBC News 24. On the radio, 5Live and TalkSport provide a fair amount of coverage, as do local stations but, again, there is a chasm between the two. And it's not just the quantity of the coverage that is different but its nature. 'It's true that in Italy there is more pressure and that, at times, it reaches absurd levels,' says Marcel Desailly. 'In Italy there are some television programmes like [Aldo] Biscardi's *Il Processo* [*The Trial*] which are unthinkable in any other country. But at least the press gives you more information. At least they generally know what they're talking about. It's not like in England, where they claim they are journalists, but in fact are anything but journalists. In fact, in England, the press have no respect for their profession. They invent things, they exaggerate and I'm afraid that, in the long run, they will kill this sport.'

He is being very hard on the English press and, while I don't fully agree, I understand why he feels that way. I don't believe they 'invent things' any more than the press in any other country, but they are prone to exaggerate, particularly personal issues. For all the invective and criticism that managers in Italy attract, you would never see headlines comparing a national team manager to a turnip, as happened to Graham Taylor, or referring to him as 'Crazy Claudio', in an article which questioned Ranieri's tactical prowess.

I think there are two main reasons behind this. The first is that the English media take football less seriously than their counterparts in Italy (and probably Spain). They see it as a 'bit of fun', so they'll satirize and lampoon far more than they would if they were dealing with, say, politics or business. You see it on television or hear it on the radio, with ex-professionals chuckling together, or read it in the press where, often, the sports pages do not seem to apply the same reporting standards as other sections of a paper. In Italy, sports, and particularly football, reporting is deadly serious.

The second, and perhaps more important reason is that English football reporting – whether television, radio or press – is based on narrative. It is told via the experiences of the 'characters' – players, managers, referees – and the more colourful those characters are, the better the story is. Thus, characters are taken to an extreme. Arsène Wenger is 'the Professor': intellectual, cultured, sophisticated, academic. Sir Alex Ferguson is an old-school motivator, steeped in traditional values, a passionate man with a quick temper who rules Old Trafford with an iron fist.

I was privileged to spend several hours with both men in researching this book. I found Wenger passionate and Sir Alex cultured. Yet these sides of their personalities rarely come across in the media. Why? Because they do not fit the stereotype. There is Wenger, the real-life person, and then there is Wenger, the character in the on-going media soap opera. The same applies to Sir Alex. A cultured, intellectual Sir Alex would spoil the storyline, as would a passionate, over-enthusiastic Wenger.

But the issue is not just the stereotyping. It's one of personalizing. Whenever Arsenal played Manchester United for most of the past decade it became Wenger v. Sir Alex. Amazingly, given the array of superstars on the pitch over the years, the 'story' – more often than not – was about the two managers. When one beat the other, it was because somebody had been 'outfoxed' and had lost the 'mind game'. Never mind the twenty-two men on the pitch. It happens with players too, of course. I've been told it's something they teach you when you become a journalist. You're told to seek out the 'human side' of the story and make it personal. If a striker scores a hat-trick against his old club it's about 'revenge'. If a team loses, it's because the manager 'failed to inspire them'. But some-times – in fact, most of the time – there is no 'human' side. No great personality turned the tide, no riveting mental battle was won, no personal demons were exorcised. It is simply the fact that one team outscored the other. Maybe they were better tactically. Maybe they were more skilful. Maybe the referee helped them. Maybe they were lucky. Maybe it was some combination of the four. But it is more than possible that the result had nothing to do with 'bottle', 'inspiration', 'determination' or any of the other dozen or so mental factors that are generally discussed in post-match interviews in England.

In Italy, of course, we are always ready to open an inquest after every match (and usually do). The difference is that we rarely chalk up the result to the kind of mental factors cited in England. Instead, we'll examine every aspect of the play in excruciating detail, harassing coaches and managers over the slightest thing. Did the left-back defend higher up the pitch in the first twenty minutes of the second half? Did the speed work in Wednesday's training session affect the quickness of the withdrawn striker? Why did Player X come on with twenty minutes to go, rather than ten?

The debate continues until kick-off for the next match. Sometimes it seems that matches in Italy are just weekly nuisances between the real sport, which is the endless chatter, debate and controversy. You can't help but feel that managers in England get off rather lightly compared to their Italian counterparts.

'It's different in England,' says Eriksson. 'The press never analyse games tactically and technically the way they do in Italy. As for television, coverage here is very different from Italy, far more patient and tolerant. It's almost always positive. No matter what you do, there is very little criticism. For a manager, it is unquestionably a huge advantage. There is no need to constantly justify yourself and your decisions.

'For example, a few years ago Manchester United were playing Fulham,' he continues. 'Sir Alex Ferguson decided to rest Ruud Van Nistelrooy, Ryan Giggs and his starting goalkeeper, Tim Howard. All three were on the bench. The game ended in a draw. If I had done something like that when I was at Lazio I would have been massacred by the press. Here in England, nobody said a thing. Nothing. It's incredible!'

Eriksson's right. The English media are less interested in the tiny detail of the game. And they reflect what the public want, so perhaps the public are not particularly interested in the nitty-gritty. In that sense, England is different from Italy *and* Portugal. 'In Portugal we have three daily sports newspapers: *A Bola*, *O Jogo* and *Record*,' says Mourinho. 'Each one has forty pages, thirty-eight pages of football and two of other sports. They want to know everything – what is the team going to be, who are the injured players, what did they do in training that day, what is the tactical analysis. For every big game, there will be six pages, player by player, with individual analysis, and the full text of the press conference. Here in England, it's practically nothing by comparison.'

This lack of analysis is a direct result of the factors we talked about earlier: in England football, like all sport, is supposed to be fun and, to many, details of training sessions and in-depth tactical dissertations are, well, boring. Also, that kind of coverage does not aid the narrative discourse, because it tells you little about the personalities of those involved, which is central to the way the game is covered in England.

'The press in England do not analyse. If things are going well, they simply hype and promote everything,' says Ray Wilkins. 'I don't know if it's because we think positive or if it's because we're ignorant and we don't see our own faults. I remember before the game with Argentina in 1998 at the World Cup, everyone was sure we were going to win and win big. Why? Based on what? They had Veron, Batistuta and so on, yet our press was certain we were going to win because they don't know any of the foreign players.

'It's a journalism problem. They never look overseas and they aren't very prepared. In Italy it's different. The Italian journalist loves football, follows the game, knows everything about it. Our journalists love the social side, the cultural side, the personality, the conflicts. But in terms of knowledge, there is no comparison. The Italian journalist is far more prepared.'

The English press is indeed quick to jump on the bandwagon if things are going well. Then the synergistic relationship between football and the media works perfectly: football dominates airwaves and column inches, confidence exudes from every pore, and it seems nothing can go wrong. Even the non-sports media are eager to get on board.

It's something you don't really see in Italy, particularly with the national team. Even when things are going well, there is always sniping, always an underlying cynicism that the good times won't last, that the team got this far because they were lucky or the opponent under-performed. I think back to the World Cup in 1990, which Italy were hosting, and even as we advanced to the semi-finals without conceding a single goal, there was a sense of imminent disaster in the media.

Part of this may be because in Italy there is always a need to find a new star as well as a new scapegoat. In 1990, the new star, clearly, was Toto Schillaci, yet, as the side advanced, there was no obvious scapegoat so there was just general talk of problems and difficulties.

As with all things, there is a happy medium and, in my opinion, it lies closer to the English way than the Italian. I don't want the media to turn into cheerleaders and forget their public duty to inform and criticize. Nor do I want them to be uninformed or deluded. But it is important for them to remember that they are covering a sport. Analysis does not mean continuous criticism, and a bit of fun in the reporting is not a bad idea.

In Italy, there is a greater awareness of what happens in football elsewhere and a greater desire to talk about the tactical and technical aspects of the game. Too great, because it can sometimes degenerate into senseless nitpicking. But managers don't seem to mind the nitpicking, as long as it's about football.

'In Italy and Spain, the press is a different animal altogether,' says Sir Alex. 'You've got three daily papers which are all about sport. That's unbelievable. At every press conference I've been to in Italy they ask why I did this and why I did that . . . In England, they don't care about all that, they just want a story. That's why I don't go to press conferences in England. [The media] don't want to talk about football.'

Perhaps Sir Alex is being a little charitable towards the Italian media. They love controversy as much as anyone. Yet most of the time it is limited to football matters. However exasperating it might be for a manager to justify for the umpteenth time why he kept this player out and put that player in, at least we're talking football. David Platt agrees with Sir Alex. 'I had far more problems with the press in England than in Italy,' he says. 'In Italy they ask you thousands of specific questions, they talk about tactics and technique, but at least what you say gets into the papers. In England they play this game where they try to get you to say something and, if you say it, that's what they will write. And that is all that they will write.

'An English reporter will leave the newsroom already knowing what he wants you to say. He doesn't care about the rest. You can talk for three hours and then the only sentence of yours that they'll use is a half-phrase you might have uttered while walking out the door. And, of course, that will be exaggerated and twisted.'

Here, the Italian media are not blameless. Far from it. They, like journalists everywhere, love getting footballers and managers to say things, preferably controversial things, which they want to hear and they think people want to read. But perhaps the difference is that, broadly speaking, in Italy it is generally about footballing matters, rather than personality clashes or off-the-pitch issues.

According to Marcel Desailly, it all goes back to class: 'In Italy, like France, football belongs to everyone, from all kinds of social extraction,' he says. 'In England it's a work-ing-class phenomenon so the discourse around it is that of the tabloids. They set the tone, not least because they sell many more copies than the quality papers.' Indeed, it's common to see a tabloid newspaper break a story and for all the others, including the 'quality' papers, to follow up the next day. It's as if the tabloids set the agenda, in content as well as attitude. While the quality papers may feature a different writing style, they not only cover the same issues, they often do it with a similar 'tongue-in-cheek' perspective ... the kind that leads them to compare Graham Taylor with a turnip.

Giving the People What They Want?

Ultimately, the media have one fundamental objective: to attract an audience. The more newspapers or magazines sold, the greater the revenue from sales and advertising. The greater the television or radio ratings, the greater the advertising revenue. (The same applies to state broadcasters like RAI in Italy or the BBC in the United Kingdom, though the latter do not carry ads. They are public-service broadcasters, and if they don't attract a decent audience, they can't claim to be serving the public.) Attracting an audience does not necessarily involve 'dumbing down' or, to use another media cliché, sinking to the 'lowest common denominator'. Often, the type of audience you attract is as important as its size. Ten millionaires who enjoy spending money are worth more than a thousand low-income misers. In fact, commercial media is all about delivering a specific audience to a specific advertiser who wants to sell a specific product.

But back to attracting the audience. The conventional wisdom is that the media cater to what the public wants. So, based on what we said earlier, the public in both countries wants controversy and criticism. In England it is personality-based and placed within a narrative structure. And, to some degree, it's tongue-in-cheek. In Italy the controversy is usually over some tactical, technical or physical detail and is taken very seriously, with no fun involved. While in England controversy is usually dealt with over twenty-four hours, in Italy it rumbles on into the following week.

Yet I am not sure I accept this: I am not sure it's what the public wants. Rather, it's what they have come to expect. I believe that the public's tastes are not immutable, that they evolve and change.

That was one of the reasons why I became involved with Sky Italia's football coverage. I liked and admired their vision: they combine the English narrative format with Italian footballing expertise. I thought Sky Italia could – if not change the way the game is covered in Italy – at the very least provide an alternative commentary, which would give as much space to the positives (a great match, a superb save, a moment of sublime skill, a touching banner from the fans) as it did to the negatives. Also, when it covered the negatives, it did so in a way that was thorough and honest, but still respectful.

It's part of the reason why you are reading this book and not my autobiography. I could have written my memoirs, a revealing jaunt aimed at showing 'The Real Gianluca Vialli'. But I chose not to because I would have had to reveal things about my family, friends and colleagues that I believe should remain private. I believe that what occurs in the dressing room should stay in the dressing room. (Within reason, of course. If someone is breaking the law it's a different matter.)

In England, it is usual for players to write 'tell-all' auto-biographies, which often expose matters that should probably remain confidential. Indeed, many write an autobiography to get things off their chest in a format they can control. They know they won't be misquoted in their own book, and, the more salacious the tales they tell, the more vitriolic the criticism of ex-managers and team-mates, the more they'll be paid. When you write an autobiography you get an advance based on what the publisher thinks he can make from serializing the book. And when you write a tell-all book packed with juicy, titillating stories and behind-the-scenes revelations, you're bound to get a hefty cheque from a tabloid newspaper.

It might be commonplace in England, but it leaves a bad taste in my mouth. If a footballer's memoirs mean violating the trust that I believe should be implicit among teammates and colleagues, perhaps the world is better off without them. Particularly if they're written by a foot-baller in his mid-twenties, as too often happens. It's something I've never quite understood: unless you're an Olympic gymnast, you shouldn't be writing your memoirs at the age of twenty-five, partly because you still have lots to achieve and partly because, most likely, you lack the introspection and the maturity to evaluate your life.

Unless, of course, it's all about money in which case, as the saying goes, 'strike while the iron's hot' – when you're at the peak of your popularity. And if you're going to do that, don't forget the behind-the-scenes stuff and a few well-placed barbs against your colleagues. It will make you lots of money. Whether it does anything for your image or for football is another matter.

In England it is accepted that a footballer will try to make extra money from the game, exploiting his name or his image. That's why this type of autobiography is so popular, as is 'chequebook journalism' – paying players and managers for exclusive interviews. It doesn't go on in Italy and, I suspect, would not be tolerated, perhaps because footballers are seen as spoiled, greedy and overpaid, and the idea that they could charge someone for their thoughts would be distasteful to most. Also, the Italian media refuse even to contemplate paying for access.

Italians and Englishmen are used to different types of coverage in terms of content and quantity. It's not as if people in Italy like football more than they do in England. It's just that the game is lived differently and a big part of it, probably a bigger part of it than in England, is through the media. Which is why there is wall-to-wall coverage in Italy, unlike England.

Of course, there is another big factor: the amount of access granted to the media in either country. In Italy, many clubs give daily press conferences but in England most speak to the media once a week (and some even less frequently). It's far easier for the media to speak to players after matches in Serie A than it is in the Premiership. From a manager's perspective, having the press around for just a couple of hours a week is bliss, at least as far as Arsène Wenger is concerned. 'I love it,' he says. 'It is much easier to protect the players from the press. And it is probably more necessary to protect them, because in England the papers are far more interested in scandals than in technical issues. In Latin countries it's the opposite. Either way, the fact that they only come once a week is fantastic, because it allows us to work in peace.'

Yet according to José Mourinho, this isolation, coupled with the English media's selective coverage, can be damaging to the clubs. 'It looks much easier in England because nobody disturbs you, the press never come to training and you only see them once a week,' he says. 'But in fact I think it is much more difficult. It is because of the coverage football receives. In Portugal, if I gave a press conference I knew that the next day there would be four pages devoted to it, carrying every single word I said. It would have to be that way, each paper has so much space to fill. That way, I know that my entire message is getting across. In England, they will only take a few words, because they are only looking for the controversial stuff. And, often, it's out of context.'

It's a valid point. In England, because there is less coverage, a manager's message is distilled to a few quotations once a week and, of course, he can't choose which of his words are used. He's in the hands of the media. 'And ultimately, it's the same everywhere you go,' says David Platt. 'Either you manipulate the media or the media manipulate you.'

I was on the receiving end of one of the most brilliant media manipulations in footballing history, although, at the time, it didn't feel that way. Cast your mind back to the 1990 World Cup. Italy were playing at home and, despite not always impressing, we had won every single game in reaching the semi-final against Argentina. We were getting a tremendous lift from the crowd at Rome's Stadio Olimpico, where we had played every match until that point. The semi-final, though, was to be held in Naples, at the San Paolo stadium. From our perspective, it was the worst possible venue this side of Buenos Aires. Diego Maradona – the Argentina captain – played his club football in Naples and, to many Neapolitans, ranked somewhere between legend and deity. The newspapers immediately began to speculate: would the Neapolitan crowd in the San Paolo dare to go against their hero, Maradona, and support Italy, their country?

Maradona answered that question, raising the stakes once and for all: 'Why should Naples support Italy?' he said. 'Italy doesn't support Naples. They don't even consider them a part of the same nation, except now, of course, when they need their singing and their support in a World Cup semi-final. The truth is that they don't care about Naples and Neapolitans, they are just using them. The people of Naples know who really loves them. I do.'

It was powerful stuff and it created a genuine club v. country loyalty dilemma for so many Neapolitans. Maradona had a point. At the time, Naples, a big city with its share of social ills, was largely forgotten by the rest of the country, particularly the wealthy north. Neapolitans were left to fend for themselves, often implicitly treated as second-class citizens. When Napoli fans travelled to northern cities to follow their team, they were often greeted with offensive banners and tasteless insults. It's not surprising that they felt alienated by Italy's football establishment.

At the same time, Maradona had been loyal to them: he had come from Barcelona, a massive club, and delivered two league titles. He had embraced Naples like few other players in history. And, although he had been born 8,000 kilometres away, he felt, acted and spoke like a Neapolitan.

With hindsight, it's perhaps not surprising that, for those of us on the pitch that day, it felt as if Italy v. Argentina was being played on neutral ground, rather than Italian soil. Compared to the support we had enjoyed in Rome, it was eerily silent for long stretches. Some of the fans booed the Argentine anthem. This embarrassed me, because I find booing another nation's anthem despicable. Yet, in their own misguided way, they were trying to show their support for us. When Toto Schillaci gave us the lead in the seventeenth minute, they cheered, but it certainly was nothing like the explosion of jubilation we had experienced in Rome. It was strange . . . like playing under water. We created lots of chances, but to no avail. And after each miss, or save by the Argentine goalkeeper, Sergio Goycoechea, there was no gasp or groan, just polite applause.

I could tell something was wrong. I had played there before for Italy – against China and Sweden – and this was not how Neapolitan fans behaved. They were normally so much more passionate. That night, it was all different.

In the sixty-seventh minute Claudio Caniggia's now infamous header looped over our goalkeeper – and my dear friend – Walter Zenga, and Argentina levelled. We were shocked but confident that we could rally, particularly since we had dominated the match. I expected the crowd to roar us on, yet all I heard were isolated shouts and a low rumble. Even now, it's incredible to me how silent 60,000 people can be. I thought they would be galvanized by the substitutions. Shortly after the equalizer, I was replaced by Aldo Serena, our target man, and immediately thereafter Roberto Baggio came on too. He had been outstanding in that tournament, capturing headlines left and right. Even Madonna had saluted him, performing in his number eighteen jersey. And yet there was . . . nothing. It was as if the crowd was embarrassed.

We eventually lost that game on penalty kicks. Argentina went on to lose the final to Germany, 1–0. Yet the memory of that crowd at the San Paolo lives on. And, to me, it was all down to Maradona and the way he sensed the public mood and manipulated the media to his advantage, planting the seed of doubt in their minds, questioning whether they were more loyal to Italy or to himself.

Maradona's genius was not limited to the pitch. But even if you're not at his level, it's useful to be able to manipulate the press to your advantage, and particularly if you're a manager. Which is why John Barnwell believes that the FA's coaching course should include more training in media relations. 'A manager needs to know how to manipulate the press,' he says. 'It is essential to know ahead of time what they're going to want, just as it is important to be prepared before each interview. These are things which can and should be learned.'

A good relationship with the media is indeed beneficial. Yet some managers do not have a particularly good rapport with them. I suppose it goes back to something our old friend Machiavelli might have said: either befriend the media or make sure they're scared of you. The few managers who ignore the press are so successful and powerful that they do not need to court it: they usually enjoy its support anyway (the media, being humans, more often than not will jump on the winner's bandwagon regardless).

As a player, I often felt targeted by the media, probably because I was one of the more high-profile guys and therefore more exposed. Sometimes I accepted the criticism – after all, I know when I play badly. But, other times, I simply felt it was excessive, unwarranted or personal. More than once, I stopped talking to the media. Just like that. I would turn down all interview requests – whether print or broadcast – smile and walk right past reporters. I could have scored a hat-trick that day or missed two sitters, but either way, during my blackout period I spoke to no one in the press.

It's not a course of action I would recommend to footballers today. First, even when criticism is excessive or unwarranted, there is no way to fight back beyond what you show on the pitch in the next game. But, more importantly, if you don't talk to the media, you attract more criticism for not speaking out. They accuse you of sulking, of being an outcast or big-headed. It's not worth it – although there are advantages.

One of the most obvious is that, if you're not speaking to the media, you're free to focus on your football: you don't have to think about what you're going to say. At the same time – at least, this was what happened to me – you gain 'street cred' with some of the fans. Many supporters are quite sharp and see right through the clichéd pre- and post-match comments and the predictable 'puff-piece' interviews. By refusing to play a part in all that, you seem more genuine to them.

But the cons of not speaking to the press outweigh the pros, particularly when you become a manager. The press wield a tremendous amount of power and it is foolish to ignore it. I learned later in my career that the best way to deal with the media is to give them what they want – within clear boundaries. When I was manager at Chelsea, I gave very few one-on-one interviews, but I made it a point at press conferences to answer every question as thoroughly as possible. Mourinho does the same. I don't think it's a coincidence that as managers we have both enjoyed a good relationship with the media.

Others go further. I know of managers in Italy and

England who will take phone calls from journalists at midnight and gladly reveal whether the left-back has recovered in time for the next day's match. They suck up to the press, who will take as much as they can get. Give them an hour and they'll want two. Take their phone call at home at eleven p.m. one day and refuse it the next – they'll crucify you in print. What I've learned is that the correct way is to understand their concerns and give them what they need to do their job well, rather than simply offering them everything they want. But what you can't do – and must never do – is ignore them altogether. 'This is especially true in Italy,' says Marcel Desailly. 'You have to make yourself more available to the press because you know they can influence the manager's decision-making. So every interview you give is an opportunity to influence somebody, to create something positive for yourself and your image. After all, everybody reads the player ratings and so you have to play your part.'

Yes, the 'player ratings', or '*voti*' in Italian. To outsiders it's a quirk of the Italian game, but to a footballer they're disproportionately important. Each of the major newspapers grades each player after each game, often devoting a paragraph or two to his performance. The same happens in some English newspapers, but the space devoted to them is minimal. 'In Italy they get the biggest names to do the ratings, they take them seriously, they're well thought-out and researched,' says Paolo Di Canio. 'In England, it's a joke. They don't matter and, frankly, they shouldn't because they're silly. A player comes on as a substitute and they give him a 2. I mean what's that?'

Indeed, in England the player ratings fit the rest of the sports coverage: they're a bit of a laugh, not to be taken too seriously. In Italy, they are like a school report, and while most Serie A players will tell you they pay no attention to them, I can assure you that they're lying. After all, it's only human nature to check out what others are saying about you. And even if you set no store by a particular journalist's opinion (and sometimes it's a good idea to ignore what they say) it makes sense to keep an eye on the ratings because they matter to coaches and fans.

'In England, it's all different,' says Desailly. 'You don't get much benefit from talking to the press. First of all, you know that most of the newspapers are not taken seriously by anyone. And it's their fault that they're not taken seriously because they are always looking for controversy and conflict. So speaking with these newspapers simply does not make sense. You know full well that it is more likely to be a negative experience than a positive one.'

Players, particularly foreign ones, often complain about the British press coverage, especially in the 'red-tops,' because it intrudes on their private lives, and the critical tone is often adversarial and hostile, sometimes insulting.

'I complain about the press all the time,' says Sir Alex. 'In England we have fewer privacy laws than on the continent. And I never agree with the press invasion of private lives. The tabloid industry is ferocious here in terms of competition. After a while of reading headlines which denigrate managers, you just stop reading. Why should I read criticism of myself? It's stupid.'

While I don't enjoy being criticized (nobody does), I understand that a player or a manager has to accept it. And you can learn from it. However, there is a difference between sharp – even harsh – well-reasoned criticism and the kind of viciousness to which the media sometimes sink. In England it's often personal criticism. In Italy, they may not attack your character but they go after your work with a gusto that sometimes seems premeditated. Worse, Italian football suffers from negative short-term attitudes. If the right results aren't delivered straight away it's a 'crisis'. A team might win eight matches in a row, follow with a draw and a loss and, suddenly, it's in freefall. Of course Italian football is about results, but when you're judging a game, common sense should apply. If a team play poorly and create no real chances but score a goal on a botched clearance, and see their opponents hit the woodwork three times, in Italy they're praised for 'hanging in there' and 'grinding out the three points'. If they play brilliantly, create lots of clear-cut chances but fail to score and concede on a single, individual error, talk of a crisis arises.

Putting it to the Test

So far, this discussion of the media has been based on impressions, not scientific data. Is the English press really more interested in controversy? Is the Italian press really for anoraks? I have always felt more comfortable with the press in England than in Italy, but perhaps I am the exception. I wanted to get to the bottom of it, so, for three months – between February and April – I logged the main story of the day in *Gazzetta dello Sport*, Italy's biggest selling sports newspaper, and compared it with the main story in three English newspapers: *The Times* (and its sister paper, the *Sunday Times*), the *Daily Mail* (and the *Mail on Sunday*) and the *Sun* (and the *News of the World*).

I felt that one Italian paper would suffice because the other 'mainstream' papers, such as *Repubblica* and *Corriere della Sera*, tend to follow what *Gazzetta* writes. In England, however, it was important to look at all three segments of the market. I noted which sport was being covered and the category of the headline and story: 'result or preview', 'controversy', 'transfer story', 'non result- or preview-related news' and 'other'.

Unsurprisingly, football dominated, with 97.8 per cent of the lead stories in the *Sun/News of the World*, 94.2 per cent in *Gazzetta dello Sport* and 90 per cent in the *Daily Mail/Mail on Sunday*. *The Times/Sunday Times* remained football-oriented, but with a comparatively low 74.2 per cent. This was unsurprising in that football in England retains working-class connotations and *The Times/Sunday Times* has a higher proportion of middle-class readers (reflected in its coverage of rugby and cricket, which represented 15.8 per cent of the lead stories); yet for *The Times* this represents a significant departure from its roots. It's a safe bet that fifteen years ago there would have been far less football coverage. While coverage of sport in general has increased over the past twenty years, the boom has been disproportionately football-related. In the late 1980s, *The Times* had three dedicated full-time football reporters; today it has thirteen. The number of rugby writers has increased from two to three, while the number of cricket journalists has gone from six to eight.

Things became really interesting when I looked at the type of story leading the day's news. *Gazzetta dello Sport* seemed actively to avoid controversy in its headlines – 'controversy'-related articles represented just 15.2 per cent of the total, less than each of the three English papers, and it usually led on results or previews of matches. Headlines such as 'Milan Masterpiece', after a Milan win, or 'Last Call: Roma and Juve', ahead of the final opportunity for those two clubs to advance in the Champions' League, were typical.

'Controversy' was a staple for the English papers. The *Sun/News of the World* went for it 47.8 per cent of the time, compared to 42.2 per cent in the *Daily Mail/Mail on Sunday*. The most striking difference was that, even on match-days, the emphasis was not on the game but its possible knock-on effect. Thus, on the day Monaco played Chelsea in the semi-final of the Champions' League, the *Daily Mail* led with a story about how David O'Leary was being lined up to replace Blues boss Claudio Ranieri if things went wrong for Chelsea. The following night, after Chelsea's shock 3–1 defeat, there was no sign of O'Leary: instead the headline and the lead story were all about Ranieri's post-match self-criticism. That Chelsea had lost was subordinate to Ranieri's *mea culpa*.

The impression you are left with is that football alone isn't exciting enough for the English press. It needs to be spiced up. Of course, controversy exists in Italy, but it's rarely the day's top story. Perhaps this is because the English media don't take football as seriously as their Italian counterparts and thus need a bit of spice to remain interested. This also explains another difference. In Italy, the same story, particularly if it's in the 'controversy' category, will rumble on for weeks. People will resurrect refereeing mistakes from the previous month, they'll reflect endlessly on matches that have already taken place. Quite the opposite from England, where issues are quickly introduced and quickly forgotten.

'Here in England the game finishes at the final whistle,' says Mourinho. 'They may complain, they may shout, but that lasts one day and then they move on. In other countries, in Portugal, in Italy, it does not finish there. The next day everyone re-reads exactly what happened in the newspaper. And then they react to it. And then the day after that they read the reaction. And then the reaction to the reaction. And so on . . . it does not end until the next game starts.'

In addition, the English press devotes more space than its Italian counterpart to smaller clubs, provided there is a juicy story. For example, Ian Walker, the Leicester City goalkeeper, made all the back pages after wrestling a pitch invader to the ground. This raised a debate about crowd behaviour, safety and security. A similar incident in Italy is unlikely to make it out of the inside pages, unless it occurred at a big club. Indeed, coverage of the big four Serie A clubs – Milan, Juventus, Inter and Roma – dominated *Gazzetta dello Sport*. I had the impression that if Juve's Alessandro Del Piero had lost his wallet it would be front-page news. On the other hand, if a Chievo player – say, Lorenzo d'Anna – lost his wallet, it would only make the news if the CIA discovered that the cash in it had been diverted to Al Qaeda via an offshore bank run by a couple of Martians who own a time machine and are visiting from the future accompanied by Shergar, Lord Lucan and Amelia Earhart. This is in keeping with the pattern we observed earlier. The English media look for good human-interest stories and they are not limited to big clubs. The Italian media are focused on results, which means they have little time for or interest in a quirky feature unless it involves the big guns. They are too busy analysing, dissecting and putting managers and players on trial.

Yet while the Italian media, particularly television, can be exceptionally tough, the relationship between journalists and football is more adversarial in England. 'We have some good journalists and we have some who are not so good,' says Ray Wilkins. 'They're the ones who are always putting words into your mouth, the ones who search through your private life, who create conflicts and controversy. Naturally this is a huge burden on any relationship.

'When I was younger, I would go to dinner or to the pub with journalists. We all did it and it was there that we would build a relationship based on trust. Today it's different. Today players are always suspicious of the press and, sadly, they are right to be suspicious. But that's not the way it should be. A journalist should be an ally, not an enemy.'

Quite right. It's a perfect example of synergy, and everybody wins. A journalist gets a great interview and the player looks good in the press. But that's not the way it works.

Instead of a virtuous cycle built on trust, we have a vicious cycle based on suspicion. Players turn down interview requests and are standoffish to the media because they don't want their words twisted and they don't want to be 'stitched-up'. At the same time, the media are annoyed that players are so difficult to get to, and that when they eventually get to interview them, their comments are usually bland and uninteresting. When a journalist gets a juicy quote, he can't resist the temptation to splash it all over the paper and make a big deal of it.

The press say they have no choice. They have to fill their pages and, because they have so little access to the players, they have no alternative but to make the most of what they get. The players, of course, say that this is precisely why they don't like speaking to the media: the risk of getting stitched up is enormous.

It's bad for both parties. And while it's not particularly good in Italy, it's worse in England. At least in Italy reporters have a slightly greater opportunity of building a relationship with a player. And that's important: if there's a relationship, both sides benefit. The player knows he can get his point across in a way that is accurate and reliable, that if he says something inappropriate, something he might regret, perhaps in a moment of anger or sadness, the journalist can tone it down or leave it out. The journalist has an inside source, who can tell him what is really going on and who is willing to share his perspective.

'I'll give you an analogy,' says Desailly. 'Football is the adult and the media are the teenage son, who needs to rebel. He does the opposite of what he is told. He thinks his parents are stupid or liars, he wants to figure things out for himself, he wants to be controversial. That's what the English press is like, far more than in Italy. And yet it's strange because if you know the Italians and the English as I do, you would not expect such a gutter press in England. After all, here in England they have a sense of civic pride. They respect people's privacy. If I'm out on the street with my family nobody comes up and bothers me. They respect my personal space. Certainly more so than in Italy. And yet, this is the weird thing, in Italy the media are more or less respectful, whereas in England they aren't. This doesn't reflect the average Englishman one bit.

The English people are civil, the English media are not.'

One can only conclude that the difference in the media is not down to its representatives being English or Italian. Rather, it's a result of the way they go about their jobs. And that is inevitably coloured primarily by access, which results from trust. Or, in this case, mistrust.

Trouble is, how do you break the cycle of mistrust? How do you rebuild? To some degree, the answer is more openness, not less. I would propose giving the media more unstructured access – perhaps a weekly 'mixed zone' after training, like they have at Champions' League matches – with the understanding that all conversations must be taped. If a problem arises and the journalist is found to be at fault because he deliberately distorted a player's words, then his or her paper is punished. And if the problem originates with the player – he said something inappropriate, which the journalist reported accurately – then the player is fined. People should take responsibility for their actions and, at the same time, build trust between these two parts of the footballing world.

In Italy, managers complain that the media wield far too much influence. In England, despite the scandals, people take it all with a pinch of salt, partly because the media never seem to take things as seriously, and also their credibility and trustworthiness, especially the tabloids', is questionable. Perhaps also it's because the English don't always react as you might expect them to. Especially the footballers.

When the media broke the news of Sven-Goran Eriksson's liaison with Ulrika Jonsson, it dominated the press and the airwaves for months. He was concerned that it might undermine him in the eyes of the players. He shouldn't have worried: 'The players here couldn't care less about what the papers write,' he says. 'I know this all too well. Before going to Korea for the World Cup I felt the need to say something to my players since I was all over the papers. They just burst out laughing. They said, "Boss, why would we care about this?" It genuinely did not matter. Welcome to England!'

Welcome to England indeed, where the louder the press scream, the less people seem to notice.

Chapter Eleven

Oxygen Shortage: Falling Attendances

If there were no football supporters you would not be reading this book. You would not be reading it because I would not have become a professional footballer. (I would probably have gone into architecture or, failing that, the military.) If there are no supporters, nobody is buying a ticket or watching a match on television, which means there is no money to support professional football. There would be no stadiums, no football on telly and probably no replica kits. People would still play football, but it would be much like going for an afternoon stroll, a popular thing to do, but not something that is going to attract paying customers. Supporters are the lifeblood of the game as a spectator sport. There is no getting round that. Particularly today, when so many clubs run themselves – or try to run themselves – as businesses, the well-being and happiness of the fans should be of paramount importance. Sadly, that is not always the case. Too often, fans are exploited and squeezed. And too many are voting with their feet.

The numbers are there for all to see. Between 1980 and 2000 the average attendance in Serie A oscillated between 30,000 and 34,000 (reaching as high as 38,872 in

1984–85). In the last five years it has fallen steadily and, as of January 2006, it stood as low as 21,635. It is the lowest average attendance in Serie A since 1964-65. The situation is no better in Serie B. The average gate in 2004-05 was 6,867. My records go back to 1962 and those were the worst attendance figures I could find.

English football is different. Indeed, taken in ten-year increments, the top-flight has been moving ever upward: from 21,080 in 1985 to 24,294 in 1995 to 33,890 at the end of 2004–05. And yet, from 2002 to the present, that figure has declined every year. Unlike Italy, where everybody agrees the situation is critical, in England opinions are mixed. But the numbers suggest a certain disaffection, at least with the game in the top-flight. Further down, it's a different story. The Championship is a roaring success, with an average gate of 17,410 in 2004–05, up from 10,882 in 1994–95. Indeed, it is the sixth best supported league in Europe, after the Bundesliga, the Premiership, Serie A, the Spanish Liga and the French Championnat. But the figures show that we have a problem – even though someone is doing things right (the Championship).

Gazzetta dello Sport published five reasons why football attendances have been declining. The first was ticket prices. Across the board, they are considerably higher than they were fifteen years ago in both Italy and England. Average prices remain considerably higher in England, although some figures are misleading. Football clubs charge what the market can bear, and because English grounds on average are smaller than Italian ones, ticket prices are higher. Italian clubs offer a wider range of tickets. At the San Siro, for example, prices for 2005–06 ranged between €17 (£11.50) and €300 (£206) for Inter matches. By contrast, at Chelsea the cheapest ticket is £35 and the most expensive non-corporate seat is £60. If you want to splurge and impress someone by getting the 'best seat in the house' it will cost you nearly three and a half times as much to do so at the San Siro than at Stamford Bridge! An economist would say that Italian grounds have more 'price points', which means they can reach a wider range of customers. At the heart of this is the fact that Italian grounds are bigger. The £11.50 'cheap ticket' option at the San Siro puts you way up in the third tier: from there, players look only marginally larger than bacteria. By contrast, the £35 'cheap ticket' at Chelsea ensures you are still close enough to the pitch to see the whites of Frank Lampard's eyes (if you have 20/20 vision).

'I don't think the problem is ticket prices alone,' says Dave Boyle, deputy chief executive of Supporters Direct. 'It's the combination of high ticket prices and unfulfilled expectations. It's worse than ten years ago. Back then the prices matched the expectation.'

Luca Locatelli, marketing director at Atalanta, agrees. 'I don't think it's down to ticket price. That's just an excuse,' he says. 'In Italy, in Serie B you can get into a game in the *curva* for as little as six or eight euros, maybe twice that in Serie A. That's not a lot these days, certainly not in Bergamo.'

Yet if high ticket prices do not necessarily depress attendances they have a different, perhaps even more dangerous effect. 'In England keeping prices high was a way of sanitizing the stadiums. The thinking was that working-class potential hooligans could no longer afford to go,' says Locatelli. 'The problem, of course, is that many more peace-loving working-class people were also shut out. I think as a football club you have to be very careful with your pricing policy. It's not just about maximizing profits, it's about being as inclusive as possible so that you can also plan for your future.'

A number of studies, several of which David Conn cited in his excellent book *The Beautiful Game?*, indicate, for example, that teenagers are disappearing from English football grounds. These kids are supposed to be the next generation of fans yet they no longer watch live football. 'It's where you learn to be an adult,' says Boyle. 'We're talking about kids at school who for the first time have to decide what to do with their pocket money. When they were younger maybe their parents took them. Now they are on their own and the ticket prices for them are just too high. Also, kids that age are spontaneous. Now that grounds are all-ticket, it means they have to buy tickets in advance and they don't do that.'

Indeed, as someone who spends a lot of time at football grounds, it's something I too have noticed. I see plenty of guys aged twenty-five or above, who got hooked on the game when they were younger and now can afford to go. I see families, too, dads with their little kids. But what happens when a kid turns fifteen or sixteen and doesn't want to spend Saturday with his father? What happens if he can't go to the match? Do we lose him for ever?

The sad truth is that we probably do. Clubs are so fixated on short-term profit that long-term concerns are hardly a priority. Teenagers, pensioners, the working poor, none of these people are particularly attractive from a commercial perspective. The stereotypes are well-known: teenagers can be unruly, old folk can be depressing, the working poor are seen as potential hooligans. Besides, none of these people have much money, which means they're unlikely to buy products in the club shop or snacks at the stadium concessions.

'The Ultras [hardcore fans] movement met with the Italian Football Association and presented a proposal to reduce prices for children, young people and pensioners,' says Carlo Balestri, who co-ordinates the work of a number of Ultras supporters groups. 'The FA agreed, but the Italian League was very clear. Prices are a matter for the individual clubs. They are the only ones who decide on such issues.'

It's the same story in England. 'When the Taylor Report came out it was very clear,' says Boyle. 'If you introduce all-seater stadiums then the supply of seats will be reduced, while demand for tickets remains the same. Which means that, according to the law of supply and demand, ticket prices are going to go up. To avoid this and to make sure that certain people could still afford to go, the Taylor report said that prices had to be capped and could only increase with inflation. Well, as you probably guessed, that wasn't done. Clubs simply ignored that part.'

Gazzetta's second reason for falling attendance was that too many Italian grounds are sub-standard, either because they're antiquated and decrepit or, in the case of newer grounds such as Turin's Delle Alpi stadium or the San Nicola in Bari, offer poor sightlines. Anybody who has been to a match in both countries can't help but notice the difference. English grounds are built for football and generally speaking they are comfortable, hospitable and clean.

The Taylor report originated from the unspeakable tragedy of Hillsborough, and contributed greatly to improving English stadiums. In Italy, it has been a different story. For a start, virtually all the grounds are publicly owned, rather than the property of the clubs. This means it is far easier to justify spending public money on their renovation, which is what happened before the 1990 World Cup, which Italy hosted. But government funding almost always comes with strings attached.

In this case, the 'strings' were that the grounds should be, wherever possible, multi-purpose. This meant installing running tracks in the new grounds that were built in Turin and Bari. It also meant building stadiums which were grandiose and looked good from a distance (indeed, both the Delle Alpi and the San Nicola could probably host the Summer Olympics) but which did not meet the needs of football fans.

The sightlines in both grounds are poor, partly as a result of the running track, partly because the stadiums were built with an architectural conceit rather than with football fans in mind. There is a reason why some of the best grounds in which to watch football – such as Villa Park or Ibrox – are boxy facilities which won't win beauty contests any time soon: they are built to be enjoyed and appreciated from the inside, not the outside. The other problem – and evidence that they were not built with the fans in mind – is that both stadiums are far too big. Bari's San Nicola seats 58,270. The season it opened, just before the World Cup, Bari were in Serie A and drew an average of 24,807 spectators. The most they have ever drawn is just under thirty-six thousand. And, in 2004–05, in Serie B, they drew fewer than five thousand a game. Imagine how five thousand fans look, rattling around in a 58,270-seater stadium.

It's a similar situation in Turin, with the Delle Alpi, also built for the 1990 World Cup. It holds 69,041, but since it opened, Juventus have never averaged more than 51,000 in a single season and, in fact, in 2004–05 drew a paltry 26,429 spectators. Equally, Torino, with whom they share the stadium, never saw their average season attendance go higher than 33,000 and, in 2004–05, averaged just 10,003. Again, as with Bari, it would not have taken a genius to figure out that neither Juve nor Torino would be able to sell out the ground regularly, as neither club averaged more than 43,000 a season in the decade before the Delle Alpi opened. Now Juventus are planning to renovate the Delle Alpi, reducing its capacity and removing the running track.

In the long term, it would be better for everyone involved if the stadiums were owned and operated by the clubs, but the clubs are not going to want to fork out vast sums to 'buy' something they virtually own already, particularly since city councils often give clubs favourable rent and maintenance deals. This, too, is a sign of short-termism. However good the rent deal, a city council is unlikely to invest heavily in renovations. In the same way, a club will not want to invest in its ground unless it gets some kind of equity in return. Perhaps the solution is for city councils to work out some long-term deal that would see grounds revert over time to club ownership.

Otherwise, Italy will continue to have embarrassingly poor grounds.

When I looked at the list of UEFA five-star and four-star venues, Britain had four five-star – Hampden Park, Ibrox, the Millennium Stadium and Old Trafford – and two four-star grounds – Villa Park and Anfield – whereas Italy had none in either category. I would hope this will change if Italy is awarded the 2012 European Championships.

For all of football's bluster in calling itself a business, when it comes to long-term investment, public money is almost always needed. This is undoubtedly true in Italy, but, as Boyle points out, in many cases it is the same in England: 'After the Bradford fire they found a newspaper under the stand,' he says. 'It was twenty-three years old, which meant that nobody had ever cleaned under that stand. The truth is that until people stop going, renovating is not an issue. Eventually the clubs were compelled by government to take action and the government provided public money. That's why the stadiums in the Premiership are all-seater.'

So, without public investment, most clubs will not renovate or improve their grounds. Many believe that, with a few exceptions, most Italian clubs fail to see the link between better facilities and bigger crowds. 'The stadiums aren't particularly good, but six or seven years ago, in those very same grounds, there were seven or eight thousand more fans per game, which indicates that it can't be that big a factor,' says Balestri.

I suspect he's right. Clean, comfortable stadiums may help attract new fans, but they probably do not affect established fans' attendance. As long as a ground is safe, fans will go, no matter how decrepit it is. You might not, however, have what the economists call 'churn': new fans replacing old ones, which is what some say has happened in England. The contention is that as some of the 'old-school fans' grew disaffected and stopped going, their absence was not really noticed because they were replaced by 'new' supporters, people who perhaps had never thought about going to a football match before but were seduced by the hype and glitz of the post-Bosman Premiership and its gleaming new grounds. In Italy, however, when the 'old school' fans left there was no gleaming new stadium to attract their 'replacements'.

Gazzetta dello Sport's third point is inherently Italian. It is known as the 'Pisanu Law' after the politician who introduced a set of measures aimed at making Italian stadiums safer. Some of its provisions are basic, such as making turnstiles mandatory to control the flow of spectators and to ensure that ticketless fans do not enter. Others are rather more extreme. Matches became all-ticket and each ticket became nominal: you had to provide formal identification to buy one. 'We organize a hundred and twenty buses of supporters for each game,' says Giordano Maestroni, co-ordinator of Milan's official supporters' clubs. 'Now, with the Pisanu Law, we have to provide a list of names and identification documents when we order the tickets, which have to be bought at least forty-eight hours before the game. For us it's a huge problem. Many people who might decide at the last minute to go to a game are now shut out.'

Maestroni's group shows how rank-and-file supporters were affected by this law. The fans in the clubs he represents hail from towns and villages all over Italy. They aren't Ultras or potential troublemakers; most are families or middle-aged supporters. 'This law was introduced without anyone consulting us or fans like us,' he says. 'We are the majority, after all. Instead they made it seem like it was all about the violent minority. And we have to pay for the actions of a few idiots.'

It is unlikely that the Pisanu Law could have been introduced in Britain, where there is a much different attitude towards privacy, as the debate over national identity cards shows. When Margaret Thatcher tried to introduce identity cards for football supporters, there was an enormous backlash from civil libertarians. In Italy, the debate hasn't been about civil liberties, though, it has been about inconvenience. For Atalanta's Locatelli, the main problem was that, like many things in Italian football, it was rushed through and supporters had no time to get used to the idea. 'It came overnight so nobody saw its good points,' he says. 'When you actually dissect it, there is a lot of good in it. And with enough time and a proper awareness campaign you could probably have persuaded most people that it's good for the game. You could have given people time to change their habits. Instead it materialized from one day to the next and everyone viewed it as an imposition. The result is that crowds are down, which means sponsorship is down, which means clubs were hurt as well as fans.' The Pisanu Law is hurting attendance, but if it improves safety, it will have been worthwhile. Indeed, the early statistics are encouraging. Violence fell across Serie A. The number of wounded fell by 87 per cent among police and 16 per cent among supporters, while the number of arrests declined by 54 per cent and the use of teargas at matches was down 93 per cent.

I should declare my bias on *Gazzetta*'s fourth point: television. I work for Sky Italia, which holds the satellite broadcast rights to the home games of eighteen of Serie A's twenty clubs and screens every one of those matches live. As a result, almost every fan of a Serie A team in Italy can watch their club from the comfort of their living room. The impact is far-reaching. In England, a rule specifies that there can be no live English football on television between three p.m. and five p.m. on a Saturday, when most matches kick off. It's common sense: because there is no football to watch on the box, a dedicated fan will go out to see his local club play. That's the logic behind it.

'When I was ten years old if I wanted to watch Serie A football I had to harass my parents into taking me to the stadium,' says Locatelli. 'Over time it ignited my passion and I fell in love with Atalanta. Today a kid can watch anything he wants on television. That's how he becomes a fan. He doesn't need to know what a football ground is like, the colour, the sounds, the songs . . . His support for a club is born and lives on through television. And, because the bigger clubs are on television more often than the smaller clubs, or, at least, they get more attention, more kids end up supporting Juventus and Milan.'

An important point. Televising games hurts smaller clubs more than bigger ones, partly because the bigger clubs have more fans so still draw decent crowds, and partly because when fans watch football on television, they are drawn to the big clubs, not the small ones. So most arm-chair supporters back big clubs. It's inevitable that if your only contact with a club is via television, you will be drawn to the glitzier teams that get the most coverage.

'At Atalanta we can "capture" fans by having them come to a game, letting them see and feel the excitement of an Atalanta match,' says Locatelli. 'We have a family stand for four hundred kids at every match with games and face painting and Warner Bros characters . . . all that stuff that kids can relate to. It's a way of getting them into the ground and then they have contact with Atalanta and our players and hopefully they develop a passion. We want our kids to grow up as Atalanta fans, after all.

'If you're a club like Atalanta you can't hatch that same passion via television,' he adds. 'We don't win the *scudetto*, we're not in the Champions' League final. People don't casually fall for us after watching us on television. We have to get them into the ground. That's when they see that live football in the stadium is a completely different product from football on television.'

To me, that is the key. Television can only hurt attendances as long as it is seen as a substitute for being at a match in person. In England, for a variety of reasons, going to a football match is one thing, watching it on television another. Both are enjoyable, yet they are seen as inherently different experiences. In Italy that differentiation does not exist. Too many people view a match on television as an alternative to the stadium experience, which hurts attendance figures. If going out or staying in is the same, why not curl up on the sofa rather than braving the elements? 'It's obvious, we Italians are a country of lazy people who can only criticize,' says Fabio Capello. 'We always want to be comfortable. Do you know that eighty per cent of Italians drive to work every day instead of walking or taking public transport? Eighty per cent! It's the same with football. It's too hot, it's too cold, it's too far . . . so they sit and watch it on television.'

But even though England has dealt with televised matches far more intelligently than Italy, the situation is far from perfect in the Premiership. Most weekends five games kick off at the traditional time of three p.m. on Saturday and another five are sprinkled over three days: two on Saturday (twelve thirty p.m. and five-fifteen), two on Sunday (two p.m. and five past four) and one on Monday night (eight o'clock). The irregularity has had a profound effect on fans, particularly those of smaller clubs. According to Dave Boyle, 'For bigger clubs it doesn't make a difference because the fans are always there, but for smaller ones it's a problem because more people are picking and choosing,' he says. 'A season ticket used to be a block purchase, you knew that every other Saturday at three o'clock you had a match to go to. Now that it's spread through the weekend, people become more selective, they'll buy individual tickets, arrange their time differently. They lose the habit of Saturdays at three. And the thing about football is that once you stop, it's hard to pick it up again. It's like an addiction in reverse. Once you're unhooked, you're gone.'

In Italy, some clubs view falling attendances philosophically: 'Well, we have five thousand fewer fans per game, but we make ten million euros more from our television contract, so it's OK.'

'It's an interesting question, whether football is something to be watched in stadiums or on television,' says Boyle. 'And when that question has been asked of the clubs, they have said, "Let's go with what television wants, because they give us more money."'

Needless to say, that is a short-sighted and foolish view.

Television executives are interested in supplying football as entertainment. Half-empty stadiums make for a poor spectacle, and if fans stop going they may eventually stop watching as well. And, of course, as Locatelli explained, televised football favours the bigger clubs.

So, what can be done? First, we have to ensure that going to a football match provides the kind of experience that television can't offer. And until that happens it's important for football to understand what economists call the value of 'scarcity'. That means working to ensure that every last fan who could be persuaded to go to a game does so. Limiting live football on television would help.

The English model, with the five Saturday non-televised games, is a rational set-up. I fear that in Italy it will be impossible to revert to that. Italians are too used to televised live football and the clubs would not accept such a change. However, there is an alternative way of doing things that, I believe, would help and, with some prompting, prove acceptable to the clubs.

I suggest that you should not be able to watch on television a live game that is taking place within fifty kilometres of your home, unless it is sold out. So, for example, if I live in Rome, my television subscription would entitle me to see the away games of Roma and Lazio, plus the home games that sell out and all other Serie A matches. In that way I would be encouraged to go and watch my local club in person when they play at home. This system is used in American football, in the NFL, and it works extremely well. It also has a wonderful side-effect: teams benefit from being on television, but they can only appear if they sell out, so those who take care of their fans and 'put bums in seats' are rewarded.

The rule encourages them not to price tickets too high and to do everything they can to make sure the spectator comes back the following week. Technologically it would not be difficult to implement. And I believe television companies would be in favour of it if it meant having better attendances at the ground: half-empty stadiums are a television producer's nightmare. Also, they would pay the clubs a little less money since the games would reach fewer viewers.

Gazzetta's final point has been much debated in England and in Italy. It contends that the quality of play has fallen and that the gap between rich and poor clubs is so great that people have lost interest. Because Serie A and the Premiership are seen as a closed shop, with the same three or four clubs winning all the time, and the others playing for peanuts, fans are deserting *en masse*.

While it's obvious that the gap between rich and poor continues to increase as the number of big clubs diminishes – Italy's fabled 'seven sisters' are now down to three, Milan, Juventus and Inter – it may not be contributing to the fan exodus. 'Ultras and real supporters couldn't care less about whether their team is doing well,' says Balestri. 'Or, rather, they are not going to stop going if their team is doing poorly. Obviously they want to do well, but they are so attached to their club that they will always be there. That's what defines them. The "normal" fan is a different issue. But I think it's more a case of people feeling cheated by what happened five or six years ago, when chairmen were talking about floating on the stock market and conquering the world. So many of those promises were not kept and the fans who were drawn to the hype are also the fans who left.'

Boyle echoes his view: 'I don't think the standard of play is so important,' he says. 'You'll put up with it. You go with your friends and you have a nice time. It's a social ritual. That's why AFC Wimbledon is successful. People said their fans would never settle for that level of football after watching the Premiership. Instead, the opposite occurred. Fans flocked to the games. It's one of the lies the Premiership tells itself, that people want to watch great players,' he adds. 'The truth is that people want to watch football and great players are a bonus.'

Not everyone agrees. Fabio Capello maintains that people are drawn to quality and that television has taken quality football into everyone's home. In his opinion, once you've seen Barcelona or Milan play, it's hard to go out and pay money to watch your local lower-division team. 'A kid is smart to not watch his local side if it's bad football,' he says. 'It used to be that people didn't know any better, but now they do. Thanks to television, people understand the way the game is supposed to be played. And the reality is that Serie B is downright depressing and you have to be on drugs to watch Serie C . . .'

Harsh words, but heartfelt. I wonder, though if, perhaps, on this issue Boyle and Balestri aren't a bit closer to the hearts and minds of the average fan. Supporters want excitement and entertainment, which can take many forms. And I think it's also worth making a distinction between the hardcore fans – and I don't just mean the Ultras in Italy, but anyone who is loyal regardless of the opposition and the place in the table – and the more casual supporters. A lot has to do with the way fans define themselves. And in Italy there is no question that many see themselves as loyal supporters but, in fact, are casual.

Drug-taking Mercenaries and the Disney Experience

I have added a sixth reason to *Gazzetta*'s list and it primarily affects the Italian game: loss of credibility. It's a certain creeping cynicism, a sense that football is run by charlatans and thieves, everyone is out to make money, and justice can be bought or sold. It's a system in which a 'normal' person often no longer feels at home. In short, instead of being a happy escape from everyday reality, football becomes a mirror of the real world, with all its ills and ugliness.

'You see it especially in Serie B,' says Balestri. 'The *curva*, where the Ultras go, is always full, because they're always there. They never abandon the team. But the stands on either side of the pitch are deserted, as is most of the visiting section. Football is no longer respected.'

Locatelli concurs: 'The main problem is that there is a disaffection with the world of football. They don't believe in it any more. The biggest difference between Italy and England lies in what fans think of the players. To an English fan, players are gladiators, who put every last drop of blood on the line in every game. To an Italian fan, players are mercenaries, who do just enough to scrape a pay cheque. Even the ones who are idolized . . .'

And it's hard not to be disillusioned, given the stories coming out of Italian football, from owners who acquire a club, bankrupt it, then move on to another, to referees who are constantly under scrutiny, from 'arranged' matches and 'favours' to accusations of doping and drug-taking. It seems at times that the Italian game is hell-bent on self-destruction.

Match-fixing is something I struggle to come to terms with. It's one thing, as we discussed earlier, to do an opponent a 'favour'. However unethical and despicable I find it, I suppose some people see it as a venial crime. But match-fixing for profit is another issue, particularly in the top flight, where so many players are millionaires. In Italy, we had two major match-fixing scandals in the 1980s, both involving illegal betting rings, which saw players and coaches receive long bans. But there have been other, supposedly isolated incidents, as recently as 2004–05. Indeed, Genoa's promotion to Serie A that year was cancelled after their president was found guilty of trying to rig their final match of the season.

I don't have much to say about it, except to point out how much shame those involved brought to the game. And with similar scandals occurring in Greece, Belgium and Finland in the last year or so, I can only urge the game to remain vigilant. This problem has not gone away.

The issue of doping and drug-taking is worth a digression, not least because I was directly pulled into it some years ago, when Zdenek Zeman, then manager of Lazio, implied that Juventus had regularly given their players illegal performance-enhancing drugs during my time at the club. Zeman did not have any specific evidence, except that Alex Del Piero and I had grown bigger and more muscular in our time at Juve. It led to a judicial inquiry and a long trial, in which many of us who had played for the club between 1994 and 1998 were called to testify. Ultimately, Juventus's team doctor, Riccardo Agricola, was acquitted on appeal but, as so often happened, the suspicion never went away.

The Juventus side that I captained to a Champions'

League crown in 1996 is still seen by many as having been drugged up to its eyeballs. Some opposing fans still call the players 'drug cheats'. And in the eyes of many, our achievements have been tarnished by the accusations. For me, the experience was very painful. First, I have always taken great pride in my training and worked hard to take care of my body. Football is a physical game. Our bodies are the tools of our trade, the machines with which we run our race, and we work very hard to keep them in top condition. To hear people say that our success is all down to popping pills is very hurtful. For me, the worst parts occurred during the trial, when Zinedine Zidane and I were called to answer questions about what substances we took on a particular day, years earlier. When we said we did not remember, some people took that as a sure sign of guilt, mocking our 'sudden lack of memory', as they put it. As if you should be expected to remember what you had for breakfast five years ago!

Confusion surrounded the affair, although the facts were simple. Juventus, as a club, had a well-stocked pharmacy, including – as the inquiry discovered – 281 different drugs. I don't know if that is a lot or a little – I never counted how many there were at other clubs. But the inquiry also revealed that every single one of those drugs was legal. In other words, not one was a banned substance, which explains why not a single Juventus player tested positive between 1994 and 1998, despite the frequent tests in Serie A as well as in UEFA and FIFA competitions.

Was I given more drugs and pharmaceutical substances at Juventus than I received at Chelsea, Sampdoria or Cremonese? Probably. Were they all legal? I'm neither a doctor nor a pharmacist, but there is no doubt in my mind that, as the evidence showed, this was the case. We were given nothing illegal. And, as far as I'm concerned, the debate should end there. Or, rather, the real debate lies elsewhere and it has to do with what level of medical treatment a footballer should receive.

A footballer is, among other things, a multi-million-pound asset of a business corporation. That corporation feels entitled to do all it legally can to keep all of its assets in full working order. That's why footballers get far better (and more expensive) medical care than 'civilians'. And it's also why footballers will more readily take painkillers and other drugs that may give them an edge in terms of helping them to recover from injury or help them play through the pain. If a postman or a teacher twists his ankle, a doctor may decide it's best for them to be on crutches for three weeks and let the ankle heal naturally. But a footballer is expected to be back on the pitch as soon as possible. Playing through pain is a mark of pride, as is gritting your teeth, putting your body on the line and going out there filled with painkillers. After all, footballers – as we hear time and again – are highly paid pro-fessionals. The show must go on. The system demands that you constantly push your body to new extremes. The result is that while there is no doubt that sport in general is good for you, the same cannot be said of professional sport. It's something entirely different.

I shake my head in frustration when I hear old-timers call today's players 'whingers' because 'back in their day' there was no squad rotation, the pitches were awful and guys happily played fifty or sixty games in a season. That may be true, but today's players are bigger, stronger and quicker than those of twenty or thirty years ago and the game is played at a higher, more punishing pace.

The reality is that we are paying a price for all this. Players can and do develop serious ailments later in life as a result of what they went through in their playing days. They also have more ups and downs throughout the season. And, as was the case in Italy at Juventus, they find themselves willing to put their bodies under great stress just to be able to compete at the highest level.

As if to add insult to injury, the Juve situation made people cynical. It led them to believe that clubs readily cheated and happily put their players' health on the line. And, perhaps the worst crime of all, it gave the impression that everyone was, to some degree, taking illegal performance-enhancing drugs. Imagine the message it sends to a young footballer.

I think back to Locatelli's words – that too many Italians see the players as nothing more than mercenaries: it's a brutal assessment. And one that makes me, as an Italian, very uncomfortable. Part of it, as we saw earlier, is socio-cultural: we tend to think the worst of people until they prove us wrong. That is our cultural matrix. Yet it is only part of the story. The other part is that those who are involved in football – players, clubs, the federation, the media, the fans, all of us – do not do enough to defend the game and to fix it.

'Italian football has a lot of problems, but every single day it is attacked by fans, the press, the clubs, everyone,' says Locatelli. 'And the institutions, the league and the football association, who should be defending it, do very little to defend the game from these routine attacks, some of which are well founded, some of which aren't. When everybody is denigrating the game, how are you going to attract more fans? In England, they understand this and they always rise to the defence of the game.' The fact that in England you can be charged with 'bringing the game into disrepute' shows how seriously the integrity of the game is taken. Any attack is repelled for the good of the game.

'Yes, but in terms of England being clean it's just one of the lies we tell ourselves,' says Boyle. 'We say we have incorruptible civil servants who don't take bribes. Of course they take bribes. They take bribes all the time. It's just that we don't call it that. Still, we haven't lost all faith the way you seem to have lost faith in Italy.'

Boyle believes that something else explains the decline in attendance in England: 'This does not apply to Italy, not yet anyway. It's the sanitization of the experience. The vibrancy of the stadium as a festival of football, a carnival atmosphere . . . That has been lost, compared to other countries. Many English stadiums are now dead, with everybody moving robotically one way or the other. Football used to be like theatre without a director, unscripted opera,' he says. 'Now it's staged. At too many grounds they play music when a goal is scored! That should be a spontaneous moment with the crowd celebrating and instead it's drowned out.'

Indeed, in that sense there are situations when things have clearly gone too far. After the final whistle in the final of the 2004 European Championship, classic rock music blared for about twenty minutes, drowning the delight of the celebrating Greek supporters. I'm sure they didn't mind, such was their joy, but for everybody else it was rather depressing, as if the stadium had turned into a roller disco, *circa* 1981.

This issue highlights the differences between Italy and England. In Italy, for better or worse, there are organized supporters groups, such as the Ultras, who help dictate the atmosphere at a ground. In England, where organization among the fans is much looser, there has been nothing to stop what Boyle calls the 'sanitization' of the game. To him, the loss of terracing was a major factor: 'It may have helped get rid of hooliganism in English grounds, but it also got rid of the vibrancy of the atmosphere. Part of it is that there is an inherent fear of the mob, a sense that you don't know what they're going to do next. Those in positions of authority like to control the people, keep them behind fences or in cages. But standing is like cannabis or homosexuality. You can pass all the laws you like, but if people want to do it, they'll do it.'

Middlesbrough's Riverside Stadium is a good example. The ground is an all-seater and the no-standing rule is strictly enforced. This is because, according to Boyle, the club is put under a lot of pressure by the local authority. The way they deal with visiting supporters who stand is by cutting their allocation for the following season. Thus, Manchester United had their allocation cut from 3,000 to 1,500 and then to 750. This is no solution. Middlesbrough FC have no choice – Boyle says the local authority has the power to shut down the stadium if the club doesn't comply – but it seems an extreme way of dealing with things. At other clubs, such as Chelsea and Portsmouth, standing is sometimes tolerated, as the stewards use greater discretion. 'That's why attendance in the lower leagues has gone up,' says Boyle. 'It's not that people want to watch the football because it isn't particularly good, it's still the usual kick and rush. But people go because it's fun. You can stand, you can dance and sing, you can move around.'

The success of FC United, which regularly draws some three thousand fans even though it is ten tiers below the Premiership, is illuminating. Here was a group of supporters who said, 'Enough!' and created a club tailor-made to their own wishes.

I wonder if something like that could happen in Italy. Because of the power of the Ultras and other supporter groups, I can't imagine football in Italy becoming sanitized to the degree that it is in some English grounds. In the 2005–06 season, when Milan played Juventus at the San Siro, Milan's Curva Sud unfurled a giant banner that read, 'Our answer to your modern football . . .' A few minutes later, everybody at that end of the ground was holding up red or white cardboard squares which formed the word: 'No!' Visually it was extremely powerful, and it was applauded by the Juventus fans at the other end of the ground. Now Juventus and Milan are probably the two most powerful and 'institutional' clubs in the Italian game. Certainly Milan fans also have the benefit of arguably the best stadium in Italy, safe, clean and relatively affordable. Yet they, too, were eager to make their voices heard, to reject what they considered to be a travesty of the game they loved: the over-sanitized, over-commercialized, over-hyped version peddled by TV companies and others.

'We in England put up with things, it's in our nature to just accept things,' says Boyle. 'It happens with ticket prices, trains, bus queues. We just don't complain.' Some might say that in Italy we complain too much. We don't know what a 'stiff upper lip' is and we don't want to know: it gets in the way of crying.

Chapter Twelve

Irrational, Unconditional Love

In 2003–04, Leeds United supporters lived through the final chapter of a nightmare. Three seasons after reaching the semi-finals of the Champions' League the club found itself relegated. Saddled with a mountain of debt, Leeds United were on the verge of bankruptcy. The fans, who had believed their club to be one of Europe's greats, saw their dreams shatter.

And yet their behaviour did not change one iota. I remember a humiliating 5–0 pounding at the hands of Arsenal at Highbury: the supporters, despite a seven-hour round trip, continued to hail their heroes, spurring them on to the final whistle, then applauding them off the pitch. Even more telling was the final home game of the season, against Charlton. Leeds were mathematically relegated, yet they were applauded on to the pitch as if they were walking out for the FA Cup final. It was an end-to-end game in which they squandered a 3–1 lead, allowing two late goals and settling for a 3–3 draw, but throughout the Leeds fans sang without pause. They were doomed, they were down, but they would not abandon their team. At the final whistle there was even a peaceful pitch invasion, with some players carried off in triumph.

No matter the pain – and it was painful, as evidenced by the sight of so many young men in tears – they were determined to show their love for the team.

When I tell this story in Italy, people assume I'm lying or exaggerating. Nobody believes fans can behave like this. And yet, while Leeds fans admittedly are perhaps at the more passionate end of the spectrum, it is common for a disappointing season to end in tears of commiseration rather than howls of anger. Arsène Wenger says, 'If we lose a game, I always look at the faces of our fans after the match as they begin to head home. And what I see in their eyes is above all pain and disappointment. In France on the other hand I would see only anger . . . rage directed at the players and the team.'

It's a similar story in Italy. When you lose, the prevailing emotion is anger, followed by indifference. What would have happened if, rather than being in Yorkshire, Leeds had been in the hills of Tuscany? For a start, there would have been no pitch invasion at the final home match because the ground would, at best, have been a quarter full. Club officials would probably have been in attendance with a police escort. The atmosphere would have been funereal, made all the more depressing by the empty seats. One area of the ground would still be full: the 'curva', home to the club's hardcore fans, the Ultras. Unless, of course, they had decided as a group to register their disapproval by not showing up or by milling around outside the ground rather than going in. Would the players have received any support? Perhaps some would, but most would have been ignored. It would depend on their relationship with the Ultras.

For the players it would be a surreal, depressing

environment. But in some ways it would offer respite from what would likely have happened shortly before, when the club's relegation became a mathematical certainty. In England, that day was greeted with sadness and shared mourning. In Italy it would have been about rage – against the club, the manager, the players. Boos and insults are the least of a relegated player's concerns. In some cases, so-called fans have laid siege to the dressing room, vandalized players' cars, even physically attacked them. Sometimes Ultras groups are behind this, at other times angry hoodlums masquerade as fans. Either way, the first reaction is of rage and hostility. Then comes indifference.

And it is that indifference which is so striking and so dramatic. One game the stadium is packed, with fans spurring you on, and at the next it is close to empty. It's as if, once the objective is lost – whether it is winning the title or avoiding relegation – the battle is over and there is no point in continuing.

This links back to what we discussed earlier in the book – the fact that, to many Italians, the joy of football is primarily derived from the result. The emotion a fan experiences from watching his side play is subordinate to the result. Once a team has failed, there is no point in continuing to watch because nothing is at stake. The battle has been lost. Even winning a game, once you have already been relegated, is nothing more than an exercise in self-delusion.

In England, when the battle has been lost, being there is a sign of belonging, doing one's duty, loyalty. 'Here in England, their patience is infinite,' says Eriksson. 'The supporters never criticize and they always applaud you. And the ground is always full. It doesn't matter if you do well or not, the supporters are always there.'

For Arsène Wenger, the reasons for this are historical. 'Anglo-Saxon culture is all about banding together in small groups, which, to survive, had to remain united and loyal to each other. If you think about it, British history is the history of thousands of years of warring clans. To survive they looked inward, fostering unity and loyalty among themselves, that was their strength. It was very clannish and tribal. Now, Italy and France were also tribal. But to survive, they did things differently. That's why our history is the history of alliances and betrayals, of the Borgias, of double-crosses, of being with one ally one year and another the next. You love your colours, but you love your own survival more.'

Put that way, Wenger makes it appear as if the French, the Italians and other Latin cultures are cowardly and the British are loyal. It's not something I fully agree with, though it's a nice theory. Yet Wenger isn't making a value judgement. And, in fact, it's not as if the passion and loyalty of the British is necessarily positive, as he explains further.

'It comes down to rationality,' he goes on. 'The Latins think more, they reason more, they are more analytical. If they find something they like, they ask themselves why they like it. And this creates detachment. The Anglo-Saxons don't do this. If they like something, that's it, they are attached to it and they will always feel attached to it with the same intensity. Maybe it's irrational, but that is the way it is. They don't question their love or their passion. This is part of the reason why I always say that if I were going to war I would want to do it alongside an

Englishman, not a Frenchman,' he adds. 'The Frenchman would think too much.'

In 2002–03, Siena were promoted from Serie B to Serie A. The tiny Tuscan club had an average attendance of 6,301 that season. The next year, with everyone excited at being in Serie A, it skyrocketed to 11,142. Siena avoided relegation, a minor miracle, and one might have thought that this would generate even more excitement among the fans. Not so. In 2004–05, despite again avoiding relegation, they lost 15 per cent of their attendance, which fell below 10,000. And, as of the winter break in the 2005–06 season, it fell again, to around 7,800. The club had lost a huge chunk of its spectator base despite its positive results on the pitch. For Siena to avoid relegation, as they managed to do for two consecutive years, was the equivalent of winning the *scudetto*. And yet, for a sizeable number of supporters, it wasn't enough. They experienced promotion, they experienced Serie A and then they left. How could they be so fickle?

Wenger might suggest that rather than being fickle, they're rational. Once the novelty had worn off, they were gone. Unconditional love, like that of the Leeds fans, is irrational: they kept going and supporting the club even when it was 'treating them badly' because they were in it for the long haul. It's a bit like being married, sticking together through good times and bad. Some might say that marriage is the epitome of the 'irrational' act.

In that sense, those 3,500 Siena fans who abandoned the club never 'married' it. Indeed, they probably never fell in love. If you will allow me a runaway metaphor, the relationship was purely physical, and once the fun went out of it, they walked away. Siena were still in Serie A but the fans realized it would never reach the next level. Siena would not turn into Juventus or Milan. And so they walked out.

If Wenger is right about English fans being less rational, it would explain one of the mysteries that foreign players encounter when they come to England: the English public rewards effort rather than ability. 'We're not as theoretical, as intellectual, we're much more visceral,' says Boyle. 'Our game is not about excellence, it's about trying. We're not focused on winning, we just want to see effort. If they just aren't good enough, that's OK, as long as they've tried.'

In a 'rational' world, you would accept that some players might be lazy yet so good that they win games singlehandedly. And you would accept that they might stand around on the pitch for much of the game, as long as they help you get all three points. In England, that's not the case. Because the measuring stick is effort, not outcome, the lazy player is rejected in favour of the one who runs around – even though his runs may be pointless and he may not have a shred of ability. 'It's because they have a sense of belonging and a sense of history, which is greater,' says Wenger. 'If you try hard, if you tried hard in the past, the fans will back you until the very end, even once your legs and your ability are gone.'

The player who tried hard in the past showed his loyalty to the fans, so the fans stay loyal to him by supporting him even when, clearly, the team might have been better off without him. Is it rational? Of course not! But it's English.

'Loyalty is the biggest word in English football,' says Boyle. 'You are loyal to the team and you expect the team to be loyal to you. The team is loyal to you by showing effort, not ability, because ability is something that is viewed with suspicion. And thus there is a big taboo about booing your own team, particularly at some clubs, like Liverpool. You'll remember how awful they were under Gerard Houllier and yet I think they were only booed once by the Kop. At every game you could tell the fans wanted to express their frustration but, somehow, they held back because it wasn't the Liverpool way.'

This is why so many players who have played for Liverpool have nothing but praise for the Kop and the rest of Anfield. That kind of constant unconditional support is truly special. And yet it's irrational, as is the way some football is played in England. 'It's the biggest difference of all between Italy and England,' says Eriksson. 'When there are fifteen minutes to go and you're one–nil up, in Italy you do your sums and you figure it's best to hang on and defend. In England you keep attacking, as intensely and as furiously as before. The fans won't accept anything else. There is no Catenaccio here!

'And often the little clubs think and act like big clubs,' he adds. 'They may play away from home against a Manchester United or an Arsenal and they'll do everything they can to win, going out there with no fear and not making any adjustments. Sure, later we can debate whether it's the right thing to do, because, ultimately, your objective is to win and gain points in the table and sometimes you have to know how to defend a lead and how to play for a draw. But for the fans, it's wonderful!'

That devil-may-care attitude is changing. Over the last few years we've increasingly seen some clubs be more speculative, more defensive in certain matches. Yet the basic sense is still there and it's a direct result of the kind of football the fans want to see. It was one of the things that struck me when I arrived at Chelsea in 1996. After fifteen years in Italy, I thought I had consolidated my way of playing football. Instead, I found myself caught up in the English spirit, and my foreign teammates were equally infected with the 'English style of football'.

'To me it is still one of the things which amazes me most year after year: seeing teams full of foreigners going out there and fighting with the same spirit and intensity as the English players,' says Wenger. 'When we at Arsenal play Chelsea there might be just five Englishmen out of the twenty-two on the pitch. Yet the two teams remain distinctly English in their approach.'

It is a magical quality in the English game. The way the fans affect the players is, perhaps, unique. In speaking to my foreign colleagues, I have come to realize just how much English football changes you, and how much of that is down to the supporters. 'I can't love Portuguese football a hundred per cent any more,' says Mourinho. 'And I don't think you can love Italian football a hundred per cent, Luca. That's because of what we have seen here. When you work in England you understand what English football means and you are never the same. Don't get me wrong, I don't accept English football as my game, I still want to influence it. But, for sure, it has changed me.'

In England one experiences a cocktail of unconditional support and the profound urge to throw yourself into battle, abandoning all calculation and rational thought. That is what the fans seem to ask of the players and, according to Marcel Desailly, it's not necessarily a good thing: 'The Italian fan is much more knowledgeable about football than the English one,' he says. 'He also thinks about it more and is more demanding. It is much harder to fool him. I'll give you an example. If a player in Italy shoots from forty yards out, unless he scores he is criticized. He is told to keep it simple, not to think he is Roberto Carlos, to pass and not be selfish, things like that. And the criticism will come from both the fans and his teammates.

'In England, when a player shoots from forty yards out, even if he completely miskicks it and the ball ends up outside the ground, he'll still get a roar of applause. Why? Because the English fan appreciates the effort and he is grateful for the fact the player tried. And he also assumes that the player, because he is a professional, knows what he's doing, otherwise he wouldn't be on the pitch. The Italian fan thinks he always knows better than the players on the pitch. The English fan has only admiration for the players, provided they show the right effort.

'In Italy your whole game gets broken down and judged and if they don't like something you did, they destroy you. In England, they just keep applauding you even when you are playing poorly . . . It may surprise you, but I actually prefer the Italian way. It's nice to be praised and applauded all the time, but somehow when they'll cheer for anyone it's not quite the same thing. When the Italian fan praises you, you know it means something, because he is knowledgeable.'

They're Just Average Joes and Average Giovannis

In fact, the admiration fans have for players is another thing that sets the English game apart. In Italy, players have to earn respect, but in England they are granted it immediately, although they may lose it if they do not show the right kind of effort. In England fans direct their displeasure elsewhere, at least initially. To Boyle, the answer is obvious: 'It's an easy excuse to blame everything on the class system in this country, but generally it's true. If things are going bad, the board is blamed or the manager is blamed, not the players. The players are seen as one of us and, when you complain, you don't complain about your own, you complain about your "betters", those in power . . .'

In fact, there has always been a certain rapport between players and fans in England, a sense of kinship and respect. Gordon Taylor tells a story that summarizes it neatly: 'It was right after the war and the players were discussing whether to go on strike for higher wages,' he says. 'A young footballer raised his hand and said, "I come from Bury, my dad works down the coal mine six days a week and he earns a lot less than we do. Are we sure it's right for us to ask for more money?"

'Tommy Banks, a veteran full-back from Bolton Wanderers, stood up and said, "Son, I hear what you're saying. I have the highest respect for your father. I too worked in the coal mines. I know it's hard work, it's dark, it's cold . . . and if your dad feels like marking Stanley Matthews this Saturday afternoon, he's welcome to try." '

To the English public, players aren't idols, they are working-class heroes, one step removed from the average Joe: they get to play football for a living, fulfilling the aspiration of many working-class men, which makes them special. Because they are 'of the masses', the masses appreciate what sets them apart.

In Italy, the supporters idolize Francesco Totti at Roma or Paolo Maldini at Milan, but they don't necessarily feel the same kinship. There is a distance, which comes from the footballer's talent, his privilege, and perhaps the fan's jealousy. When the player performs badly, the crowd turns on him because it's as if he's squandering his gift, and because they do not feel that the player is one of their own.

Arsène Wenger highlights another reason why fan loyalty is so high in England: 'It's simple,' he says. 'Clubs in England treat their supporters better than clubs in France or Italy. It's part of their global vision. Fans are an integral part of the club, like the players, the coaching staff and the board. Look, it's easy to be cynical about this and it's obvious that, in theory, every club would like to be like this. But in England they take it very seriously. And, most importantly, the fans really feel this and believe in it.'

When I was managing Watford, the club hosted regular fans' forums and made an effort to answer their concerns, whether it was to do with the food at the concessions, technical issues with the playing squad, or kick-off times, which we pushed back for midweek games from seven p.m. to seven forty-five, to give people time to get to Vicarage Road after work.

When I asked Locatelli if such efforts would be worthwhile in Italy, his response was far from encouraging: 'Right now a fan forum in Italy is not possible. I am all in favour of dialogue, but it has to be founded on a basis of respect and, I'm sorry to say, that basis of respect does not exist right now. The fans do not respect the clubs. And when we clubs can prove to the fans that we are worthy of their respect, only then can we have an open and peaceful dialogue.'

Why is there such an adversarial relationship between fans and clubs, I asked, and why, unlike in England, do so many fans refuse to back their club – even though they may back the players?

'There is a major cultural difference,' Locatelli explains. 'The English fan feels a sense of belonging to the club. He considers himself part of it. The board, the players, the manager, they are all on the same side. The Italian fan is different. For him it's not about identity, it's about faith, it's quasi-religious. His faith is towards the club as an abstract ideal. The "physical" club – the players, the board, et cetera – are just the current caretakers of that ideal. And, as such, they can be criticized.'

I find Locatelli's point fascinating. And I think his religious analogy is fitting. In the same way that some people believe in God and have a strong faith but dislike or criticize the Church, the physical manifestation of that faith, so too do some fans adore their club, while possibly rejecting those who physically embody it, such as the chairman and the players.

That explains not just the adversarial relationship fans have with many club boards, but also why they are so quick to criticize players, who are charged with preserving something sacred, the club itself. If they fail to do so, the fans feel entitled to make their opinions known.

In England booing your team is almost like booing yourself. That's how far the English fan identifies with the club. And that's why we so often hear fans sing: 'I'm Boro/Villa/Chelsea/City till I die!' It's an issue of identity. In Italy, the fan is outside the club. His loyalty is to an abstraction so he can voice his disapproval freely. After all, he is not part of the club.

I was reminded of this in the summer of 2005 when the Italian FA found Genoa and its chairman Enrico Preziosi guilty of match-fixing and relegated the club to Serie C. It had won promotion to Serie A, but a series of phone taps revealed that Genoa had paid off Venezia, their opponents on the final day of the season. Naturally, Genoa supporters, who had been out of Serie A for a decade (a long time for one of the most successful clubs in the Italian game), were gutted. But their despair soon turned to anger – not towards Preziosi, who, as chairman and owner, was ultimately responsible, but towards the Italian FA for punishing the club, and therefore its supporters. They accepted that match-fixing is wrong and needed to be dealt with, but it was Preziosi's crime and therefore he should pay, not Genoa's supporters. The fans had done nothing wrong and were now being punished.

Demonstrations erupted all over the city, with supporters blocking railway lines, fighting running battles with the police and venting their fury. It was a singularly Italian way of dealing with things. The Genoa supporters viewed Preziosi and the 'physical' club as an entity unrelated to them and the 'abstract' club they supported. In most 'normal' countries, the fans' fury would have been directed at Preziosi: after all, it was on his watch that the club tried to corrupt another club (and got caught), which cost it promotion. Yet Genoa supporters simply did not make that connection. They felt they were being made scapegoats for Preziosi's crime.

The Ultras: In a League of their Own

The embodiment of this attitude – loyal to the colours,

the crest, the 'abstract' club, suspicions of the 'physical' club, the players and the board – the Ultras are one of the more controversial elements in the Italian game. To many in England, the term 'Ultra' is a synonym for 'hooligan'. In many Italian papers, 'hooligan' is a synonym for 'travelling England fan'. Both views are ignorant.

Ultras groups began to appear in the 1970s and really took off in the 1980s. To an outsider they are passionate fans who band together with banners and logos and vaguely aggressive names such as Juventus's 'Arancia Meccanica' (Clockwork Orange), Milan's 'Brigate Rossonere' (Red and Black Brigade) or Roma's 'Fedayn'. These groups of young men meet in often tense circumstances, and violence or chaos is often a by-product.

Yet they also devote time and energy to something in which they believe, and follow a code of conduct:

1. Love your colours unconditionally.
2. Be prepared – within the limits of your ability, not your convenience – to make sacrifices well beyond the average fan in supporting your team.
3. Have a sense of territory and of belonging. Your seat in the stadium is not just a numbered plastic seat, it is your territory and you shall defend it.
4. Be part of the group but always maintain your own individuality and think for yourself.
5. Know how to distinguish passion from greed. Be prepared to give without receiving. And never profit financially from your club.
6. Weigh up the pros and cons of all your actions, in terms of what is advantageous not only to you but also to your group.

7. Wear your colours with pride.
8. Love your city and your neighbourhood and be proud of who you are.
9. Do not turn the other cheek.
10. Do not stop supporting your team even during the most humiliating defeat.

On the surface, apart from point 9, it looks harmless. So why do Ultras have such a poor reputation?

Part of the problem is that some Ultras groups embrace the symbols and slogans of the far left or far right. While their political views are rarely at the heart of their clashes with police or opposing fans, too often their banners and slogans create an ugly, intimidating atmosphere. Also hoodlums and troublemakers often hide among the Ultras, using as cover their numbers and clout.

Even when politics are not an issue, the Ultras, by their nature, are difficult for the world of football to deal with. Their point of pride – that, come what may, they will follow their team everywhere, in total independence – makes it difficult to include them in the football process. They harbour resentment for the people who run football, who they feel are motivated by money and greed, politics and personal ambition – anything but love of the game.

'There used to be this idea that footballers were attached to their clubs. Now many are seen as mercenaries,' says Balestri of the Progetto Ultras. 'There used to be a sense that chairmen were benevolent father figures, supporters at heart who treated the club like an extension of their family. Now these men are seen as greedy fly-by-night opportunists, looking for money or popularity. Money is the new deity. It's what it's all about. And they reject that. Just as they reject the star system, the hype, television.'

Curiously, this rejection of commercialism and 'football-as-business' is just as much a hallmark of Ultras groups on the right and far right, as it is, predictably, those on the left. Their brand of right-wing politics is – economically at least – nothing like the Thatcherite free market and far closer to the anti-globalization protesters seen in Nice, Genoa and Seattle. It's what Italians call *destra sociale* ('social right') and they share the far left's loathing of a US-led *laissez-faire* capitalist world order based round institutions such as the World Trade Organization, the World Bank and the International Monetary Fund. In fact, Carlo Giuliani, the anti-globalization protester who was shot and killed by Italian military police at the G-8 riots in Genoa, was a Roma fan, and was buried with the club's flag over his coffin. Even though he was a self-described Communist, Lazio's right-wing fans saluted him with a large banner shortly after his funeral.

English supporters are far less politicized, but they share similar sentiments, at least in the sporting sphere. There are plenty of old-school fans who don't like the way the game is going. But the Ultras are far more powerful and better organized. Potentially they could be a tremendous force for change, a genuine voice representing a large group of supporters.

Yet several facts make their inclusion difficult. The first is that, despite the best efforts of certain people, including Balestri, the Ultras reserve the right to resort to violence when they feel under threat. Various Ultras groups have added to the code, specifying, for example, that 'civilians' (non-Ultras) must never be involved in violence, that weapons such as knives and chains must not be used and that violence is only acceptable when the opponent is in equal or greater number. 'Look, this is about limiting violence and being realistic about what they are and are not willing to do,' says Balestri. 'Obviously, they are Ultras, not pacifists. But they also know that violence is dangerous and counterproductive. There are countless examples of teams with massive rivalries and grudges to bear where, thanks to some mediation and some goodwill, violence was averted. I think in general they try to avoid violence. But if it finds them, well, like I said, they are neither saints nor pacifists.'

To compound the problem, many young men in Italy, as in England, enjoy getting into fights and breaking things. I don't think it's a cultural thing – you need only visit an English city centre at pub closing time to see that it's common among youths across Europe. For those who choose to link their fighting to football, the Ultras provide a convenient smokescreen. And because the Ultras will fight back when attacked or threatened, a handful of troublemakers can wreak serious havoc. That's why, in this context, even people like Balestri believe that eliminating violence is not realistic. 'You can't avoid reality,' he says. 'If a politician comes in and talks of eliminating violence altogether he is not being realistic. But if he wants to come and talk of limiting violence, well, that's another story . . .'

Balestri does some important work and I understand his point about realism, but I can't agree that we should accept a level of violence in our stadiums, which is what 'limiting' rather than 'eradicating' violence means. The Ultras are doing themselves a massive disservice by leaving the option of violence on the table. I think most of them realize that violence only leads to more violence and more repression. And a lot of negative press.

Some genuinely don't seem to care what others think, but the Ultras are not a separate race. They are simply very passionate fans who make certain choices and who eventually get married and start families, retreating to 'civilian' life. The way football is going, there is a genuine risk that Ultras culture will be wiped out, as terrace culture was eradicated in England. And that is not what the Ultras want. Already they complain about what they see as a growing repression, in the form of strong-arm policing and legislation, such as the Pisanu Law. As Balestri says, 'It doesn't work for a number of reasons. What they should do is get to know the *curva* and, above all, demilitarize the grounds. Our stadiums look like bunkers, like some kind of obstacle course with the moats and the fencing. That just creates an atmosphere of tension and intimidation. And, of course, the police don't help. In the north of Europe they are discreet, in Italy they show up in full riot gear twirling their batons. And there is also this belief that the travelling supporter is a potential criminal. Instead of welcoming him as a guest, he is treated as a threat. It's no coincidence that so many travelling supporters, especially English ones, have had problems with Italian law enforcement.'

We would indeed do well in Italy to re-examine how football matches should be policed, and we could learn a thing or two from what has happened in England. But before we can go any further, the Ultras must reject violence. Only then can the powers-that-be start dealing with them on equal terms. And only then can they truly start effecting change in the areas that are important to them, such as kick-off times, the commercial exploitation of the game, television, etc.

I suspect some Ultras feel that the minute they renounce violence, they will lose whatever clout they have in the game. If that is so, they underestimate their own power. The Ultras represent 15–20 per cent of the stadium-going public (and the figure is far higher at certain clubs), and they are the loudest, most passionate, most visible supporters. They can vote with their feet whenever they want and make their voices heard. But only if they have the credibility and the moral high ground that comes from renouncing violence.

That aside, there is another reason why the Ultras are reluctant to get directly involved at an institutional level: working more closely with the clubs, the league or the FA would cost them their independence. By staying 'outside the system' they can criticize and owe nothing to anyone. Were they to come formally into the fold, they would be part of the system – the system they so often rail against. That is why the approaches have so far been tentative, more of a sounding-out than anything else. 'The FA and the league know who we are and know the main Ultras groups,' says Balestri, 'and there have been informal meetings and consultations, but, for now, it's a low-key relationship.'

If some Ultras groups are reluctant to get too involved at institutional level, at certain clubs they are a little too involved for the wrong reasons. It is known that some clubs bankroll Ultras by paying for their away travel and their tickets. In exchange, the Ultras perform the odd 'favour' for the president. For example, if he wants to sack the coach but doesn't want to look like the bad guy, he might have the Ultras insult the gaffer at every match, turning public opinion against him. That way, he can sack him saying, 'I had no choice.' The Ultras are also convenient if the president wants to put pressure on certain players, perhaps to sign a new contract or accept a loan move or simply to perform better. Such cases are not the norm but they have been known to happen. Genuine Ultras are disgusted by this because it is the polar opposite of what they stand for. Indeed, many codes of conduct specify that members must be financially independent of the club. Yet the sad truth is that Ultras themselves can be manipulated, whether covertly or overtly.

Ultras groups reject what they call 'modern football', yet they have not taken the necessary steps to be real agents of change. They are concerned that 'modern football' will wipe out Ultras culture. If it does, it will be a sad day. But they will have to bear some of the responsibility for refusing to be part of the solution.

Chapter Thirteen

Too Much for a Mere Mortal: the Disappearance of the Old-style English Manager

Clubs are the focal point in football, where managers and players, fans and the media meet. They are the hub of the footballing world, and over the past twenty years, they have changed more than any other element of the game. That's why it's wise to take a step back and reflect on the consequences, because these changes have had massive knock-on effects.

The main change is that football clubs are now big business. Or, rather, they act as if they are, which means balancing their hunt for success on the pitch with fiscal responsibility. Once upon a time clubs were clubs, with no profit motive; everything was re-invested and the main point was to play football. It was in that context that the English figure of the manager ruled supreme. He was ideally suited to that type of football. Back then, there were no massive sponsorship contracts to worry about, no stadium securitization deals to negotiate, no shareholders to appease. The club secretary would tell you how much was coming in and how much was going out. Based on the difference between the two amounts, the manager would handle contracts and transfers. That system is disappearing.

'I think it's inevitable that it will go,' says John Barnwell, of the League Managers' Association. 'Every club has two objectives, a commercial objective and a sporting objective. You need a person to reconcile the two. A person who can mediate between balancing the books and the needs of the playing squad. The sporting goals should be prioritized, of course, but clubs also need to answer to their shareholders.'

The solution, it would appear, is a system similar to the Italian model, with a manager who is really a first-team coach and a sporting director (or general manager, or director of football) who handles transfers and contracts, and liaises with the commercial side. In fact, it's a necessity because the manager's job has simply become too big. 'When I was managing Nottingham Forest I went mad because I had three thousand things to do,' says David Platt. 'I had to buy players, sell players, negotiate their contract extensions, scout potential signings, talk to the press, meet with local politicians and community leaders, answer correspondence and have endless meetings with the chairman and other board members. There was so much work that there were days when I did not have time to go on the pitch and take training. In fact, it happened quite often – I'd say at least a few times a week. Of course, I would have loved to handle training and be out there with my players. But a manager has so much responsibility that there simply was no time for it.'

It sounds like a paradox: a coach who does not coach. But that's the reality at many English clubs where the assistant manager runs training.

'I think the Italian system is far more logical,' says Eriksson, 'because English managers have to do two jobs.

And how can you have a training session without the manager?'

The other drawback with the English system is that managers can often find themselves in a difficult position when it's time to renew contracts. 'How do I look a player in the face, tell him he's worth fifty widgets, not a hundred, and then, the following week, motivate him fully, convince him he's capable of achieving great things?' says Platt. Not to mention the potential conflict of interest. When the person negotiating the deals is also the man working closely with the players every day, there is clearly scope for impropriety. This explains why England is moving towards a set-up in which, as in Italy, the sporting director is as important as the manager.

Arsène Wenger is one person who disagrees with that trend. For starters, he does not believe it's important for a manager to run training sessions: 'I am convinced anyone can run training,' he says. 'Out of two thousand managers, at least nineteen hundred could run my training session as well as me. There are no particular secrets, it doesn't take much. Because the secret of success isn't in training your team. It is in building your team, choosing the right players. I like to say that if things go well for me in June, they'll go well for me the entire season. If, on the other hand, we have problems in the summer, if we don't get the players we want, we struggle later on.'

His position is antithetical to the long-established norm in Italy and France, where the chairman and sporting director choose and buy the players. In that context a good manager is the one who can perform best with the players bought for him. Wenger selects the players himself. While he does not negotiate contracts or transfers, he nevertheless plays an instrumental role in bringing footballers to the club. Imagine the manager as a chef: the Italian chef would be like one of those guys on *Ready, Steady, Cook* who has to make do with whatever ingredients are supplied to him. Wenger would be the kind of chef who would get up early and go down to the farmers' market, select the best ingredients and then throw them together nonchalantly. 'I am very lucky because at any other club I would be having to make compromises constantly,' he says. 'I know how things work. Chairmen and sporting directors feel the need to sign big names, players to satisfy the media and the fans. Of course, those types of players generally cost more than unknown ones who could do the same job for a lot less money. So you have less money left over for other signings. But by signing the big name you win the approval of the press and calm the fans down, so that's what many clubs do.

'In reality, however, it's counterproductive because it limits your options,' he adds. 'A few years ago I signed a young defender named Kolo Toure. Nobody knew who he was. Within a year he became a regular at Arsenal and one of our key players. Now, I am sure that if I had been managing Juventus at the time, they would never have allowed me to sign a player like that. Why? Because he's not famous, because he is a risk. And at Juventus, like all clubs run by committee, with a manager, a sporting director, a chief executive and so on, they don't like to take chances. Taking risks like that would involve everyone. Here at Arsenal if I want to buy Kolo Toure I can do it. The decision is entirely mine, the risk is entirely mine.

I am the only one who faces the consequences if it does not work out.'

Wenger underscores the best aspect of the English system. When just one person is responsible, the buck stops with him. He makes the personnel decisions and, that way, there are no conflicts. In fact, the system works because Wenger does not operate on his own but with people whom he trusts. His scouts point out players to him, and the club's executive vice-president, David Dein, swoops in on Wenger's targets, then negotiates with agents and other clubs. If these people did not take some of the pressure off him, Wenger really would be working forty-eight-hour days.

While this arrangement works well for Wenger at Arsenal, Marcello Lippi, for one, is sceptical about how it would function elsewhere: 'Wenger is true to himself and his system,' he says. 'He plays a certain way and he buys players who fit into that vision of football. I like the way he actively chooses the players himself. But in the rest of the world, it's all different. And I don't think most clubs would allow him to work that way, choosing players according to his own vision of the game. Because the simple truth is that if you have the chance to sign a good young player at the right price or maybe a superstar on a free transfer, you'll do it even if perhaps it does not fit your system or your style of play. You worry afterwards about how to fit him into your team.

'At least, that's our philosophy in Italy,' he adds. 'And I think we train coaches to be good at doing just that, being flexible with players and formations so that you can succeed with whatever you have to hand. If the club buys you a good player, it's up to you to make it work.

Otherwise you're not doing your job. I can understand the club's position. They can't just make every transfer decision on the manager's wishes.'

It's interesting because in the old English system the manager was omnipotent. But I do feel that there *is* too much work for one person. Having said that, how you divide up the job is a matter of personal choice. Wenger spends a little less time on the training ground, a little more scouting potential signings and none in negotiating with clubs and agents. When I managed, I spent more time coaching, which I enjoyed and felt was important, and less scouting players. What I did not do at all, like Wenger, was negotiate transfers – it was not something I felt comfortable with. To operate in that sphere, you need a range of contacts with agents and clubs around the world. You also need a fair amount of legal expertise for the contractual side, as well as financial nous. I am not suggesting that a traditional manager can't do the job, rather that to do it properly you need either experience or specific training of a kind that most coaches are unlikely to have.

The trouble with having split responsibilities, as is the case in Italy, is that there is less accountability than in the one-manager system. It seems to me that, particularly in Italy, the coaches get all the blame when things go wrong, even though the problem might have been a result of a poor summer-transfer campaign. Or maybe the negotiators failed to sign the guys the coach wanted, or spent too much on some and then could not secure others. Sporting directors are rarely held accountable to the same degree as coaches.

Mastery of the transfer market is as important as it ever

was. Nobody has an unlimited budget, which means that for every signing there is an opportunity cost. A player might be a steal at £2 million plus £1 million in wages a year, but a complete waste at £4 million and £1.5 million in wages. That's how tight it is. Clubs would be wise to recognize this and place greater emphasis on the role of sporting director. We have already seen Chelsea do this when they attracted Frank Arnesen, one of the best in the business, from Tottenham Hotspur. And, indeed, at Chelsea the role is further divided: Mourinho selects the players he wants, but chief executive Peter Kenyon negotiates the transfers – similar to Arsenal, where Wenger and Dein operate as a team.

Going beyond that, the next step is to treat managers and sporting directors as a team, perhaps hiring and/or sacking them as a pair. Just as today some managers take their assistants with them wherever they go, perhaps sporting directors should go with them too. It makes sense. The manager would be working with someone he trusts and who, presumably, is on the same wavelength. He would feel comfortable in delegating responsibility, which would allow him to focus on technical matters. At the same time, the sporting director would have more freedom to operate: because he knows the manager and what he wants, he could make decisions more quickly – if an opportunity arose out of nowhere, he could grab it. Would the clubs want such a system? Perhaps not: if the sporting director remains separate from the manager he can provide continuity year after year, if the manager is sacked or moves on to another club. Also, a long-serving sporting director would know the club inside out, and would be able to make the kind of long- and medium-term plans that a manager/sporting director combination would be reluctant to implement.

Then again the chairman and chief executive can supply continuity – though this is only desirable if you're getting good results. If you need to sack your manager, presumably it's not the kind of continuity you want to maintain. Under the system I propose, a club would treat the manager and the sporting director as a team, which would mean sacking them both if necessary. They share responsibility so they should both be held accountable. Football has entered an era where a great sporting director – like Frank Arnesen or Fiorentina's Pantaleo Corvino – is worth nearly as much as a top-tier manager. It's time that we recognized the good ones and held the others account-able, just as we do with managers.

Selling Football Dreams

Player transfers and contracts have always been im-portant, but never more so than over the past decade or so because they are far and away a club's biggest expense. In the mid-1990s many started to believe that top football clubs could actually increase their revenues and even turn a profit – which they had not done since the days of the maximum wage. At the time, television revenues were booming and merchandising was all the rage – clubs were convinced that you could slap a logo on any old bauble and fans would buy it. Marketing types talked of 'maximizing revenue streams' and 'captive audiences'. Everybody was spending money, convinced that they were 'building a brand'. Those who didn't have enough borrowed it, either from the bank or by floating on the stock exchange. Back then, financial institutions had bought into the hype and were throwing money at clubs with the zeal they had reserved for dotcoms.

Everyone knows what happened next. Virtually all the extra money raised in TV income went to the players in wages. Consumers showed they were a little more clever than previously believed: they weren't going to buy junk at a mark-up simply because their club's logo was on it. And as for the 'additional revenue streams', when football clubs got into other businesses – from hotels to mortgage-lending – in most cases they found that consumers had no brand loyalty. Or, rather, their brand loyalty applied to football, but did not extend to financial advice. And clubs lost money. Huge amounts. Transfer spending sky-rocketed, wages ballooned, and there was no equivalent increase in revenue. Those clubs who had wealthy patrons – like Inter and Milan in Italy – weathered the storm thanks to the owners' largesse. Those who did not have generous benefactors (or whose benefactors turned out to be less wealthy than they first appeared) – Lazio, Parma and Fiorentina in Italy, Chelsea, Leeds and Sunderland in England – found themselves reeling under mountains of debt.

Interestingly, two clubs, both English, managed to avoid the financial meltdown: Manchester United, in the rarest of football phenomena, turns a sizeable profit year after year, thanks to its commercial might; and Arsenal's acumen in the transfer market, particularly in selling players, is without parallel. In the nine years since Wenger's arrival, the club's cumulative transfer balance is around negative £10 million, which is exceptional for a club of that size. When you consider Arsenal's sales – £30 million combined for Emanuel Petit and Marc Overmars, £23 million for Nicolas Anelka – you realize just what an outstanding job they have done in that department. And you understand how important a good sporting director (or his equivalent) is.

However, the rest of football suffered a disastrous financial blow. And with the euphoria of the late 1990s gone, clubs woke up to the obvious: it is nearly impossible to make money in football. Of course, the game had known this for most of the twentieth century but in the heady post-Bosman days, when everyone and their mother tried to float on the stock market, it had been forgotten.

This begs one of the most serious questions now facing the game: if you can't make money in football how can we support so many professional clubs? Indeed, there are 132 full-time professional teams in Italy, and a hundred-odd in England. How do all of these clubs make any money at all? Down at the bottom of the league structure, the share of the TV contract is tiny, so most of the income comes from gate receipts, which in England are reasonably healthy. In Italy, they are appalling. As I write this, Macclesfield are the bottom club in terms of average attendance in the 2005–06 season, with a median gate of just under 2,000. As low as that figure is, it is higher than sixty-three of the 132 professional clubs in Italy can boast. Think about it. With gates that low, how can you run a professional football club and break even? And what kind of people would get involved in such a business venture, knowing they'll haemorrhage funds? Indeed, why do we even talk about investment in football when, in fact, with few exceptions, there is no return?

The answer, sadly, is that too often the wrong kind of people are involved. Some do it to boost their ego or for publicity. Others think they can make money, usually by illicit means, whether money-laundering or accounting fraud. We've seen it all in Italy – we've even had a Mafia boss own a football club. (And, to prove an earlier point, after he was found guilty of racketeering, fraud and extortion and his club was wound up, fans were protesting in the streets, arguing that they should not have to pay for his crimes.) We have had club presidents who owned two, three, even four clubs, sometimes three at a time! We have had presidents who owned a club that went bankrupt, then somehow bought another. You can imagine what this does for the credibility of the sport. 'That's the thing, with football the way it is, there are presidents who are in it just for themselves, who speculate on the game and suck money out, using it for their own interests,' says Giordano Maestroni, of the Milan Supporters' Clubs. 'We all know this. But then we fans are weak. We see these hucksters come into our clubs, hear them make empty promises, then watch them build up debt and ruin our club. Yet we allow it because they tell us what we want to hear. We too want to win, we want to live the dream.'

Live the dream.

Sounds familiar? It's what former Leeds chief executive Peter Ridsdale famously said he was doing when the club was spending big in an effort to become a European power. It was a strategy that backfired spectacularly, of course, because it was predicated upon continuous improvement: qualifying for the Champions' League each year and earning more money every season to meet the rising wage bill. As soon as Leeds faltered on the pitch, things fell apart financially and the house of cards collapsed.

'Ridsdale lived his dream with someone else's money,' says Boyle. 'Nobody was ever really honest about their situation. Nobody said, "OK, it's a big gamble and it's only going to work if we do well in the Champions' League each year." Nobody said, "Are we sure [David] O'Leary is the right man or is he just going to buy Danny Mills, [Robbie] Fowler, [Seth] Johnson and [Michael] Duberry?"

'Most of all, nobody came out and said what would happen if things did not work out. The risk was potential extinction. Getting it wrong meant taking ten to fifteen years to recover.'

Fans are just that: fans. They don't like to hear about financial responsibility or balanced books. If somebody comes along waving money around, even if it is not his money, that's good enough for most. This is especially true in Italy where too many fans view a wealthy, free-spending club as a kind of birthright. If the club does not spend, if it doesn't generate some kind of enthusiasm by bringing in players, they are not interested. The best example of this is probably Napoli. Everybody knows that in the Diego Maradona years, the San Paolo was packed with 75,000 spectators most weeks. At the time, Napoli fans were widely praised for being some of the most passionate in Italy. The club's golden era yielded two league titles and a UEFA Cup – at a price. Napoli accumulated so much debt that, by the mid-1990s, they were no longer a force and at the end of the 1997–98 season they were relegated to Serie B. A new owner,

Giorgio Corbelli, promised to restore the past glory. Napoli were promoted back to Serie A in 1999–2000 and the club brought in some big-name players, none bigger than the Brazilian Edmundo. The fans flocked back to the San Paolo, Napoli averaged 38,890 spectators in 2000–01 but, alas, the team was relegated. Once again it was discovered that the club was crumbling under a mountain of debt. Had it avoided relegation, the situation might have been salvaged, since Napoli had an excellent television rights contract – but that was conditional on the club remaining in Serie A and, when it went down, its value plummeted. So, too, did attendances, hitting rock bottom in 2003–04, when the club attracted an average of just 14,603 supporters.

What happened next may seem amazing to some, but is typically Italian. The club went bankrupt and, under an Italian law known as the 'Lodo Petrucci', the debts were wiped out and a 'new Napoli' was created from scratch, one division below, in Serie C1. That 'new Napoli' was bought by the wealthy film producer Dino De Laurentiis (whose credits include, among others, *Conan the Barbarian*). He ploughed money into the club and the fans returned virtually overnight. Despite being in Serie C1, two levels below the big-time, Napoli drew more than 37,000 per game, a tremendous achievement for what is essentially third-tier football. Napoli lost in the play-offs that year, but De Laurentiis promised even more investment and that they would be in Serie A within two years. And yet, bizarrely, the supporters dried up again. The 37,000 average became, as of January 2006, a paltry 22,600.

To me, Napoli's attendance roller-coaster means several

things. First, unlike their English counterparts, Italian fans need hope to show up at the stadium. If they don't feel that a better future lies ahead, they will not support the team. And yet, because they want to believe, they are eager to overlook an owner's track record (and there are some real snake-oil salesmen out there) if he puts money into the team. Just as they'll overlook where that money comes from and whether, in fact, it exists. De Laurentiis was different; his investment was genuine but still didn't win over the fans.

The second conclusion to be drawn is that fans get bored very quickly. As with Siena, an owner can promise instant results and back it up with money, but if success isn't immediate the fans will walk out.

Italian clubs know this. And that's why chairmen are so eager to manipulate public opinion and make promises. It is also why few clubs make long-term plans. With fans who are liable to walk out, why worry about the future?

It is a similar story in England, though perhaps not to the same degree. Clubs such as Leeds, Ipswich and Derby County, all of whom hit hard times financially, illustrate the dangers of short-term thinking to appease the supporters.

One of the most widely held clichés about football supporters is that, because they are fans, they are naturally free-spending and irresponsible when it comes to their club, but it isn't true. This has been shown in England by the success of initiatives such as supporters' trusts, where groups of fans band together to buy equity stakes in their clubs. Far from spending freely and throwing caution to the wind, the trusts have shown themselves to be fiscally responsible, probably more so than most traditional owners. 'It was said in the past that if you put fans in charge of clubs they'll want to spend big, they'll get carried away and be irresponsible,' says Boyle, whose organization, Supporters Direct, facilitates the creation of such trusts. 'In fact, that's not the case. It's when you have egotists and self-promoters in charge, that's when you get into debt! Of course, not all people are like that – some people are just ambitious for the club.

'When the local supporters' trust put Brian Lomax on the board of Northampton Town, the other directors complained that he was too fiscally conservative and that he wasn't behaving "like a fan", because he did not want the club to sign certain expensive players. Lomax replied, "I'm a fan, I love the club, but I want my club to be here for my kids." There's a certain realism that sets in when fans take over.'

Today, supporters' trusts run four league clubs directly – Brentford, Chesterfield, Rushden and Diamonds and Stockport County – and they are represented on the boards of another twenty-one. They also run eight non-league clubs, most of which have been saved from bankruptcy and extinction. They are legal entities with strictly audited books and their representatives are democratically elected.

'A businessman would never give a million pounds to a club without representation on the board . . . why should the fans?' says Boyle. 'Because that is exactly what fans do. They put money into the club in so many ways, from tickets to merchandising to television. Without them there is no income at all. They are the ones who are really investing in the club, week in, week out. Why shouldn't they be represented?'

The flipside, of course, is that clubs run by fans are financially hamstrung. It is difficult for them to obtain credit lines and they can't run up debt. This makes it difficult to gamble and 'live the dream', as Peter Ridsdale might say. And perhaps that's not a bad thing: it forces clubs to stay within their dimension, spending only what they take in. But it makes serious capital investment difficult, since obtaining loans is tough. And, most of all, it would be a hard sell with the fans, particularly in Italy. Many Italian fans prefer the thrill of the rollercoaster ride (and the tears that follow) to the safety (and boredom) of fiscal responsibility.

For all the damage that was caused by the financial mis-management of clubs like Napoli and Lazio, their supporters will always treasure the *scudetti* they won. No bankruptcy tribunal could ever take that away. If they could go back, would they make different choices? Would they want to swap their current plight – Napoli in Serie C1, Lazio in a financial coma in mid-table obscurity – for a decade of mid-table security, on the pitch and on the balance sheet?

Probably not. The short-term thrill is worth everything to many Italian fans. It's an attitude I fail to comprehend, particularly in light of Wenger's 'Latins are rational, Anglo-Saxons are irrational' argument. Surely winning a title and having four or five years near the top isn't worth bankruptcy and oblivion? Surely, like Lomax, they would want the club to be there 'for their children'?

Or maybe it makes sense – because in Italy the harsh truth is that the risk of bankruptcy and oblivion is minimal. In England clubs occasionally go under, like traditional businesses, but in Italy it hardly ever happens, thanks to the Italian FA's 'Lodo Petrucci'.

'Lodo Petrucci': The Victimless Crime?

In the past when football clubs went bankrupt, they were wiped out. A new club could be formed but it would have to start near the foot of the pyramid, at amateur level. In the 1980s, this fate befell some important clubs, including Palermo and Catania, who had been as high as Serie A. The next high-profile bankruptcy came towards the end of the 2001–02 season, when Fiorentina went under. This time, however, the authorities treated it differently. Taken on their own, Fiorentina's books would have been OK. It was just that the club's owner, Vittorio Cecchi Gori, had used the club's shares as collateral to obtain loans to prop up his other ailing businesses. When those businesses went under, they took the club with them. Thus the courts 'went easy' (at least, that was how it appeared at the time: knowing what we know now, it was hardly the case) on Fiorentina, although cynics might suggest it had more to do with the club's size and ranks of supporters. Rather than disappearing from the football pyramid, the new Fiorentina was given a place in Serie C2, two rungs beneath the old Fiorentina. The club's right to participate in C2 was given to the mayor of Florence, who solicited bids from local investors and eventually turned the club over to Diego Dalla Valle, who still owns it today.

The powers-that-be realized they had set a dangerous precedent with Fiorentina as they had effectively broken their own rules. And with another string of bankruptcies coming up, something had to be done. They decided to turn Fiorentina's 'exception' into law, thus creating the 'Lodo Petrucci'. The rule applies if a club has been in the league for at least ten consecutive years (or twenty-five years overall) and is excluded from its division for economic or financial reasons (usually bankruptcy or being unable to meet the league's minimum requirements). Instead of dropping down to amateur football, the club is disbanded and a new one created in its place, one division below. The new club has to be from the same city as the old one and its creation is handled by the city's mayor who solicits bids from potential owners. Anyone who had more than a two per cent stake in the old club is barred from bidding for the new one. The bidders have to pledge to pay any outstanding wages owed to players or managers (but, interestingly, not other creditors) and illustrate their plans for the club. Based on this, the mayor decides who takes control of the re-formed club.

The 'Lodo Petrucci' has been immensely popular. Indeed, last season no fewer than four Serie B clubs took advantage of it, in what turned out to be one of the most comical (or embarrassing, depending on your point of view) epilogues to the Italian season. Torino Calcio won the promotion play-offs, but was declared bankrupt. Thus, promotion was cancelled and the club was re-formed in Serie B as Torino FC. AC Perugia was next in line for promotion, but it, too, was declared bankrupt and re-formed in Serie B as Perugia Calcio. Salernitana Sport finished in mid-table, went bankrupt and was relegated to Serie C1, with a new club, Salernitana Calcio 1919, replacing it. Finally Venezia AC finished second bottom and was relegated to Serie C1. It, too, went bankrupt and popped up a division below, in Serie C2, as SSC Venezia.

(And let's not forget that Genoa, who actually won the Serie B title and promotion to Serie A, was banished to Serie C1 for match-fixing, as mentioned earlier.)

Given all this, is anyone surprised that Serie B has less credibility than Saddam Hussein's press attaché, the one who said that Baghdad was not under threat of invasion even as US tanks rolled past behind him? Apart from the alphabet soup of letters – AC, FC, SSC – has anything really changed for the fans of those clubs? Does bankruptcy mean anything? Is it a punishment or a blessing?

Take Torino. Its promotion went up in smoke, but now, instead of a perpetually cash-strapped owner like Franco Cimminelli, it has a new patron, Urbano Cairo, who seems ready to splash the cash. And, best of all, Cairo takes over a debt-free club, which means he can spend even more money, since he doesn't have to worry about servicing old debts. For Torino fans, spending one more season in Serie B is not a big price to pay in exchange for a debt-free club and a wealthy, enthusiastic new owner.

And that's the problem with the Lodo Petrucci. It is simply unfair to those who play by the rules, the clubs that pay their taxes on time, that don't accumulate excessive debts, whose books are in order. It's not fair that they should be penalized. The former president of Bologna, Giovanni Gazzoni Frascara, described the cavalier attitude of certain clubs as 'financial doping'. And clubs get away with it because even if the authorities step in (as they did, to their credit, last summer, forcing out those four Serie B clubs) the Lodo Petrucci means it won't make much of a difference to the supporters. They'll just wait for the new club to be formed in place of the old one.

Thus, Italian fans don't have the same incentive to band

together to save their club as the English do through the supporters' trusts. This is another negative aspect of the Lodo Petrucci: it robs fans of the connection to their club. All that happens when a team goes bankrupt is that another replaces it: similar colours, similar crest, just a few different letters in front of its name. One is as good as the other.

That's why I'm in favour of abolishing the Lodo Petrucci immediately. Bankruptcy must mean something or it is no deterrent to mismanagement. And the more mismanagement and financial chicanery there is, the more dubious characters will be attracted to the game for the wrong reasons. Needless to say, the more dubious characters become involved in football, the more people lose faith in the game and its institutions, and the more honest folk are tempted to cheat, whether it's 'cooking the books' a little or making a call to their 'friend' on the opposing team before a crucial match.

At the same time, and to avoid having clubs go under every year, Italy needs to impose rigorous financial oversight and very tight controls, limiting the amount of debt a club can accumulate, as well as placing restrictions on what owners can do with their shares in the club (to avoid, for example, asset-stripping).

But that's only the start. Fans have already shown that they are more vigilant than many owners. That's why we should, wherever possible, favour the creation of supporters' trusts and help them get a representative on their club's board. Would Torino now be in Serie A if there had been a true representative of the fans on the board, with access to the club's books and full knowledge of the situation?

I am not suggesting there was any wrongdoing by the previous owners, but a big part of Torino's problem was that, with the club already heavily in debt, they spent more money to try to gain promotion to Serie A. This wasn't because they were stupid: they were under pressure from the supporters who felt their club 'deserved' to be in Serie A. The same supporters who made their feelings known, on more than one occasion, by becoming violent. When the club's owners pleaded poverty, the fans did not believe them. Would they have felt differently if their representative had been on the board and able to explain the situation to them? I think so. In fact, what if a Torino supporters' trust had taken over the debt-ridden club at the start of the 2004–05 season? Would they have spent money they did not have? Or would they have fought tooth and nail to preserve their club, the club of Loik, Gabetto and Valentino Mazzola, Superga and the five consecutive Serie A titles? I think I know the answer.

Supporters' trusts, in England as in Italy, would help to keep some of the more unsavoury characters out of the game and would bring to bear the degree of financial responsibility that the game badly needs. The knock-on effect will be a reduction in the number of professional clubs. To have 132 is absurd, particularly when so many fail to draw any significant support. Some of those clubs would be much better off downshifting to semi-professional status. The same applies in England.

If people want to put money into the game to support clubs that wouldn't otherwise exist as a professional entity, that's their choice. But if the clubs are deceiving people – beginning with their own fans – or skimming money from other parts of the game, something should be done. Football has always been about clubs at the top of the pyramid subsidizing those below. The game is an important social catalyst and I am not advocating that this should change, but it seems clear that clubs which are not viable on their own should not be bankrolled for the sake of it. I am not suggesting that they should fold, just drop a division or two, or become semi-professional. You can preserve football's place in a community and its social function at grassroots level without the local club having professional status. AFC Wimbledon and FC United have proved that this is true.

Creating a New Ruling Class for Football

To me the current financial situation underlines the importance of vigilance and compliance in football. We may not be comfortable with the idea of football as a business – especially as part of the entertainment business – but we've gone too far in that direction to pull back. Our clubs, at least in the top flight, have to be run in a professional manner and according to the rules and practices of business. And that is why we need not just serious rules and stringent oversight but also willingness on the part of the game to enforce them. A law that is not enforced or, worse, enforced selectively is pointless. It gives rise to lack of belief in the authorities. What football needs, in both countries, is strong leadership from people whose main interest is the game, not outside concerns. It is hard to fathom why the same people run the game, year after year. And, sadly, it seems there is little accountability.

It's a similar story in Italy and in England. People make

mistakes, in good faith no doubt, and are rewarded with bigger and better jobs. As I look at the Championship table, I see Ipswich Town and Sheffield Wednesday, two sides with an important past in the Premiership but now facing hard times, particularly in financial terms, as they struggle with tremendous amounts of debt. The former Ipswich chairman, David Sheepshanks, went on to become chairman of the Football League, while his colleague at Sheffield Wednesday, Dave Richards, is chairman of the Premier League and the Football Foundation, as well as a director of the FA.

In Italy, the situation is even worse. It seems that the same group of people, Franco Carraro, Antonio Matarrese, Gianni Petrucci and Adriano Galliani, have been involved in making decisions for the good of the game for most of the past twenty years. How is it possible that there are no real alternatives, that the same faces keep moving around at the highest levels of the game, without any real change? I am not attacking them as individuals. I am sure they are clever men. But I wonder where the next generation of leaders will come from. Why can't football draw its leadership from within its own ranks? Why can't we have footballers in those key positions?

I know the reason why. Most footballers lack the education. Most of us barely study after the age of eighteen and you can probably count on one hand those who have a university degree. It's the way the game is. Our energies are taken up with playing from an early age. When we reach the end of our careers, at thirty-five or -six, it's not realistic for us to go back and do a degree course, then start from scratch and work our way up through football, whether at league or FA level, as forty-year-old junior bureaucrats.

It seems clear to me that the game would benefit from a whole new class of administrators, ideally drawn from the ranks of ex-footballers. I would propose a kind of masterclass for ex-players, a two-year programme that would combine basic law, business and management, hosted by one or more universities. There would be a work-placement element in which students would rotate through internships in various departments at various institutions, from the league to the FA to the Olympic Committee. Obviously the course would not be for everyone: you would be admitted after an exam and an interview and, where necessary, a bursary would cover the cost. I wouldn't expect more than a dozen or so students to start each year. And, perhaps, the various institutions could have a 'fast track', reserving a job for a graduate of the programme each year.

To make it work, it would have to take only the best and brightest, drawn from all levels of professional football, and they would have to be people with a genuine interest in pursuing a career in sports administration. Then we'd be getting executives who have come purely from football. People who have been there, in the front lines, sweating after a ball on the pitch.

Television: Friend, Foe or Chainsaw?

Who runs the sport at institutional level? Brian Barwick, the chief executive of the English FA, comes from television (among other things, he was responsible for bringing the Premiership to ITV as well as overseeing ITV Digital . . . not his finest work.) The FA's executive director, David Davies, also comes from television: he was a BBC presenter and reporter. The FA's director of corporate affairs, Simon Johnson, formerly headed the legal department at ITV.

Thus, of the FA's ten-man management team, three (including the two in the most important positions) come from television and one, Trevor Brooking, from football. In Italy, we have even fewer athletes – the exception is the president of the Italian FA, Franco Carraro, a three-times European water-skiing champion – but television is just as well represented, if not more so: the head of the Italian league is Adriano Galliani, who was at Mediaset, Italy's largest commercial broadcaster.

I point this out to show how television and football are, for better or worse, closely linked. I know some traditionalists yearn for the kinder, less commercial world in which football existed without worrying about television. But that world no longer exists (and has probably been extinct for a very long time). Football and television are thoroughly co-dependent. Television funds football. Football provides content for television. There is no escaping this. From football's perspective, television is like a chainsaw; used properly you can cut yourself a lot of firewood for the winter; used incorrectly (or by a homicidal maniac), it can slice your family to bits.

How do we use television correctly? First, look at its impact. The biggest charge is that television has inundated the game with money, most of which has gone to the players in the form of wages. But the money was not distributed evenly and the result is a widening gap between rich and poor.

The gap widens on two levels: between the top tier and the lower divisions, and between bigger and smaller clubs in the same division (particularly in Italy). Until 1992, English television revenues were divided according to the '50:25:25 rule': if that rule applied today, the Premiership would get half of the revenue, the Championship a quarter and Leagues One and Two would share the remaining 25 per cent. But in 1992, famously, the top flight broke away and the Premiership was formed. This allowed the top-tier clubs to sell their television rights independently of the lower three divisions. Which, of course, meant that top clubs grew richer and richer (helped by the fact that the value of television rights boomed in the mid-1990s) while the rest of professional football suffered.

In Italy, the situation was less extreme until recently. Through 2006, Serie B clubs received a guaranteed annual bonus payment of at least 103 million euros (£71 million) from their colleagues in Serie A, in addition to whatever they could raise from the sale of their own rights. That arrangement, however, will be gradually phased out and Serie B will be left largely to fend for itself, much like Serie C (which has been in that situation for years) and league clubs in England.

Premiership and Serie A clubs are easy targets for those in the lower divisions. They are seen as wealthy millionaires who won't share with their brethren at grass-roots level. Many traditionalists yearn for the old days when the top of the football pyramid shared its wealth with those further down.

It's a nice idea, but we have to be careful. First, I endorse the importance of grassroots football – but what does that mean? Consider twenty full-time professional footballers in a League Two or a Serie C2 club drawing three thousand fans a game. Is that grassroots football? If so, would it be any less grassroots if those same players were amateur or semi-professional? Would anything really change for the supporters and the community? Lower-league football is important but nowhere is it written that it has to be professional. If today lower-league clubs are struggling with wage bills, I am not sure that transferring wealth from the top to the bottom is a long-term solution. One thing the recent past has taught us is that every time there has been a boom in football revenue, most of it has gone straight to the players in wages. If League Two or Serie C2 clubs suddenly found themselves with an extra million or so per year, where would it go? To pay players. Hardly grassroots football. (It's another reason why I support greater involvement from supporters' trusts, especially in the lower leagues. They have shown themselves to be fiscally responsible, they have no interest in receiving footballing 'welfare', but rather want to stand on their own two legs, and they know that the financial health of their club is more important than a new right-back.) And before we try to force the Premiership or Serie A to share all (or even most) of their pie with their poorer brethren, we should remember that there is no legal reason for them to do so. You can't coerce a football club: you have to convince them that it is in their interest to do something. Or, at least, convince a majority of clubs that it is in their interest: they can coerce the rest (unless the rest simply break away, which was what the Premier League did). For better or worse, we live in the European Union and it is a free market. To think that a football association or even a government can step in and order the top clubs to divide their money in a certain way is fanciful. Not even UEFA or FIFA can do it. If they tried, we would likely see the formation of that fabled 'breakaway European Super League', which is occasionally talked about. In fact, Europe's Antitrust Commission has looked at the issue of football rights on more than one occasion and it is quite clear that, in their eyes, even the current system is far from ideal. Some say it amounts to a cartel and that rights should be sold individually by each club.

Which brings me neatly to the next point: uneven distribution between clubs in the same division. In Italy, this has happened since 1999, when clubs were allowed to sell the rights to their matches individually. This means that broadcasters have to negotiate with each Serie A club and, since some clubs are more widely followed than others, their rights are worth far more. So, for example, in the 2005–06 season, Juventus earned around £53 million from television and mobile-phone rights, while Treviso, the smallest Serie A club, earned approximately £7.5 million. These figures incorporate Serie A's 'mutuality' – a subsidy from bigger clubs to smaller clubs – which represents around 18 per cent of the total value of the rights. In the Premiership, rights are divided far more equally. While in Italy the biggest slice of the television cake (Juventus's) was seven times as large as the smallest (Treviso's), in England the slices were cut far more fairly: Chelsea received the biggest payment in 2004–05, around £30.7 million, which was less than twice as big as the smallest, Crystal Palace's £18.3 million. That's because television rights are sold collectively by the Premier League, which splits the revenue along far more equitable lines: 50 per cent is divided equally among all clubs, 25 per cent is apportioned based on league position (with the last-placed team getting one-twentieth of the first-placed) and the remaining 25 per cent is awarded based on the number of live television matches shown each season.

To me there is little question over which system is better, both ethically and for the good of the game. And it is certainly not the Italian system, which is so weighted towards the bigger clubs that it causes an enormous imbalance. Three clubs – Juventus, Inter and Milan – earn nearly as much broadcasting revenue as the other seventeen combined. Obviously that is not healthy.

It's not just a question of bigger clubs being able to afford more in wages and transfers. They also become disproportionately powerful within the league. Again, this is especially true in Italy because the bigger clubs have huge squads and regularly send as many as a dozen players out on loan. They are generally either gifted youngsters who need experience or established veterans (usually foreigners) who want regular playing time. For some smaller clubs, their survival hinges almost entirely on the players they can get on loan. And they end up beholden to the clubs who have loan players to offer . . .

What all this leads to is a competitive imbalance, where the same teams triumph over and over again. We've all heard the stats. Since the creation of the Premier League – and thus the creation of the competitive imbalance in England – only four teams have won the Premiership: Arsenal, Manchester United, Chelsea and Blackburn Rovers. The latter two were bankrolled by outrageously wealthy men who broke the bank to build their success, while the fomer two won the other twelve titles and, not coincidentally, were the biggest earners in that period. In

Italy, the last four years have seen the same two clubs – Juventus and Milan – dominate.

A fairer distribution of television revenues is therefore essential. But the question is, what is fair? From a sporting perspective, the answer is clear. Everybody should be given the same amount of the pie, so that all can be on an equal footing. That way, competition would be based on ability, not simply how many superstar players clubs can go out and buy.

But that rationale ignores two key points. First of all, it's utopian; it may work in a parallel universe, but it ignores the history and culture of our sport, which has alway had large and small clubs. Second, while it may be fair from a sporting perspective, it is decidedly unfair from a business perspective. And whether we like it or not, the game is no longer merely a sport. The line was crossed a long time ago, from the moment clubs began listing on the stock market and attracting investors looking for a return. When football, in its hunt for new investment, began turning to people who were in it not for the idealistic love of the game but because they hoped to make money from it, the rules changed. And in a free market society, companies have to look to maximize profits. This is not because they are greedy, it's because that's how the market works. When you have pension funds and institutional investors putting money into football clubs, they need to see a tangible return on their investment.

It may make us uncomfortable, it may be dangerous for the game, but it's too late to go back. Now that clubs are businesses, they are governed by the laws of business. And if the biggest clubs were to go to court to demand a bigger slice of the pie based on the fact that they generate more revenues than the smaller ones, they would probably win. That is the basis of the so-called European Super League which occasionally rears its head.

Think it can't happen? Think again. A breakaway Premiership seemed unthinkable too not that long ago. The simple harsh truth that nobody wants to hear is that clubs are businesses and business will tend to gravitate to where it can make money. And, in football at the highest level it's potentially an NFL style European Super League, with teams allocated to cities based on catchment areas, no promotion and relegation and no UEFA to preserve the notion that this is something other than just another branch of the entertainment industry.

If we don't want to see that – and I certainly don't – then we have to find a business model that works and is fair to everyone. And that includes the big clubs.

Conclusion

In 1848, two Cambridge students, Henry de Winton and John Charles Thring, met with representatives of various English colleges and, after a meeting lasting seven hours and fifty-five minutes, laid down the Laws of the Game. If they could be with us today they would probably be shocked by the evolution of the sport they helped to create nearly 160 years ago. One thing they would agree on, I hope, is that football needs to grow and evolve with the times because it is no longer just a sport. It is business and it is entertainment. It is high culture and it is gutter populism. It is sacred and it is profane. It is nationalism and it is globalism. It is so many things to so many people, which is why we have to be prepared to allow it to evolve, because that is what has enabled it to survive for the past century and a half.

The first set of football rules, from 1848, have been lost, but there is a copy of the 1862 rules, laid down and revised by Thring. If you read his 'Rules for the Simplest Game' you realize just how much things have changed.

1. A goal is scored whenever the ball is forced through the goal and under the bar, except it be thrown by hand.

2. Hands may be used only to stop a ball and place it on the ground before the feet.

3. Kicks must be aimed only at the ball.

4. A player may not kick the ball whilst in the air.

5. No tripping up or heel kicking allowed.

6. Whenever a ball is kicked beyond the side flags, it must be returned by the player who kicked it, from the spot it passed the flag line, in a straight line towards the middle of the ground.

7. When a ball is kicked behind the line of goal, it shall be kicked off from that line by one of the side whose goal it is.

8. No player may stand within six paces of the kicker when he is kicking off.

9 A player is 'out of play' immediately he is in front of the ball and must return behind the ball as soon as possible. If the ball is kicked by his own side past a player, he may not touch or kick it, or advance, until one of the other side has first kicked it, or one of his own side has been able to kick it on a level with, or in front of him.

10. No charging allowed when a player is 'out of play'; that is, immediately the ball is behind him.

Just four of Thring's rules, one, three, five and eight, have survived, although some players – and I speak here as a striker – still ignore number three ('Kicks must be aimed only at the ball'). Imagine if rule two were still in effect, if we could grab the ball with our hands and then kick it, like a 'mark' in Aussie Rules. Or how about rule four, which prohibits jumping and kicking the ball at the same time? Imagine how much duller the game would be without bicycle kicks . . .

It goes to show that football has always changed with the times, yet hasn't lost sight of what makes it special: its simplicity. If we are going to make it a better game, if we are going to understand it fully, we have to be open to change, just as were those who came before us.

Each of us finds courage, wisdom and inspiration in different places. For me, the words of Paulo Coelho resonate:

A warrior of light knows his own faults. But he also knows his qualities.

Some of his companions complain all the time that 'other people have more opportunities than we do'.

Perhaps they are right, but a warrior does not allow himself to be paralysed by this; he tries to make the most of his virtues.

He knows that the gazelle's power lies in its strong legs. The power of the seagull lies in the accuracy with which it can spear a fish. He has learned that the reason the tiger does not fear the hyena is because he is aware of his own strength.

He tries to establish what he can truly rely on. And he

always checks that he carries three things with him: faith, hope and love.

If these three things are there, he does not hesitate to go forward.

When I set off on this long journey to the heart of football I was not sure what I would find. As I shared my thoughts and picked the brains of some of the smartest, most experienced men in the game, I found some answers. And yet for each answer I found half a dozen more questions, many of which had never previously occurred to me. That's probably why this book is now twice as long as it was originally supposed to be.

And then there are those issues which I did not get a chance to address. Racism, as in the 'real' world, remains a lingering problem in the game, both among some supporters and in the entrenched attitudes of some in the game's power structure. Fixture congestion – a direct result of financial pressures – is leading footballers to play far too many matches. Technological advances in everything from shoes to kit to the ball itself are changing the game as well. And there is the way our competitions are set up: the Coppa Italia is obviously moribund, but we need to ask ourselves whether and how we can improve, in terms of structure, the Champions' League, the League Cup, even the Premiership and Serie A. Then there is the role of players in determining how the game is run. In March 1996 I helped lead the first (and, to my knowledge, only) professional footballers' strike, to protect the pensions of unemployed players at all levels of the game. I still believe players can and must play a larger role: without them football would not be the massive business it is today. I would have loved to examine all these topics in greater detail, but there is only so much I could cover. You'll just have to wait for the sequel.

Looking back, though, I don't think it's necessarily a bad thing. Finding an answer means your journey is over. Uncovering more questions means your search for the truth goes on. And, ultimately, it's that search which keeps us alive. I hope this book helps provide a talking point and, maybe, an inspiration to those who love this game to go on and continue the search.

I still don't know if I prefer Mary or Veronica. But I do know for sure that I can no longer imagine life without one or the other. Which means that, footballing wise, I'll just have to be in a permanent *ménage-à-trois*.

Postscript

The hardcover edition of this book was published in the spring of 2006: I could never have imagined that, in the space of a few months, Italian football would be hit by two diametrically opposed events, both of which would have a massive impact on the game. The world media – as they often do – tried long and hard to find the link between the 'Calciopoli' influence-peddling scandal and Italy's triumph at the 2006 World Cup in Germany. As with all subjective things, if you look hard enough, you can come up with a tenuous connection – perhaps one could say that Italian players are at their best when they feel cornered and under pressure – yet aside from that these are two independent and unrelated events. The only common thread linking them was geographic and tempo-ral, and that was merely a coincidence.

I say this because Italy's success in Germany was a syn-thesis of everything that is good, everything that works, everything that we can be proud of in our football. In the preceding pages we talked of professionalism, of the work ethic, of preparation: qualities which set us apart on the pitch, though less so off it (at least in the football sphere). At the same time, we displayed tactical versatility and the ability to read matches and react creatively, changing things around at the right time. Much of the credit must go to Lippi, of course, but the players deserve their share as well: they were the ones who were able to interpret his instructions in the best possible way.

In my mind, there is one moment which best epitomizes all this: the semi-final against Germany in Dortmund. With the score deadlocked at 0–0 in extra-time, Lippi sent on two additional strikers – Ale Del Piero and Vincenzo Iaquinta – to replace midfielders Simone Perrotta and Mauro Camoranesi. This was a stroke of genius, pure and simple. Lippi flew in the face of convention and stereotype as we played the final sixteen minutes with four strikers – Iaquinta, Del Piero, Alberto Gilardino and Francesco Totti – on the pitch. Plus Andrea Pirlo – hardly a ballwinner in the Claude Makelele mould – in front of the defence. Plus two aggressive attacking full-backs like Fabio Grosso and Gianluca Zambrotta.

Lippi's move was bold, but it was a calculated risk, the fruit of experience and analysis. The match had been a played at a very high tempo and both teams were clearly tired. Yet Germany were the hosts, spurred on by a noisy and intimidating home crowd, so their natural propensity was to pour forward and attack. At the same time, because fatigue had set in, both sides were stretched on the pitch, the defenders tended to sit somewhat deeper and the strikers did not track back as much as they might have earlier in the game.

By sending in Iaquinta and Del Piero, two forwards, Lippi managed to take some of the attacking impetus away from the Germans. You can't simply bomb forward when you're playing against four strikers. At the same time, with the teams being stretched, spaces were opening up throughout the pitch. And anyone who knows football will tell you that, when you've got room in which to play, the more technically gifted players have an edge and both Del Piero and Iaquinta are skillful strikers.

But that's only part of the story. The tactical part, if you will. Del Piero and Iaquinta aren't just talented players, they are also extremely hard workers, with a strong sense of team ethic, guys willing to sacrifice themselves for the common good. While they are very different as players (Del Piero is a creative number ten, Iaquinta a strong and physical target man) both are very much athletes who take great pride in their ability to do the less glamorous dirty work: tracking back, tackling, helping out, making countless runs into space. In that sense, they are typically Italian, they've been indoctrinated into that kind of thinking and playing.

Of course, other nations produce forwards with a high work rate, guys who will sacrifice themselves for the team. But my impression is that those players tend to be born that way. Their aptitude for self-sacrifice is a result of their personality. Wayne Rooney works hard because that's the kind of player he is, not because he was taught to do it. But, looking back over the years, I can only think of a handful of Italian international strikers who did not work hard off the ball. I don't think this is a coincidence. In Italy, if you're a forward who is not prepared to run himself into the ground, unless you're phenomenally gifted, you won't get far.

Much of this book speaks to the fact that, historically, our football has been obsessed with results. I'll be the first to admit that it's a double-edged sword. On the one hand, it has caused us to lose – at least some of the time – an appreciation of beauty, creativity and enjoyment on the pitch as we sacrifice style and aesthetics on the altar of the outcome. On the other hand, it has also helped us recognize that 'beauty' can't be its own reward. It has to serve a higher purpose. Put another way, 'art' on the football pitch has to be functional, it can't be a case of 'art for art's sake'. And only when it is accompanied by results does it reach its fulfilment.

I think that players like Del Piero or Totti – guys who represent both quality and quantity, who can both conjure up the creative flourish and sprint thirty yards to make a crucial tackle – are the way they are precisely because they were born and raised in Italy. We'll never know for sure, but I believe that, had they been born in England or Brazil, they would have developed into entirely different players. I can't say whether or not they would have been better (perhaps they would have been – freed from defensive duties, their attacking instincts might have developed even further), but undoubtedly they would not have fitted as seamlessly into Lippi's vision of football. In that sense, perhaps, Lippi, like the Italy managers who came before him, had a slightly easier task in that his players were not just gifted, but also tactically versatile and willing to sacrifice themselves, just as his brand of football demanded.

I know all too well that clichés are the currency of footballspeak and, as such, Italy will be stuck with the 'defensive' label for a long time to come. But in reality it's an outdated view. Rather than describing us as defensive, I would say we're pragmatic. Or, better yet, Chameleon-like. We can adapt to any situation. We can sit back and defend in numbers as tenaciously as anyone. But we can also push forward and break down opponents with technique and guile. Yet always with an eye on our objective: getting the result we want.

I'm generally hesitant to draw broad conclusions from a competition like the World Cup which, after all, lasts only a month and where the margin between winning and losing is often miniscule. That said, there are some basic truths which emerged. For a start, once again we've seen that the best squad does not always win (in fact, it rarely wins). Brazil's experience proves this eloquently. I think there are a number of reasons why they underachieved, but in my view the one which sticks in my mind is their pre-tournament preparation. It reminded me of Apollo Creed's training in the Rocky films: lots of hype, lots of glamour, but not much substance, almost as if the players felt invincible. At the same time, on the pitch, Brazil looked as if they had just been thrown together, without any sense of balance, as if talent alone could be enough to crown the world champions. The tactical scheme itself, the much-discussed 4-2-4, seemed based solely on the fact that it was the one formation which allowed the manager to cram as many of the superstars into the starting XI as possible. And, while superstars can undoubtedly win you games (sometimes singlehandedly), in the long run, if you don't have a balanced structure in which they can operate, you may find yourself paying a steep price. Think of the Brazil side that won the World Cup in 2002. Yes, they had Ronaldo, Rivaldo and Ronaldinho up front. But they also featured three central defenders plus a ballwinner like Gilberto Silva. That's what allowed them to get away with the three attack-minded frontmen, all of whom had essentially a free role. In 2006, the balance was all wrong. They removed one of the central defenders and added a new forward in a free role, which may explain why this was Brazil's most disappointing World Cup since 1990.

Overall, the World Cup showed that the game is still evolving tactically, though there are a few common threads. Most sides relied on a back four, with a holding midfielder just in front of the defence and one central striker. Beyond that, the variety was impressive. Holland and Portugal used two genuine wingers, Spain had two men in a free role behind a lone center forward. England used a withdrawn striker in virtually free role, while Argentina sent their second striker out wide and ran most of their possession through an advance playmaker like Juan Roman Riquelme. Lots of different interpretations, virtually all of them predicated on a holding midfielder and a central striker. The exception in all this was Italy, but, as we said, the strength of the Azzurri in this World Cup was the ability to adjust tactics and personnel match-by-match. Rather than following the tactical trends, Lippi preferred to pick and choose on a case-by-case basis. This was a luxury afforded to him by the fact that he had one of the deepest and most versatile squads around.

Of course, the party did not last long for Italian football. The 'Calciopoli' scandal brough to light the absolute worst not just in Italian football, but in Italy as a country. Corruption obviously exists everywhere but the most painful realization was the impression that in Italy it wasn't the individuals (or, rather, not 'just' the individuals) who were corrupt, but the system as a whole.

And that is the most worrying aspect. Because it's one thing to punish and eradicate those who break the law, quite another to heal a rotten system. Especially when the whole system seems to be composed of three types of people: those who are dishonest, those who are honest but don't realize others are dishonest and those who tolerate the dishonesty of others, perhaps because they themselves don't feel as if they can change anything. Maybe people are fundamentally honest before entering the 'system' and they genuinely believe they can change it. Once inside however, they tend to fall into one of the three categories listed above.

Some say our football has always been that way, that we've always looked to gain whatever slight edge we can, whether it's influencing match officials or the league or opponents. I don't know if this is true, but what I do know is that once football became awash with cash, the temptation to cross the line and do something unethical or illegal became that much harder to resist. Clubs are now businesses, they have bottom lines like corporations and often, shareholders to answer to. These shareholders got involved in the game because they wanted to profit from it. And profit can be had in different ways. You can do it honestly, by developing your commercial division and attaining success on the pitch, thereby increasing your prize money and TV rights revenues. Or you can do it dishonestly: bungs, bribes, intimidation, pressure, fraud, etc. Often these two approaches are intertwined. The 'dishonest' methods can help you gain success on the pitch which, in turn, allows you to profit from the 'honest' revenue streams.

It hurts me to say it, but football is a world tailor-made for those who are unscrupulous and dishonest. It's true in both Italy and England, but in Italy we have an added problem: we are so cynical that we always think the worst of others, assuming that everyone steals and everyone is bent. As a result of this, we assume that those who are honest are fools (and this goes beyond football, the same applies to those who pay their taxes in full). And therefore we are more likely to tolerate certain things if not engage in them ourselves. That's why if Italy is ever to become a 'normal' country, we have to work three times as hard. We have to deny a part of who we are, we have to learn to trust each other and we have to remain ever-vigilant. Because the sad lesson of the Calciopoli scandal is that we are all, at the very least, guilty of tolerating certain things, things which, even when they weren't illegal, were certainly unethical and immoral.

Do you know the story of the frog and the pot of water? If you took a live frog and put it in a pot of boiling water it would immediately try to jump out and get away. The frog would immediately realize just how hot the water was and that, if it didn't get out, it would be boiled alive. But if you took the same live frog and put it in a pot of cold water it would just sit quietly, contented and happy. And it would continue sitting there, even as you turned on the gas and gradually turned up the heat, minute after minute. It simply wouldn't realize that it was being cooked alive. Even as the water boiled, it would continue sitting there, entirely inert.

This, to me is the greatest threat we face in football. Once we begin to accept the breaking of rules, or even just the lack of sportsmanship and fair play, we lose a sense of what is happening to us, just like the frog. It doesn't matter if we're not directly involved, the mere fact that we tolerate certain things makes us complicit. For every little episode we let slide, our sense of what is 'normal' and 'acceptable' gets distorted. That's what allowed Calciopoli to happen, we had become desensitized to certain misdeeds and failed to realize or react when they escalated into serious fraud and corruption.

Despite all this, I am not entirely pessimistic. The fact that the Calciopoli scandal was exposed shows that we are not entirely blind to injustice and corruption. We can, in fact, react, even if it took extreme circumstances for this to happen. Some say that the justice meted out in the summer of 2006 was incomplete, but at least it showed that nobody, not even huge clubs like Juventus or Milan, was untouchable and that the system could change. And this is not something to be underestimated. Because, to me, a bad system is better than a monolithic and immutable system. At least the former leaves you with the hope of a change for the better.

Italian football, at least as far as players and supporters are concerned, has shown a wonderful ability to grow, adapt and renew itself. We saw it both at the World Cup and with the ongoing success at youth level. And the love of the fans is evident every weekend when, despite all the difficulties and hurdles placed before them, millions continue to suffer and make sacrifices for their club. These are the real resources of football. And these are the foundations on which to build the future.

Appendix

Let's look at how our quadrilateral might apply to four fictional footballers. Bruno Bidone is a top-flight midfielder. He is what you would call an all-round player, with no obvious weaknesses, though perhaps he doesn't excel in any particular area. Most top-flight footballers fall into this category.

Carlos Kickaball has one major shortcoming: 'balls'. He doesn't react well to setbacks – whether it's an opponent kicking him early in the game or being left on the bench – and he sometimes lacks the confidence to take charge on the pitch. Yet he is technically sound, is a good athlete and has an excellent understanding of the game. The total area of his diagram is not much smaller than Bidone's. Yet he's inconsistent, which is why managers often feel they can't rely on him. There are a few players like that in the top-flight, but not many: teams won't take a chance on them.

Harry Hacker has everything bar technique and, because of his lack of skill, plays in Serie C or League 1, or even lower. At that level, his other attributes – courage, workrate, understanding of the game – might paper over his shortcomings. Yet increasingly, players like him struggle to find a place in the professional game.

Lorenzo Lento, on the other hand, would be a decent player if only he weren't slow and physically weak. You won't find him in Serie A or the Premiership; in a few cases he may survive in the second tier, but only if the

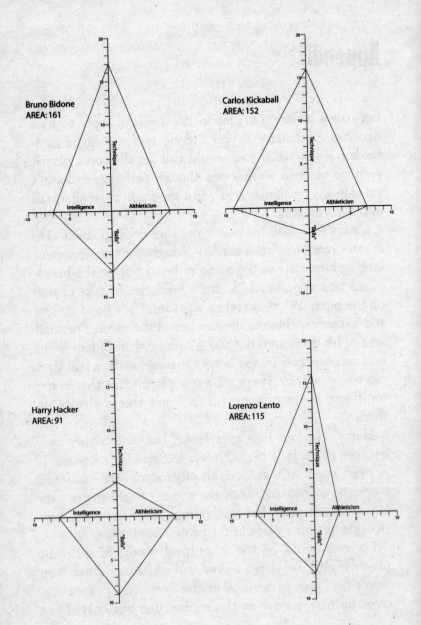

Bruno Bidone
AREA: 161

Technique
Intelligence
Althleticism
"Balls"

Carlos Kickaball
AREA: 152

Technique
Intelligence
Althleticism
"Balls"

Harry Hacker
AREA: 91

Technique
Intelligence
Althleticism
"Balls"

Lorenzo Lento
AREA: 115

Technique
Intelligence
Althleticism
"Balls"

team is built around him and other players do the running and tackling for him. That's why the total area of his diagram is greater than Hacker's. Even then, you're more likely to see Lento lower down the football pyramid, particularly in countries where the pace is lower and the football is less physical.

Bibliography

Mark Baldwin, *The Ashes' Strangest Moments: Extraordinary But True Tales from Over a Century of the Ashes*

Gianni Brera, *La Leggenda dei Mondiali e il Mestiere del Calciatore*

David Conn, *The Beautiful Game?: Searching the Soul of Football*

Franklin Foer, *How Soccer Explains the World*

Malcolm Gladwell, 'The Sports Taboo', *The New Yorker*, 19 May 1997

Jon Entine, *Taboo: Why Black Athletes Dominate Sports and Why We Are No Longer So Afraid to Talk About It*

Niccolò Machiavelli, *Il Principe* (trans. W. K. Marriott)

Sun Tzu, *The Art of War* (trans. Ralph D. Sawyer)

David Winner, *Those Feet: A Sensual History of English Football*

Index